Early Praise for *Happy As*

'Oh look, it's very sweet, but you're not going
to win a Pulitzer'
Sylvie, wife

'Book? You're writing a book???
You've never read a book in your life!'
Nicki, sister

'Will there be enough food at the book launch
or should I bring a tray of sandwiches?'
Faye, mum

'HAHAHAHA, you're writing a book,
oh wow, I hope there are plenty of pictures'
Robbie, mate

HAPPY AS
LARRY EMDUR

Stories of summer, childhood and the magic of family

HarperCollins*Publishers*

We gratefully acknowledge the permission granted by copyright holders to reproduce the copyright material in this book. All reasonable attempts have been made to contact the copyright holders; the publisher would be interested to hear from anyone not acknowledged here, or acknowledged incorrectly.

Larry Emdur is represented by:

Michael Cassel Group
Tel: +61 2 8006 1334
info@michaelcassel.com
www.michaelcassel.com

HarperCollins*Publishers*
Australia • Brazil • Canada • France • Germany • Holland • India
Italy • Japan • Mexico • New Zealand • Poland • Spain • Sweden
Switzerland • United Kingdom • United States of America

HarperCollins acknowledges the Traditional Custodians
of the land upon which we live and work, and pays respect
to Elders past and present.

First published in Australia in 2022
by HarperCollins*Publishers* Australia Pty Limited
Gadigal Country
Level 13, 201 Elizabeth Street, Sydney NSW 2000
ABN 36 009 913 517
harpercollins.com.au

Copyright © Emdurtainment Pty Limited 2022

The right of Larry Emdur to be identified as the author of this work has been asserted by him in accordance with the *Copyright Amendment (Moral Rights) Act 2000*.

This work is copyright. Apart from any use as permitted under the *Copyright Act 1968*, no part may be reproduced, copied, scanned, stored in a retrieval system, recorded, or transmitted, in any form or by any means, without the prior written permission of the publisher.

A catalogue record for this book is available from the National Library of Australia

ISBN 978 1 4607 6228 8 (paperback)
ISBN 978 1 4607 1506 2 (ebook)
ISBN 978 1 4607 4406 2 (audiobook)

Cover design by Mark Campbell, HarperCollins Design Studio
Front cover image and spine image from the Emdur family archive
Back cover image by Hugh Stewart
Internal design by Mietta Yans, HarperCollins Design Studio
Bondi map on page vi by Emily O'Neill
Unless otherwise credited, all photos are from the Emdur family archive
Typeset in Bembo Std by Kirby Jones
Printed and bound in Australia by McPherson's Printing Group

WARNING:
This book *may include facts.

*may not

BONDI ACCORDING TO LARRY, 1970S–1990S

CONTENTS

PART I: Foam Surfboards and Shagpile Carpets   1
KFC and Bleeding Nipples   3
The Battle for Cork   11
Becoming an Egomaniacal Wanker   20
'Young Man, Get Your Hand Off My Balls!'   26
'Too Much Tongue!!!'   42
The Perfect Cure for a Bluebottle Sting   49
Paul Hogan Made Me Spew But Saved My Life   58
The Mix Tape   66
Our Superyacht   70
How Did I Get Here?   81
Bad Boyfriend   87
The Bondi Spectator   93

PART II: A Cheap Watch and a Shiny Suit   101
The Moment   103
If This Van's A-Rockin' ...   112
News Overnight   121
The Watch   126
Toga, Toga, Passion Pop, Toga!   136
Death Knocks and Dingoes   144
Hairy Nipples and Her Majesty   153

Yoko Oh No	*159*
'MUM! It's Jason Bloody Donovan!!!'	*171*
'How Many Fs Appear in the Word "Dolphin"?'	*181*
No More Mr Nice Guy	*187*
Don't Drink and Bid ... Or Do	*198*
My First Time	*208*

PART III: The Bondi Boy and the Polish Goddess — 215

I Should Be So Lucky	*217*
Whitegoods-Inspired Lust	*230*
Placki Kartoflane	*244*
There's Something About Mary	*253*
Three Weddings and a Femoral	*258*
The Lighter Side	*269*
Sniffing Molly	*282*
'Emdur, You're a TV Slut!'	*286*
'Two Hundred Cheeseburgers, Please, and YES, I'd Like Fries with That!'	*295*
Larry Time	*302*
Those Tattoos Over My Heart	*311*
Mum's Menu	*317*

AFTERWORD: Bye for Now, and Keep Smiling (Patent Pending)	*328*
Acknowledgments	*339*
Picture credits	*342*

PART I

FOAM SURFBOARDS AND SHAGPILE CARPET

BONDI DREAMING

1970s–1980s

*'I love you,
I'm so proud of you!'*

Faye Emdur

KFC and Bleeding Nipples

1972

It's 2022. I'm standing on the promenade at North Bondi overlooking the iconic kiddies' pool. I'm wearing drop-crotch denim shorts, Birkenstocks and a linen shirt, and I'm sipping a double-shot skim macchiato that I just bought at Speedos Café across the road for $4.40 ... and I'm thinking, 'What happened to me? When did my life become this wanky?? Because when I was growing up and swimming in this pool, life was incredibly simple and so, so much fun.'

It was half a century ago ...

WAIT! STOP THE BOOK!!! That's how an *old man* would start his first chapter. Has my life been going on for so long I need a 'half a century' reference in there? Oh, deary, deary me ...

Oh, SHIT!!! There's *another* thing an old man would say. This book was a stupid idea – all it's doing is proving that I've accidentally become an old man.

Going off on a tangent is *also* something an old man would do, so maybe I should get on with the story before this old man gets so far off course he forgets what this story is about.

Back in the day, the beach was our backyard and the North Bondi kiddies' pool was our favourite hang. My sisters, Nicki and Martine, and I were all under ten, and we would splash around in this pool all day.

Would I get out and run the two hundred metres to the public toilet to go for a wee? As if. Back then we thought the water temperature was increasing naturally as the sun got higher and the air warmed up, but now that I know more about science and stuff, I think I can safely say that the more kids weed in there during the day, the more it heated up.

It's a tidal pool, and at high tide you could jump off the pool wall into the deeper end – not so deep, really, maybe a metre. On days when there was a big surf, the waves would smash against the wall and spray up and over, and we'd hang on to the railing, which was just a rusty chain, and swing back and forth as the waves smashed into us. At low tide, the pool would get one big flush that exposed a large patch of sand, where we would spend hours building sandcastles and just messing around.

All I remember from these days was laughter and happiness and sunburn, and ouchies when peeling the red sunburnt skin off our noses and shoulders.

Weekend breakfasts were my favourite. My mum, Faye, would make her speciality, which she called Bunny in a Hole.

She would heat the frying pan up to high – but not just *any* old frying pan. My dad, Dave, was a travelling salesman, and at the time he sold fancy pots and pans, so naturally Mum got a brand-new set.

A mere description of Mum's awesome Bunny in a Hole recipe from the 1970s would cause any nutritionist of today with a completely healthy heart to have a heart attack, maybe multiple.

Once the frying pan was heated up to high, Mum would put in more butter than any health institute around the world would recommend, then get a couple of slices of white bread – fresh or past its use-by date, didn't matter.

(Actually, according to my best writing companion Wikipedia, use-by dates for food in Australia didn't really kick in until 1978, which means before that we'd just keep eating the white bread until it went a little bit mouldy, then you could just kind of cut or tear the mouldy bits off and keep going. Those there were dangerous times.)

Mum would use a cup to press a hole in the middle of the slice of bread then throw the bread into the sizzling butter and let it fry. Once it crisped up a bit, she'd crack an egg into the hole – wait, wait, I almost forgot: first she'd put another *table*spoon of butter into the hole, more sizzling and spattering, *then* put the egg in and cook it good, cook it real good.

Now the egg is perfectly set and the toast perfectly fried. Thank you, butter.

In writing this, I'm trying to remember the scene exactly and all I can think about is how much wrong stuff, by today's standards, was happening in our house at that particular time. We just didn't know.

Mum's cooking our breakfast with half a tub of butter, Dad's walking around chain-smoking, including at the brekky table, we're all unwittingly filling up on butter and passive smoke and we're about to go to the beach *all day* in the middle of summer with no shirts, hats or sunscreen – in fact, there might even have been some coconut oil applied to get a deeper tan and fry the skin, in a similar fashion to how the butter had fried the egg an hour earlier at home. If only we'd known then what we know now.

On other very special days, if Mum thought maybe we should have a break from the butter and white bread, we would have fruit, because apparently fruit was good for you. But instead of real fruit we'd have 'froot', in the form of a very awesome breakfast cereal called Froot Loops. I never questioned why they spelt 'fruit' differently on the box. I knew this awesome cereal was from America and I thought that was how you spelt it in American.

Now, I'd seen lots of those food charts and I knew I had to eat froot, so I loaded up that bowl with as many Froot Loops as I could. Toucan Sam was on the box and he looked like a happy, healthy toucan. Surely if Froot Loops were bad for you then he'd be fat and sad, but NO, he had bright eyes and shiny feathers.

I should've known when Toucan Sam said, 'Start your day with a good breakfast *including* Kellogg's Froot Loops' that he meant have a healthy breakfast first and *then* you can have a handful of Froot Loops. But when he said that Froot Loops were full of niacin, vitamin B6 and riboflavin, he made them sound great, like when Eva Longoria says 'hya-lu-ronic' in the L'Oréal commercial and you go, 'Wow, that sounds really good for you and a whole lot of fun to say. I believe it and I want it, and I'm going out to buy it right now.'

Back then, the kiddies' pool was the centre of our universe. On really hot days, the whole family would head off early and walk barefoot in our cozzies down the hill from our house at 161 Hastings Parade, Ben Buckler, North Bondi.

We just took our towels; we didn't need anything else. We never took any supplies; bottled water wasn't a thing, but we wouldn't have taken it anyway, because there was a bubbler. Why would we carry our own water when we could easily go and put our mouths on a bubbler that ten thousand other beachgoers had slobbered all over?

Sometimes it had good pressure and you could keep your mouth a safe distance from the layers of cold sores, gum disease, influenza, E. coli and giardia. At other times, when the pressure was low, you'd have to bring your cracked, sunburnt lips close to the water hole and keep them there long enough to get a mouthful of water and quite possibly legionella.

One day there was a dad pushing his kid around the kiddies' pool on a fibreglass surfboard – a proper, grown-up surfboard. The little boy, about my age, was standing up and the dad was running behind him, pushing the board along in the water as hard as he could.

This looked like *so* much fun. They were very friendly days and everyone spoke to each other, so when the other father had run out of puff from pushing his kid around the pool, Dad asked if *he* could borrow the board and push *me* around.

This was my very first surf. It was a hoot.

'Look, I'm surfing!' I delightedly squealed as I zipped past Mum and my sisters. I'm sure Mum put her hand on her heart and mouthed the words 'I love you, I'm so proud of you!'

I found I had really good balance. I was having heaps of fun. Dad, on the other hand, wasn't sporty and was a heavy smoker, so I'm guessing he wasn't having quite as much fun as I was. In fact, he probably thought he was going to die.

He couldn't keep this up for too much longer, but I came up with a new idea. It was possibly the first time I realised I would one day get to a point where I didn't need my parents.

It was low tide, so there was the usual mound of sand at the entrance to the pool, gently sloping down towards the centre. I placed the board on the edge of this little sandbank so that most of the board was floating. I walked back about ten steps, then ran at the board as fast as I could, jumped onto it, and surfed off into the middle of the pool. I felt like I was surfing forever, but in reality I probably got three, maybe five metres before the board stopped dead and I fell off.

But now I was hooked on surfing. And where does a young boy who's desperate to keep surfing go to buy his first surfboard?

A surf shop?

No.

A sports store?

No.

The *Trading Post* (like eBay, but an old-school newspaper)?

No.

Correct answer: Kentucky Fried Chicken on Bondi Road, where, for a limited time only, if you bought a family bucket of chicken, then for just $1 extra you could buy your own surfboard.

Now, you're probably dying to ask me, 'Larry, what sort of surfboard would you get for just one single dollar?'

And the correct answer is: 'A shit one.'

It was made of polystyrene foam, and had a huge picture of Colonel Sanders' face painted on the deck.

It's really hard for me to put into words exactly what it was like grinding my tummy and chest over this rough polystyrene board all day, so let's do a little practical experiment to make sure we're on the same page. It's what I like to call 'immersive storytelling', sort of like they do on *Play School*, but for grown-ups. It will help you fully engage with this chapter. OK, here we go …

Grab a piece of sandpaper – the rougher the better. Now start rubbing it over your left nipple – not slowly and gently, with force and for a long time. Once the nipple starts bleeding, start grinding your *right* nipple. If the sandpaper wore down on your left nipple, for a fully balanced Sensaround experience, get a new piece of sandpaper for your right nipple. Grind until the nipple starts bleeding.

Once both nipples are bleeding equally, pour one hundred grams of tapwater into a beaker then add thirty-five grams of table salt. Stir clockwise until dissolved, and you'll have a close-to-seawater concoction. Pour homemade seawater onto bleeding nipples. After the initial pain subsides, rinse and repeat till the sun goes down and you have to go home for dinner.

(Please consult your doctor before conducting the above experiment. If you're too busy to get to the doctor and you trust my medical advice, please don't try the above. Unless the last book you read was *Fifty Shades of Grey* and you've been meaning to try this sort of stuff but just haven't got round to it yet.)

That's what a day surfing on the KFC foamie felt like. Yes, the foam was like sandpaper, and the places where the red paint of the Colonel's face had dried were even rougher against your skin.

They were happy days, unless you were a nipple.

But at least now that I had my own board I was allowed to venture out of the kiddies' pool and splash around in the little waves on the beach just outside the pool wall. This was the natural progression of a Bondi grommet: first, pushed around the kiddies' pool on a borrowed board by your parents, then your own KFC nipple-ripper foamie in the northern corner, then eventually you'd end up down the south end on a fibreglass 'grown-up' board.

Soon nearly every kid had one of these KFC boards; the northern corner was full of them. You could always tell who had a KFC foamie, because they had terrible board rash all over their tummy and chest. It was a special little club. We'd spend hours and hours paddling around on those things.

If you caught a big wave or you fell onto the board, it would snap. The bins around the beach were full of broken KFC boards. In later life a snapped board was a tragedy, but when your KFC board snapped it was actually a joyous occasion, because it meant you and the family would soon be heading back up to Bondi Road for another bucket of KFC.

And this, ladies and gentlemen, is where my KFC addiction and my constant yearning for Sylvie to bite my nipples began …

Joking – I don't really have a KFC addiction.

The Battle for Cork

1973

Long before Bondi Airbnb owners worked out how to squeeze ten to twelve broke backpackers into an attic, Mum had lovingly designed a completely cramped yet somehow functional living space for three kids, all under ten, in a small bedroom with an even smaller sunroom attached.

It was our second Bondi home, in Hastings Parade.

This was how we lived. Nicki and Martine had small single beds on opposite sides of the bedroom. There was a thick strip of ribbon on the floor, over which neither girl could cross onto each other's sides. Nicki was on the same side as the door, so she had easy, carefree access. Martine was on the opposite side and had to jump from the bedroom door to her side without touching the ground on Nicki's side. Martine was an excellent gymnast, so this was no problem for her.

Then there was another kid's bed in the adjoining sunroom, which magically became a tiny bedroom, and the occupant, me, could only access his room by accurately walking along the ribbon through the girls' room.

If I accidentally stepped *off* the ribbon, then I would technically be in either Nicki's or Martine's bedroom, and that would be a breach of the strict privacy terms and conditions of the arrangement. The ribbon on the floor was like the border that separates North and South Korea: to step off it or to cross it was illegal. So I would walk along that border like a drunk driver in America taking the 'walk the white line' sobriety test.

OK, now that you've got the surveyors' geographical map of our bedroom and are familiar with the laws of the land, you're probably wondering how we got through that stage without killing each other.

Actually we got on really well. In fact, it was a pretty cruisy household, full of love and happiness. Both my parents were kind and considerate; I don't remember either of them ever raising their voices at us.

I don't remember any huge fights with my sisters either. I adored both of them. I've always felt blessed to have these two fierce, fantastic, funny, creative and beautiful women in my life. Nicki and Martine have played a massive role in who I became, they've featured in a lot of my big decisions, and I'll still regularly lean on them for guidance and advice.

But back then, of course, there was a *little* bit of sibling rivalry.

Mum loved her Physical Culture. Physie was really popular, a mix of dance and aerobics, and both girls jumped right into it. Martine started doing very well at Physie and gymnastics competitions. She was a natural, and was soon bringing home prize ribbons.

THE BATTLE FOR CORK

Before this, I remember the corkboard in the corner of the kitchen was relatively well balanced. It had each of our school photos on it, a couple of pics of the family at the beach – me with my foam surfboard – and some notes from school.

But when Martine's ribbons started coming home, well, the board seemed to lose its equilibrium. Martine was getting more corkage … This did *not* feel right.

And so, The Battle for Cork began.

Nicki is the Emdur family's 'smart' contribution to the world. The only one to care about education, the only one ever to even think about going to university. Perfect student, self-confessed goody two-shoes.

We're very close; we were even born in the same year. Nicki was born on 9 January 1964, and I was born eleven months later to the day, on 9 December. (I'm going to take it for granted that you can do the maths on this one without me having to write about my parents having sex soon after arriving home with a newborn. Please move on, there's nothing to see here.)

We are of the same ingredients, the same DNA, yet Nicki be so smart and such a deep thinker, and I be so stupid and *so so* painfully shallow.

You'll probably be able to tell as you make your way through this book that this family relies heavily on Nicki. She's sharp, funny and beautiful, the organiser of the family, the checker-upperer and our resident psychologist. She fixes everyone's fractured emotional stuff, puts us back together when we're broken, helps mend relationships and sorts out work dilemmas. If only she had a dollar for every time someone in this family asked her, 'What should I do?'

In any conversation, she's never interested in talking about herself, she only wants to talk about you. Which suits me perfectly. She has given us all such incredible emotional support over the years and all I've ever given her is a *Main Event* T-shirt and a *Price Is Right* board game.

I do, however, intend to give her a copy of this book, and I'll sign it with a personalised inscription in big thick Texta so she can't re-gift it like she probably did with the *Main Event* T-shirt and the *Price Is Right* board game.

Martine, born nineteen months after me in July 1966, is the Emdur family's contribution to the arts. Creative and self-driven, she sees the world differently from everyone else. She's our unicorn-riding dream-chaser, whose artistic mind works in such magnificent and mystical ways to produce the most beautiful, mind-boggling paintings.

Martine is hard to describe, like one of her paintings – google 'Martine Emdur paintings' and you'll see what I mean. She's an abstract thinker, who generates light and love and wonderment. An early childhood around the Bondi pools and surf has filled her mind with beautiful images of water moving and sunlight playing on the ocean, and she has somehow worked out a way of magically capturing them on canvas.

And *I* would be Mum and Dad's contribution to bad television.

Nicki was our shining star at school, so all her wonderful test results and school reports started to creep up onto the corkboard alongside Martine's Physie ribbons. I had nothing going on, so I'd look at the corkboard, starting to get layered up with Nicki's reports and Martine's ribbons, and think maybe one day I'd get on that corkboard, maybe one day I'd be able to stand in that kitchen a proud boy instead of the pathetic little corkless loser I was.

Perhaps this was the first sign that I expected the world to always be about me. Which I still truly believe, and which is precisely why, while telling you a story that's obviously meant to be about my sisters, I'm still going to start the next sentence with 'I'.

I think Mum put a photo of me up there out of pure sympathy. It meant nothing – it wasn't a great school result, it wasn't a sports ribbon, it was just me with my new bowl haircut.

Yep, an *actual* bowl haircut. Mum would put an *actual* bowl over my head and cut around it with scissors. Not sharp haircutting scissors – why on earth would she go and buy expensive haircutting scissors when there was a perfectly good pair of heavy-duty craft scissors sitting next to her sewing machine? They could easily cut through denim, so she knew cutting hair with them would be a breeze.

Maybe the bowl-cut pic on the corkboard wasn't even *about* me. Maybe it was about Mum doing this great haircut, like when a hair salon puts a picture of a beautiful model in the window that screams: 'Come inside, I can do this haircut, I did this!'

I would win a couple of race ribbons along the way from North Bondi Nippers. Later I was sponsored by a board manufacturer and started taking part in local competitions, but nothing that secured me good corkage.

When I was thirteen we moved down the road to 20 Brighton Boulevard. The corkboard of course came with us, but it was still out of balance.

It wasn't until I became an accidental reporter for the local paper when I was seventeen that I started to reclaim my rightful third of the corkboard – although the stories I wrote were usually just small columns, only about the size of a first-place Physie ribbon.

A copy of Nicki's science degree with a major in psychology went onto the corkboard in 1986 in the coveted centre spot.

I had started in TV by then, and thought this would be good therapy to help me to get over my corkboard fascination. Sure, Nicki's degree was in the centre of the corkboard but *I* was on *TV*!

But if being on TV was so damn fabulous, why was I still jealous of my sisters' corkboard real estate? In the years ahead, I would draw on every chapter of Nicki's psychology thesis to understand my corkage obsession.

Then, WHAMMO, in 1997, Martine, who'd been making a real name for herself doing chalk murals and menu boards in cafés around Bondi, decided she'd try her hand at selling some of her art. She'd walked past the small art gallery at the back of Bondi Pavilion, and something inside just made her book the next space available. Then she raced home and started working on her first-ever show.

The opening was *such* a beautiful night. The paintings were a few hundred dollars each. Mum was walking around offering guests sandwiches from a platter, Nicki and I were walking around with trays of drinks, and the little red dots symbolising that a painting is sold were flying up all over the place.

Watching Mum that night was hysterical. She would work the room, gathering intel, and subliminally bully people into buying paintings. Like a lioness stalking then attacking a wildebeest, she'd drift around the room in hyper-stealth mode, then she'd see someone on their own admiring one of the paintings and she'd pounce.

'Aren't they beautiful paintings? This is one of the last ones available, you know. Nearly everything else is sold. I've seen five other people interested in buying this, you should act quickly. What about this artist, isn't she amazing?!'

Martine needed absolutely no help selling those paintings, absolutely no help whatsoever, but if she did, Mum would be the best marketing person since the actual Wolf of Wall Street.

It made complete sense when Mum caught Martine's eye at one point and mouthed the words, 'I love you, I'm so proud of you!'

(It's such a cliché for a son to say his mum is the best mum in the world, but I actually believe that. How did Mum support us all in such varied endeavours and directions? How did she focus on us all equally, and know exactly what each of us needed? How did she know the answers to the girls' questions about Physical Culture and *my* questions about karate? How did she know the answers to the girls' dating questions and *my* questions about fishing bait?

She must've been making it up as she went along, because there's no book on how to raise a successful psychologist, a game-show host bimbo and a world-famous artist all at the same time.)

Martine's first show was the start of her CBD – CorkBoard Domination. After this, the invitations to her shows got prime spot.

She has gone on to become a hugely successful artist with sell-out shows, and we are all desperately proud of her and desperately pissed off we didn't buy more of her paintings when they were cheaper.

Then pictures of the grandkids started flooding the corkboard. The Battle for Cork was getting brutal. At one stage I even suggested to my wife, Sylvie, that we have another baby after our kids, Jye and Tia, were born, just to reclaim some corkboard space. (Yes, you're right, just another poor attempt at talking my wife into sex.)

But then some of Martine's big paintings started appearing around Mum and Dad's house. These gazumped anything and everything else. Sure, maybe I could talk Sylvie into having more sex with a view to perhaps getting a photo of a new grandchild up on the corkboard, but the only way I could ever really compete with Martine's beautiful paintings would be to come around to Mum's house with the entire *Price Is Right* crew – lighting, cameras, models and our announcer, Cossie – then when she gets home from shopping I get her to put her groceries in order from least expensive to most expensive on the kitchen bench. *Beat that, arty-farty Marty!*

Now there are some beautiful new *great*-grandkids on the scene: Leon, Billie and Clementine. COVID-19 has kept us apart in these early days of your lives, but I can't wait to be a great great-uncle to you all for the rest of my life.

I hope one day you read this book and feel just a *little* bit guilty that you knocked all us oldies off the corkboard. You're all so cute but SO selfish!

That said, with all *your* photos on the corkboard, well, I surrender. How can I compete with *that*? I was recently on the cover of *TV Week*. Thirty years ago that would've gone straight to the middle of the corkboard; now it's lucky to get a spot on the shelf under the coffee table. Wow, being famous isn't what it used to be.

Once upon a time, newspaper articles about my TV shows would get up there too, but there was one rare time I had to ask Mum to take an article *down*. It was when *The Main Event* got axed in 1992, and it included a huge pic of me on the beach with our dog, Grinner.

I said, 'Mum, can you take that one off? It's a really shitty story about horrible ratings dragging down the network.'

She said, 'Yes, maybe, but it's *such* a lovely photo.'

I *love* it that our mum is hardwired only to see good.

Becoming an Egomaniacal Wanker

1973

Long before becoming a fully fledged, card-carrying, self-centred, egomaniacal TV wanker, I was just a normal, freckly-faced, toothless little kid at primary school who apparently, upon reflection, always craved attention. I realise that's hard to believe.

I knew I didn't really stand a chance at the annual Rose Bay Public School marching parade. There were some very good marchers there. A lot of the girls were into Physie like Martine, and they all looked magnificent, marching around the playground like they were in Trooping the Colour. Most of the boys looked pretty stupid, but some had clearly been to the library and found books on how to march. Bloody cheats.

During practice, my socks kept falling down, I was a[lways] out of step, and my thumbs looked like two little undercoo[ked] frankfurters blowing in the breeze. I was a limp, out-of-time mass of jelly, jelly that hadn't quite set yet.

But something deep inside me wanted that podium finish. That trophy that would prove to the world I was better than everybody else. A deep-seated ego and self-importance were bubbling away just under the surface of this nine-year-old who would one day grow up to absolutely love himself sick on TV.

The night before The Big Day I marched on the spot in front of the mirror, practising my thumb work. The hands had to be tightly cupped into a strong fist, thumbs pointed accurately downward with purpose.

The right arm swung forward together with the left leg, and then came the challenging bit: the left arm swung forward together with the right leg, all in one fluid motion, and all while trying to remember to keep the hands cupped tight and thumbs pointing directly down.

The temptation when clenching one's hands to make a fist is to stiffen one's arms, but this would ultimately lead to one's instant elimination. The arms must appear to hang straight down, unstiffly, and swing naturally.

Mum could see I really wanted this, and made a fine contribution to my Olympic-esque marching campaign. She had a shoebox full of sewing stuff on the floor under her sewing table, right next to the foot pedal for her Singer sewing machine. She grabbed a roll of elastic, then ran her measuring tape around my legs just under the knee. She lovingly cut two bits of elastic off the roll; I've always had skinny little chicken legs, so she didn't need much. Then she tied them into two little stretchy circles – yep, that's right, she didn't run them through the sewing machine for ten seconds, just tied them with a lumpy knot. These elastic circles were to keep my socks up.

She had no other advice for me. Her high-impact, world-beating, tender contribution was to help me keep my socks up.

Competition day arrived. I was ready, my thumbs were ready, and my socks were locked in position so tightly I could barely feel my toes.

We all marched around the playground in a perfect rectangle. My thumbs were so stiff they were almost pointing backwards. Such was my dedication to the thumb component of the competition that my double-jointed thumbs and I very nearly made the transition from primary-school marcher to traditional Thai dancer.

I nailed the turns at every corner of the playground, working particularly hard around the top of the rectangle where the judging panel of teachers was sitting. As I got close to them, I puffed out my little chest and unstiffened my little arms, while adding stiffness to my little thumbs. My little chicken legs firmly forced my little feet firmly into the asphalt with each step.

I had Bata Scout school shoes, with a lion pawprint on each sole and a compass in the heel. I guess the idea was that if I got lost on the way home from school, the cops could find me by following the lion pawprints along the street. Alternatively, if I lost my way between the classroom and the school pick-up line, then I could always navigate the sixty-metre straight line across the schoolyard using the compass in my heel. I was so excited when I first got them, but as it turned out, I never needed to use either of these innovative options.

As I marched on, I could feel the little compass click every time my foot hit the ground. It was like my own little metronome, keeping me focused and in time.

I was now full of confidence. Mum's secret elastic bands were keeping my socks perfectly in position, even if they were so tight I could feel my circulation being cut. After all, farmers use this elastic-band technique to castrate sheep: they snap the elastic band on and eventually the testicles just fall off. But numb legs that were potentially going to fall off by day's end were a small price to pay for marching glory.

I could see the boy in front of me losing his rhythm, his left sock sliding further down his leg with each step.

'See ya later, loser!' I muttered as he was tapped out by the teachers.

The line of contestants was thinning with each lap, as the teachers picked off the weak and the frail. I was getting some sort of lactic-acid buildup where my thumbs joined my hands, but I hung in there.

Could this be happening? Was I about to do a Steven Bradbury even before Steven Bradbury did a Steven Bradbury?

Suddenly I was the last man-boy standing. *I'd won the trophy!!!*

I never got to win the Mirrorball Trophy on *Dancing with the Stars*, so this would be the highlight of my achievements in the performing arts. There I was, up on the podium, looking down at all the losers with their floppy thumbs and their socks round their ankles. Enjoying my time in the spotlight. I realised this was where I always wanted to be: the centre of attention, with everyone looking at me.

My newfound hunger for showing off escalated quickly, and I yearned for another chance to draw attention to myself.

*

Being chosen to ring the school bell at lunchtime was a real honour. Of all the kids in the school, the deputy headmaster had chosen *me* to leave class two minutes early, go out into the playground and ring the bell.

(I've never won a Logie, so I don't really know what that feels like, but I imagine it's pretty similar.)

OK, to be very clear, and in the name of factual reporting (said no one about anything I've ever written in my career EVER), *every* kid got to do this at some point, and I was probably one of the last in my year, but don't you dare try to steal this moment from me.

With my classic Little Lazza 'one sock up, one sock down' look on my skinny little hairless chook legs, my shirt half untucked (or half tucked in, YOU get to decide in this interactive book), and my little freckly-faced rebel swagger, I strode across the playground, firmly focused on the bell pole and knowing it was my time to give this dong the best dinging it had ever had.

Not a *ding dong ding dong*, or a *dong dong dong ding dong ding*, oh noooo, this was going to be a special moment in the history of the bell.

I reached up and grabbed Sally with both hands.

Did you know a bell rope is called Sally? I really hope you didn't, so you can say you've learnt at least one thing from reading this book, apart from the fact I had a semi-permanent erection between the ages of eleven and thirteen.

Well, today I was going to pull Sally with such enthusiasm and creativity that I would reimagine the entire bell-ringing tradition. I was going to change the tune to such an extent that they might even change the name of the bell rope from Sally to Larry, and from that day forth, every man, woman and child who was chosen to ring any bell anywhere in the world would have to reach up and pull Larry.

I danged and donged and dinged and pulled harder, faster, slowed it down, sped it up, did a few little rapid-fire pulls and paused for dramatic effect, then Sally and I exploded with a toe-curling tsunami of a dong, swirling to an operatic crescendo that would've had neighbours within a one-and-a-half-kilometre radius of the school weeping with joy.

I was *really* getting into this! All the kids from all the classrooms had their faces pressed against the windows, watching this performance. I was the centre of attention again, this was my happy place, this was how I wanted to spend my life, performing, bringing joy and delight to those watching me …

Suddenly the deputy headmaster put his head out of his office window and screamed across the playground: 'OY!!!!'

Surprisingly, this was the last time I got to ring the bell, but the seeds of ambition and lifelong yearning to be in the spotlight had been planted – despite the fact that the bell rope is still called Sally.

'Young Man, Get Your Hand Off My Balls!'

1975

We were two strapping young men in Speedos, and we needed cash. We were desperate enough to head down a dark path of dirty crime and dirty money. We were good kids from good families, but this is the regretful, shameful tale of where it all came unstuck.

I just wanted you to hear this from me first, before you heard it on some crime podcast, where they've used modern technology and new DNA science to crack unsolved mysteries from decades ago.

I feel ashamed to say this now, but my best mate Robbie Mayer and I started grabbing balls for cash.

You see, we had an addiction to Surf Shakes from Jimmy's Milk Bar at the North Bondi bus terminus. Jimmy had invented this shake, the thickest thickshake known to man. Take a big, tall, steel milkshake cup, milk, unflavoured ice cream, a giant scoop of malt and a generous bloootch of your favourite flavour, then let the four-shaft stainless-steel mixer work its magic.

You needed every muscle in your face to work at full throttle to get that malty murkiness through the paper straw and into your mouth. The best bit was right at the bottom of the huge cup, but it was almost impossible for a human to suck this up – for this you'd need a bilge pump.

Jimmy said McDonald's stole his idea, and we believed him.

Jimmy would leave the thickshake thickening long enough to walk across the black and white chequered linoleum floor to the lolly counter and grab me a bunch of the two-for-one-cent lollies. I'd usually go for the Cobbers and the Snakes.

We'd save up some of our pocket money, or find some in the ashtrays of our parents' cars or down the back of the couch (both of those references are code for 'steal from their drawers or handbags'), and if we didn't have enough money for *two* Surf Shakes, we'd get one and share.

But then one day a pinball machine appeared in Jimmy's Milk Bar, and this changed our world. We played it a few times and got just a *little bit* addicted. Now we had a Surf Shake addiction *and* a pinball-machine addiction, and now we also had a funding issue – as in, we had no funds.

Robbie lived on the corner of Military Road and Hastings Parade, and his house backed onto the North Bondi golf course. There was a little hill at the end of his backyard that was the edge of the golf course, and you'd regularly hear balls fly past and land nearby with a thud.

Golfers would rarely venture into the rough to retrieve a lost ball. And the hill at the end of Robbie's yard was pretty bushy terrain, kind of a graveyard. If your ball had gone in there, you'd leave it for dead.

So Robbie and I started collecting them. We got a bucketful and thought we'd take them to the pro golf shop to see if they wanted them back.

The guy in the shop said he'd give us $5 for the bucket. Five dollars! Holy crap, had we just won Lotto? Was this what it felt like being rich? Let's buy a Rolls-Royce! Let's buy a superyacht!!! Five dollars – that's five hundred cents, or a thousand lollies from the two-for-one-cent jars at Jimmy's. At this rate we'd be retired before we got pubic hair!

We *had* to go back and get more balls!

Soon enough, though, the legal supply of voluntarily abandoned balls dried up. We'd crawled through all the dense scrub along the back of Robbie's row of houses and retrieved every long-lost, forgotten ball.

We had to ramp up our innocent little operation; we had to go next-level. We had to think like criminals. *We had to steal balls*.

We were like the Bonnie and Clyde of Bondi, just with more balls, *buckets* more balls.

Until now, our field of operation had been the bushes where golfers dared not venture, but once we made this commitment to a life of crime, we decided we'd jump out and steal the balls when they landed just *in front* of the bushes, while still on the golf course and still very much in play.

We decided we'd hide in the oleander bushes at the top of the first hole.

It wasn't till nearly fifty years later, when I entered 'oleander' into Google while researching this book, that I found out oleanders are actually poisonous. Oh, well, I guess I'll put that

'YOUNG MAN, GET YOUR HAND OFF MY BALLS!'

in the 'Thank God I'm Still Alive' file, along with that time I picked up a really pretty octopus with bright blue rings in a rockpool at North Bondi and said, 'Look, Mum, look how pretty this octopus is with its bright blue rings, these rings are so bright and so blue, I've never seen such a pretty octopus, can we take it home?'

We'd go to Robbie's house after school and stay in our school uniforms, thinking the khaki would be good camouflage in the lower shrubbery of the oleander bushes, sort of around where they are at their most poisonous. We'd crawl up under the oleander bushes till we were nearly on the golf course, then wait for the balls to land close to us. We were about a hundred and thirty metres away from the first tee, which ran up a hill.

A ball would land close to us, and when we thought the time was right, we'd crawl out a few metres on our tummies, grab it, quickly crawl back into the bushes, and wait for the next one.

The golfers who knew they'd hit their balls close to the bushes would look in from the edges and give up, thinking their balls had just rolled down into the impenetrable thick stuff. We'd try not to giggle as they beat around the bush with their clubs.

We got *very* good at this. We'd get a bucketful of mainly stolen balls and take it round to the pro shop and get our $5, then cross the road to Jimmy's to get a thickshake and have a game or two on the pinball machine.

One time, a golf ball landed just near us, but further back in the bushes. I crawled back and grabbed it, then a voice boomed from the green: '*Young man, get your hand off my balls!*'

We laughed and scrambled on our hands and knees down through the bushes to Robbie's yard at the bottom of the hill. There was no way a grown-up was following us through there. A grown-up was smart enough to know that he'd never catch us — and, more importantly, smart enough to know those oleander bushes were poisonous.

It's difficult to confess that as an eleven-year-old I made money grabbing strange men's balls, but hey, it's a cruel world and a boy's gotta do what a boy's gotta do, am I right?

I'd like to take this opportunity to sincerely thank my editor and publisher for talking me out of my initial idea for the title of this book: *I Made Money Grabbing Strange Men's Balls.*

I believe that was a prudent decision.

Once I got seriously into surfing in my early teens, I needed money for surf stuff. You could pick up a cheap, second-hand, bashed-up fibreglass surfboard for about $40 or $50, but the new ones were $100 or more. So I needed to find another employer who was happy to exploit children for a few bucks here and there.

All my friends had part-time jobs; I was the lazy one who didn't. All I wanted to do was surf, but I could see they were all pretty pleased with the teeny, tiny amount of money pimply-faced teenagers were getting per hour back in the 1970s.

I'd washed Mum's and Dad's cars as many times as I possibly could for $1 a pop. Now I needed to get a *real* job, and earn some proper cash to fund my obsession.

Most days after a surf we would all walk up across the park and across Campbell Parade, the main drag that runs along the top of Bondi Beach. If our mums had given us some lunch money, we would get some fish and chips, or sometimes just chips. Otherwise we'd all lay our boards on the footpath outside Vallis's Milk Bar and go in and play the pinnies for a while.

Thinking back, Campbell Parade was in a horrible state back then: rusty shop awnings literally falling down, cracked paint and tiles on the shop fronts, a wonky footpath … nothing worthy of the world's most famous beach.

I do remember the smells. As you walked past the fish and chip shop, you'd get that waft of deep-frying batter and vinegar over hot chips; as you walked past Vallis's Milk Bar, you'd get the smell of burger patties sizzling on the grill; then you'd head past Nino's or Papa Giovanni pizza for that classic melting-cheese, garlic-seafood and burning-Meat-Lovers' smell.

Years ago, Wikipedia reported that my first job was walking up and down Bondi Beach handing out pamphlets advertising my dad's Turkish kebab joint. I still get asked today if I'm of Turkish descent – which I'm definitely not – but I *did* spend a heck of a lot of time at the kebab joint at Bondi.

It's worth noting that Wikipedia has twice reported my death. My favourite version was that I drowned in my own vomit after a three-day drug binge in a gay sex den on Oxford Street. (I may revisit this later in the book, in the grown-up bit. As we're now in the early-teens bit, I really don't want you distracted with vomit drownings, drug binges and gay-sex-den stories. Kind of off track in this chapter, yeah?)

Anyway ... as I walked with my mates along Campbell Parade, I could see Dairy Queen being built – well, you never knew exactly what was going on behind the plywood, but you could hear and see that something new was coming. This was common along Campbell Parade; not many businesses survived the winter. A new ice-cream or burger place would open up before summer and go gangbusters, then you'd see the 'For Lease' sign up the next winter as business dropped to zero.

Soon Dairy Queen was starting to look pretty flash. Apparently it was a big American burger chain that had made its way to Australia to give Macca's a run for its money. The fitout was looking bright and loud, a real standout against the milk bars, newsagent, fish and chip shop and pizza shops.

Up went the sign: 'Staff Wanted'. And I thought, 'Well, I love burgers and it's a couple of hundred steps from the surf – I can do this.' It wasn't burning ambition – more like 'Ho hum', because I wanted a new surfboard.

It was the same feeling of half-cocked motivation I had when they asked me to host *Celebrity Dog School* and I said NO, but Sylvie wanted a new kitchen so I said YES.

So I put my surfboard on the footpath outside the shop and went in – barefoot, wet boardshorts, no shirt, long hair, pimples, the full *Puberty Blues* package.

Before I said anything, the boss snapped: 'Don't put your board there, you've blocked the door to the shop.'

It wasn't blocking the door at all, he was just being a dick, and now we're off to a pretty bad start.

'Have you got any casual jobs going?' I asked.

He was wearing a ridiculous uniform – I don't remember how it looked exactly, but monkey-vomit yellow with a hint of tartan rings a bell – though to be fair I was in no position to judge anything or anyone. He kind of looked around behind me at the trail of sand my feet had left on his new tiles and sniped, 'Well, one of your first jobs could be cleaning up your own mess.'

This job interview wasn't going so well, and I didn't really care. But he said I could start the next day, a Friday, at 5 pm for a four-hour shift. This fitted into my busy lifestyle perfectly: home from school, straight down to the surf then run up to my new job.

I filled out a form, then he gave me a shirt and slacks on a coathanger, along with a cap – a ridiculous cap that perfectly matched the ridiculous uniform.

I said, 'Thanks, see ya tomorrow!', and walked out. There were still waves to be caught, so I grabbed my board and ran back down to the beach. On the way, I took the clothes off the hanger and rolled them into a ball with my towel.

The next day, home from school, I grabbed the uniform ball off the floor and jammed it all into my backpack then raced down for a quick surf.

I jumped out of the surf about fifteen minutes before my new career was due to start and raced up to Dairy Queen, put my board on the footpath outside, got a towel out of my backpack, ripped my boardies off, gave my Speedos an extra wipe to dry them a bit more, pulled out the ball of Dairy Queen uniform and threw it on.

It was completely crumpled and wrinkled, nothing like the freshly preened package the boss had handed me the day before.

I put on my Dunlop Volleys and went inside. I was salty and my hair was matted and crazy, but I don't remember ever *not* feeling that way in those days. I would always surf before school and sometimes not have time for a shower, so I just remember this feeling of being constantly entombed in dry, salty seawater.

I must've looked ridiculous; in retrospect, *I* would've sacked me then and there.

The boss was disappointed, but he only had four kids working and he needed two out the front and two behind, so he had to keep me on.

He told me I had two jobs: doing the soft-serve cones and sweeping up after anyone had come in with wet or sandy feet. I mean, who'd be disrespectful and bratty enough to do that? Honestly.

He gave me about a five-minute lesson on the soft-serve machine. It was pretty simple: hold the cone underneath the nozzle, pull the handle, make sure the ice cream goes into the cone, move the cone in small circles to get that whole Mr Whippy swirly shape, then when the machine clunks that means the serve is done. You give it a little twist for that decorative pointy shape at the top, turn to the customer with a big Dairy Queen smile, and that's it.

'What if I mess it up?' I asked.

He said, 'Well, you can give that one to the customer free of charge, but it'd be better if you *didn't* mess it up.' It definitely wasn't rocket surgery.

Mum and my sisters were the first customers to appear. They stood at the door watching me 'work'. They couldn't believe I actually had a job. I looked up and saw Mum, and she put her hand on her heart and mouthed the words, 'I love you, I'm so proud of you!'

They came in and Mum said something about my crumpled uniform. She couldn't believe they would hand out a uniform without ironing it first.

Then they ordered some burgers and I got to make them a soft serve each. I was still very new at this, so of course I screwed one up, and they got it for free. OK, so now I'm Mum's favourite child, scamming the system and saving her twenty-five cents.

It was a busy shift and soon I was getting pretty slick on the old soft-serve machine. I don't want to say I was absolutely brilliant at the little decorative twist at the top of the ice cream, but yeah, I was.

Then my mates came in, five of them. I made three soft serves perfectly, then unfortunately I really *really* messed up the last two. So I called the boss over, apologised and gave two of my mates their free ice creams.

The boss wasn't happy, but it wasn't about how happy or unhappy *he* was, it was clearly about how happy *my mates* were. I had just been elevated to Best Friend status and word soon got out that I was the go-to guy for free ice creams at Dairy Queen.

What? First Little Larry stole golf balls, now he's purposely messing up soft serves so his mates get them for free? I'm more than slightly worried this smart side-hustle of authoring books could land me in prison on historical 'ball grabbing' and 'fudging soft serve'.

Now, according to my mate Wikipedia, Dairy Queen ice cream isn't even ice cream. To be classified as ice cream, the product needs to contain at least ten per cent butterfat, and Dairy Queen's has just five per cent. It's only *half* ice cream.

So by giving away *half* the orders, I was really just doing my bit to balance up nature.

I was the Robin Hood of Bondi, stealing from the rich Queen to give to the poor surfers. I was heroically guilt-free as I lavished broken blobs of butterfat on my merry men.

I was handing out soft serves like Oprah handing out cars, and they were lining up outside, sandy feet as far as the eye could see, a huge pile of surfboards blocking the entrance to the shop. It was a beautiful sight.

At the end of the four-hour shift, I got my $10. 'This is great,' I thought, 'this is going to change my life. A few shifts a week and not only will I be able to buy a new board, I'll also be the most popular guy in Bondi.'

So I rocked up again the next day for my shift, feeling pretty pumped.

But just after I walked in, he sacked me.

Wait! What? I didn't understand.

I'm only new to this whole 'employment' thing, but you're telling me that turning up unshowered with long, wet, matted hair and zinc cream on my nose and lips, wearing a crinkled uniform with the wetness from my Speedos seeping through the Dairy Queen trousers, then giving away half the evening's profits by way of fraudulently faulty soft serves is *sackable*???

This grown-up legitimate work world is crazy. I want to go back to an easy life of crime, stealing golf balls. I was my own boss, worked my own hours; no uniforms, no butterfat issues.

'Hey, Dad, can I wash the car for $1?'

'No, mate, you washed it on Saturday and twice on Sunday, and it's only Tuesday so it should be right for a while.'

'Damn!'

I needed work. I'd had a taste of money and I wanted more. I'd had that sweet, sweet feeling of five- and ten-cent coins jingling around in the secret coin pocket of my Golden Breed boardshorts and it was a good feeling. I was going to write 'greed is good' here, but due to copyright issues I'll go with 'greediness is great'.

Nino's Pizza was on the corner of Campbell Parade and Hall Street, the priceless corner position where the Hotel Ravesis is now. There was a proper pizza battle between Nino's and Papa Giovanni just a bit further down Campbell Parade.

Nino's pizzas were classic, traditional.

There was never any internet debate about whether pineapple should be on a pizza or not, it just *was*. It was called a Hawaiian, which meant people in Hawaii must've eaten it that way, and we were all watching *Hawaii Five-0* back then and it was really cool, so pineapple on pizza was cool.

There was never any Auspol survey as to whether anchovies should be on the pizza with the capsicum and pineapple and bacon and mushroom. If anchovies were good enough for the ancient Romans because they were cheap and easily preserved, then those were exactly the same qualities I wanted on my pizza in the '70s: cheap and easily preserved. So chuck as many of those little hairy fish on there as you can.

One night, my mate Dobbo and I went into Nino's to grab a Hawaiian Pizza. We were in there quite a bit and they knew us well. Back then, Bondi was a nice, close community; the kids felt safe roaming the streets at night, and all the locals knew each other.

We waited for the pizza to make its way through the oven on its little conveyor belt, chatting about nothing in particular. (Well, actually, we were probably chatting about surfing, that was all we knew. I know for sure it wouldn't have been an intellectual conversation about politics, world affairs or whether pineapple belongs on pizza.)

As the pizza got towards the end of the conveyor belt – the bit where the edges of the base get crispy and the cheese starts to burn and bubble, like the skin on my nose after six hours in the surf – one of the guys asked if we wanted a job.

We were definitely chasing money, and we definitely loved pizzas. And ever since I'd stood on that podium at Rose Bay Public School and been awarded that marching trophy, I'd yearned to once again stand before a huge crowd of admiring fans and be the focus of their adoration. That guy standing at the front of Nino's masterfully kneading the dough then tossing a spinning pizza base into the air until it somehow stretched into a perfectly round pizza shape was mesmerising. Everyone would stop to watch; he would flirt with the female customers, and if he did an extra-high spin the little kids would clap. Perhaps this pizza shop was the obvious next step in my pursuit of a career as a professional show-off?

Yeah, I want to work at Nino's Pizza; yeah, I'll take that rockstar job!

Next minute, Dobbo and I are sitting in the very back corner of the restaurant, folding and stapling pizza boxes.

It wasn't exactly the glamour gig I'd had in mind. You're not seeing *that* on any guy's Tinder profile, are you? 'I work in the back corner of a pizza joint, folding and stapling pizza boxes.' He would be the second-most swiped-left-upon guy on Tinder, close behind the guy with 'I won the marching competition at primary school, it's all about the thumbs' on his profile.

Girls were *not* coming up and flirting with us, kids were *not* watching us fold then staple boxes and clapping and saying, 'Wow, can you do that again?!'

The guy set us up with a huge pile of flat boxes. Dobbo would fold them in half to form a top and a bottom, and fold the corners inwards, as per the perforations, then he'd slide them across the table and I would staple them and put the completed boxes in a pile up against the wall behind me.

Dobbo and I were like a well-oiled machine – a well-oiled, underage, underpaid, child-labour-ish type machine.

I wasn't competitive, but I like to think *my* job was the more important. Any monkey could fold cardboard along perforations, but it was the strategically placed staples that would maintain the boxes' structural integrity. If I didn't do my job properly, pizzas would be sliding out of those boxes every time the car in which they were travelling home to a hungry family took a sharp left turn.

We got really good at it, and in no time at all the stack of flat boxes was folded and stapled and piling up everywhere. At one stage the guy told us to slow down, as our mountain of freshly built pizza boxes was encroaching on the restaurant.

Then I heard 'Larry, Larry, Larry!' and looked up to see Mum at the front door of the restaurant. The place was full and there were plenty of tables of diners between us, and in getting my attention she'd also managed to get the attention of every single person between the front door and where we were at the back.

So now everyone's looking at Mum as she puts her hand on her heart and mouths the words, 'I love you, I'm so proud of you!'

I shooed her away. This was more than a bit embarrassing. How proud can a mum really be of a son who's stapling pizza boxes? Seriously?

I didn't see Charmaine, *Dobbo's* very proud mum, yelling out across a crowded restaurant: 'Oh, darling, I'm so proud of you for perfectly folding those corners in! You're doing an amazing job, even though all you have to do is follow the perforations, so technically it's impossible to screw up, clearly Larry's job is much more challenging, complex and difficult, but I love you anyway, I'm so proud of you!'

Now, if the mother of the pizza-spinning guy at the front of the shop came past and did that, it would make a lot of sense. But a mum saying she's proud of her son stapling, it just doesn't.

When we'd first heard the deal, it sounded great. We'd get $5 each for the night and all the pizza we could eat. Yes, the money was important, but it was the second part of the proposition that *really* got us excited.

That first night I said to Dobbo: 'When they ask us what pizza we want, let's go for the Supreme *and* the Hawaiian.' So we kept folding and stapling and waiting for someone to come and ask us what we wanted for dinner.

Then, on his way back from clearing a table, the boss walked up with a big round tray with two leftover slices of pizza on it and said, 'Here ya go, boys.'

When someone says 'all the pizza you can eat', would you automatically think they mean nice fresh pizzas, or would you automatically think they mean slices of pizza coming back to the kitchen that customers haven't finished?

We got to taste pretty much everything on the menu that night. I'd never tried the Number Eight with Extra Pepperoni before, and I'd never had the Spaghetti Carbonara or the Cannelloni. But now I was getting to sample everything, even if it was just cold, soggy leftovers.

At one point, a few slices of Margarita and a few slices of Meat Lovers' Pizza landed on our table, so we creatively spread some meat over the Margarita to create a Meatarita. We thought this was brilliant, but in fact all a Meat Lovers' Pizza really was, was meat on a Margarita anyway, so by taking the meat off the Meat Lovers' to put on the Margarita we'd just accidentally turned the Meat Lovers' into a Margarita. Had we just reinvented the wheel, twice?

We got to try *so* many things that night – quite possibly including, but not limited to, hepatitis A, B, C, D and E.

Didn't matter, it was forty-five years before COVID.

We only did a few shifts, then the surf got really, really good and I think we just didn't turn up one afternoon. Pizza-stapling career over.

'Hey, Mum and Dad, can I wash your cars?'

'Too Much Tongue!!!'
1976

I'd tell her I loved her over and over again. I never even looked sideways at another woman. I was completely devoted to Abigail.

I would think about her day and night, and would bore my friends stupid telling them all about her. They'd be like, 'Ohhh, no, not *another* Abigail story!' as I'd regale them with yet another brilliant Abi tale. Sometimes I'd tell them about the sex, sometimes I'd tell them about what she'd been wearing last night, or maybe just about something funny or adorable she'd said. Although they'd never met her, my friends felt like they knew her.

She was everything I'd ever wanted or needed in a partner. It's probably the only time in my life I've looked at someone and immediately thought I could spend every day of the rest of my life with them, no question, no doubt.

Abigail was the ultimate sex siren. I loved her like I'd never loved a woman before.

'TOO MUCH TONGUE!!!'

After going to bed on school nights, I would sneak back out to the lounge room at 8.30 while Mum and Dad were watching TV. I'd kneel silently, stealthily behind the couch like David Attenborough stalking a screaming hairy armadillo in Paraguay. Our lounge setting was bamboo, and there were just enough gaps between the bamboo stems and the cushions for me to catch glimpses of the show they were watching.

Number 96.

Abigail was the star of the show, and my girlfriend, although she didn't know about our relationship. But that didn't bother me too much.

An incredibly raunchy show for its time, it had boobs and bums aplenty, and lots of passionate kissing. In fact, it had everything a prepubescent boy needed. I'd sit quietly, pressing my face between the bamboo in anticipation of Abigail's arrival on screen.

After a drawn-out and particularly one-sided romance, I finally, tragically realised we probably had no future together, so I built up the courage to break up with my beloved. It was a pretty sad moment but, as they say in the classics, it wasn't her, it was me.

I'm ashamed to admit it, but if I'm being totally honest with you, in reality I'd already started cheating on Abigail with my new love, Raquel Welch.

She was everything I'd ever wanted or needed in a partner. It's probably the only time in my life I've looked at someone and immediately thought I could spend every day of the rest of my life with them, no question, no doubt.

I was eleven, single and ready to mingle; she was thirty-five and a huge Hollywood superstar. We were perfect for each other, and to me, it just felt right. She had stolen my heart; I would've given her my entire collection of Hot Wheels cars, that was how much she meant to me.

I didn't know too much about kissing, only what I'd seen Abigail do on *Number 96*, and only what I'd practised by rubbing my face on the Raquel Welch poster in my bedroom. But as an eleven-year-old, I was painfully shy around *real* girls.

I'd seen boys and girls kiss behind the school sheds and near the car park. How did those boys get so close to those girls? They were kissing like in the movies, with their tongues and stuff. I was like, 'WOW, I wonder when *I'll* get to do that!'

Some kids my age were right into Kiss Chase. It was a schoolyard game where girls would chase a boy around the playground, and when they caught him they would kiss them. They were always very quick, clunky, tight-lipped kisses, probably not long enough to pass on a cold sore, but perhaps long enough to trigger a little bit of movement in my too-tight shorts.

From memory, most of the guys being cruelly targeted by these Kiss Chase assassins would have their shirts fully untucked in readiness to conceal any prepubescent razzle-dazzle in the groinal precinct.

For some reason, Kiss Chase at Rose Bay Public School soon morphed into a not-so-romantic fusion of *Gladiator* and *Squid Game*.

For some reason, one fateful day, I was targeted by a Pash and Dash squad. A group of highly efficient young girls who hunted in a pack.

Using stalking techniques developed by velociraptors over eighty million years ago, they were inescapable. You remember the scene in *Jurassic Park*? It was just like that. One cute little velociraptor would flirt with you while the others hid in the bushes and behind the buildings. As the cutie distracted you

'TOO MUCH TONGUE!!!'

with her big eyes and adorable slow-motion blinking, the others would move in from every direction, then their hunting trap would tighten with deadly, razor-sharp precision.

Today, however, the Pash and Dash squad weren't acting alone. I don't know how many Vegemite sandwiches or Space Food Sticks it cost them, but the girls somehow made a deal with my friends to trap me. Who knew girls could get guys to do whatever they wanted them to?

Robbie Mayer and a couple of other mates grabbed me, backed me up to the bell pole and held my hands tightly, while the girls grabbed Diana Strum.

I liked Diana a lot – as a friend – but now the scrum was pushing her and her puckered-up lips across the playground towards me at a great rate of knots.

I was trapped firmly in place. I was nervous, but I was nimble. If the *Matrix* had've been released by that point I probably would've tried one of those classic Keanu moves where he throws his legs up over his head, and in doing so twists the arms of the two bad guys in a knot that ultimately smashes their heads together, so they fall to the ground and he escapes.

But the movie wasn't out yet, so I didn't know that move; the only great escapes I'd ever seen were on *Road Runner* cartoons.

Diana was coming towards me fast, her lips focused on mine like one of those laser missiles homing in on its target.

She got within a metre, and I ducked.

It was too late for her friends to stop – they just had a ridiculous amount of smooch momentum. I heard Diana's nose break as her face smashed into the pole just above my head.

I felt *so* bad for my friend. I would never have intentionally hurt her, she knew that. It was just a silly split-second impulsive move that ended badly.

We all got the cane, and deservedly so.

I recently found Diana on social media and requested her permission to tell this story. She replied, 'Yes, of course you can, but I think you still owe me a nose job.'

*

Deep down I knew I still wanted to kiss a girl one day, but I didn't know how and I didn't know who. Which, when you think about it, are pretty much the top two vital ingredients in the whole kissing thing.

After a while, the cold, hard reality set in: I was shy and awkward, and I was never just going to walk up to a girl and say, 'Hey, do you wanna kiss?', which was what other boys were doing.

No no no, that wasn't for me, so instead, I would somehow have to insert myself into one of those ancient witchcraft-esque ceremonies of Spin the Bottle.

For those of you who don't know Spin the Bottle, firstly get a life, secondly it's friggin' awesome. A bunch of guys and girls sit round in a circle and take turns to spin a bottle in the middle. When it's your go you spin, and when the bottle stops you kiss whichever girl the top end is pointing to.

I know what you're thinking: 'How romantic, if not ever-so-slightly unhygienic.' (But I'd survived putting my mouth near the water bubbler at the North Bondi kiddies' pool, so I reckon my lips were like something out of *The X-Men*, germ-repellent and lizardy.)

We were in the park behind Dover Heights Girls' High School, now Rose Bay Secondary College. My mum and both my sisters went to school there, and now I was about to lose my kissing virginity there, so it's a very sacred place for us Emdurs. I dare say I wasn't the *only* Emdur to have a pash in this park.

Of course, each person in the circle that day had most likely already chosen the person they *actually* wanted to kiss. Each of us knew we would probably have to kiss a few people we didn't necessarily want to along the way, before the bottle eventually stopped at our dream option. By the time this happened, your dream girl might have kissed five or six other boys, so maybe the appeal had less appeal than it had when you first sat down.

By the time it was my turn, a few others had had a go, so I'd got to see up close how it was done. I was still pretty nervous, but I felt ready. I was cocked and loaded and my tongue was bursting to jump out of my mouth and into someone else's gob.

My tongue had been hiding in its dark, moist cave for twelve years, busting to get out and play with another of its kind. I had trained it and tamed it, it had been doing push-ups and sit-ups, yoga and Pilates – and this is where I'd ideally aim to insert a *Karate Kid* reference, but to avoid copyright issues, for this next bit I'll be replacing the word 'wax' with the word 'cumquat'.

I was like Mr Miyagi and my tongue was like the Karate Kid. I was teaching it poise and patience. Cumquat on, cumquat off ... we'd go through it over and over again, and now it was Fight Night ...

My tongue was a bit like a bull at a gate, and as I got close to her, I'm pretty sure the bull jumped prematurely. So from where she was sitting, she would've seen my tongue already out of my mouth and darting around like an echidna eating a whole nest of ants. I was coming towards her with unbridled enthusiasm, zero class and less-than-zero romance, tact or breath mints.

We connected, and immediately she pushed me away.

'Too much tongue!!!' she yelled.

How the hell would I know how much tongue was the right amount? Was there an international body that dictated tongue depth and pressure? Was there a Tonguethagorus's Theorem or a book I should've read? I'd only seen a few other couples do it and I thought I had it right.

Apparently it's meant to be more gentle-lollipop-licking and less All-Black-front-rower-doing-the-Haka. Who knew?!?

Nowadays you just google 'How to tongue-kiss'. Masterclass. com offers this impressive, um, masterclass:

> **Initiate a French kiss.** After a few tongueless kisses, begin lightly brushing your tongue along your partner's lips … If you receive the green light to deepen the kiss, part your lips and gently use your tongue to stimulate your partner's lips and tongue. Run your tongue along their lips or slide your tongue along theirs. Take it slowly and gently, allowing the intensity to build as you match your partner's energy and movements.

I did none of that. I wish I'd had Google then – but I also wish I'd bought every apartment in Bondi when they were $30,000, so lose–lose.

We tried again, and out of pure embarrassment I may just have kept my big mouth shut for the second attempt. It progressed to a very special and memorable kiss.

The kissee was lovely and very helpful, and I learnt a very important lesson that day: *always, always, always* untuck your shirt or tie your jumper around your waist before you French-kiss for the first time. *Always.*

The Perfect Cure for a Bluebottle Sting

1977

My mates mean the world to me.

They're the ones who don't care about the TV ratings or the negative press. They're the ones who will always say, 'Pull your head out of your arse!' at the first sniff of a wanky story.

Here are the guys who have always been there, from the start. The guys who are never *not* there.

Robbie Mayer, who's already featured in this book, is my oldest and dearest friend. We were best mates at Rose Bay Public School at five years old and have been inseparable besties ever since. I think I initially gravitated towards Robbie because even at five he looked like a thirteen-year-old, and that was the sort of protection I needed against the school bullies.

Robbie is one of the most loyal and generous guys I've ever known. You'll read plenty more about him in this book, but it represents just a fraction of the thousands of memories we share. I don't think he's ever even seen me on TV, he only watches TV for the footy. He still thinks I work on *Sale of the Century* on Channel Nine, which of course I never did.

By the time we got to high school, Robbie was very much into the North Bondi Surf Club. But I was a surfer, and there was a little bit of friendly rivalry between the clubbies (lifesavers) and the surfies. So Dobbo stepped up as my high-school bestie and surfie mate. (You've already met him too.)

Dobbo and I made a pact that we would literally surf *every single day of the year*. It was a silly twelve-year-old boy thing, but we were floating around in the surf that day and we actually leant in and shook hands on it.

It was a deal, a dare of sorts. Regardless of what our three mothers put in our way – his mother, my mother and Mother Nature – we would paddle out *every day*. It didn't matter if the waves were massive and dangerous, if they were really small or even if there were no waves at all. Yep, even if it was completely flat we would paddle out, float around for a while, have a laugh and paddle back in. We'd get back onto the beach and congratulate each other for going out when no one else would.

In howling nor'easters, or when the beach was being hammered by the legendary southerly busters, we'd still paddle out. Even if – and this is the big one – there were *bluebottles*, we'd jump in and paddle out.

We told ourselves that being stung by a bluebottle was a

THE PERFECT CURE FOR A BLUEBOTTLE STING

badge of honour. We'd scream and yell when we got stung, then proudly compare our stings and rashes at school the next day.

I'm not sure if the perfect cure for a bluebottle sting has been invented. I think vinegar is the current trend. I remember Mum pouring loads and loads of calamine lotion cream onto mine. It would dry into a thickish, pinkish crust but wouldn't really do anything. If I had a bluebottle sting across my face, then sure enough I'd end up at school the next day with a dried-up pink crust all over my face. It was a strange look, a look I would never be brave enough to wear out in public today.

The other rumoured cure for a bluebottle sting was urine. Dobbo and I were, and still are, the very best of mates, but I could never piss on him, as much as my friends at Wikipedia would love to add that to the 'Personal Life' section of my entry.

Bondi was, and remains, one of the most famous beaches in the world, and with that title comes massive crowds. Summers were hectic in and out of the water. For Dobbo and me, the end of summer was a celebration of sorts: it was when we'd get to claim our beach back from the tourists and visiting surfers.

So, ironically, the colder it got, the more we loved being at Bondi. In fact, the colder it got, the tougher we thought we were. Sometimes the weather was so miserable we could virtually be out in the surf on our own. Those were great days.

Every single day, no exceptions. That was our deal.

We couldn't afford wetsuits. In winter I would surf in a woollen jumper and boardshorts, and Dobbo would surf in his Bondi United footy jersey. We looked like a couple of clowns out there, but no one could ever question our commitment.

I couldn't work out a good way of saving money for a wetsuit. Dobbo nailed it. Most days his mum would give him $1 for lunch from the school tuck shop, so instead of eating he'd go without lunch and put the money into his wetsuit fund. He was smart, though a little bit hungry.

Dobbo and I made another pact as we caught the 380 bus up to Bondi Junction on a Thursday night to ride our skateboards through the mall. We swore that one day we would *buy* this 380 bus, fill it full of cushions and beanbags and surfboards, and just drive around Australia, surfing.

Now we're both nearly sixty, we could probably buy that bus and do the trip, but because of our bad backs, knees, hips, necks and shoulders, we'd need to take a masseuse with us, and also someone to wee on us in case of bluebottle stings, because *I'm* not doing it. Despite what you may read on Wikipedia.

*

Dobbo is one of the three Marks who've been in my posse since high school – Mark D, Mark W and Mark S. It'll make it very easy to remember their names when I'm old and start to forget stuff. We got up to *so* much mischief, you could've found us chasing two-for-one drinks all over Sydney on any Friday or Saturday night.

Once I started to get a bit of a profile on television, Mark W decided it was his role to get us free drinks, which usually involved convincing a bar manager it was my birthday. We lost track of how many times we did this and where, so occasionally we'd get into a bit of strife when we went into a bar and forgot we'd already used the birthday line there a few months earlier.

Mark W was a prestige car upholsterer, so all our cars and lounges had perfect upholstery. I once bought a classic old VW beetle and Mark W offered to cut the roof off, spray-paint the car bright white and do all the upholstery and interior in bright white to match. It was supposed to make us look like a bunch of cool surfer dudes, but it's my belief the car was more akin to something Snow White might use to drive Sneezy, Dopey and Grumpy to the nail salon.

Mark S is a legendary guy, an accident-prone funster who is plainly lucky to be alive. He's the one with the classic stories like 'I got a kebab and was sitting in the gutter when a taxi reversed into my head.' Or 'There was a redback spider trapped in my wetsuit when I was diving, and it bit me five times.'

'Bloody hell, are you going to be OK?' I asked when he told me this last one.

'I don't know, the doctors don't know, no one has ever been bitten five times before,' he replied.

We think he's either a cat with nine lives or a cockroach who'll never die.

It was on my buck's night that Mark, Mark and Mark showed me and the world what true friendship looks like. They'd obviously planned a big night, but I had to pull them up earlier in the week and say: 'Now, boys, you know about the public decency clause in my contract. As much as I'd love to run naked through the Sydney Harbour Tunnel, or be strapped to a signpost in Kings Cross and covered in sump oil, you know I have to behave, yeah?'

They convinced me to relax, it was all going to be OK.

Yeah, right. At that point I should've run straight outta there and caught a freight train to Darwin then a slow boat up through Indonesia and hidden from them for a year or two.

As we prepared to jump in the bux-bus and hit the road for a buck's night that wouldn't breach my public decency clause, Mark D – Dobbo – grabbed his bag and pulled out a clown wig and a mascara pencil. The three Marks used the mascara pencil to draw a moustache and beard on me and then put the clown wig on my head.

'There you go, no one will ever recognise you!' said Dobbo, pretty happy with his artistic creation.

Well, I've never been more looked at or more recognised in my life. It was a relatively big evening, and yes, if you're thinking that my fiancée, Sylvie, didn't believe that was where the mascara all over my face came from, then you would be, as I say on *The Chase Australia*, 'COOOOOOOORRRRECT!!!'

*

My mate Danny and I started out together doing some work with a freelance production company. He was an ambitious and talented young cameraman who had his sights firmly set on a big career in movies. He knew I had stories to tell and has pushed me to work up two feature-film scripts.

He's followed his dream all the way to Hollywood and is now working on some of the biggest Netflix and Apple blockbusters. But he's such a great mate that during a break from shooting mega-million-dollar movies, he came back to Sydney and shot my short film *Larry Time*.

Any time we're together, we talk about doing a feature film together, and I reckon one day we just might – if I can afford him, that is.

Anthony Bell is another great mate who went on to become my business manager. We share a love of boats, pizzas, motorbikes and fun.

Belly is a great dealmaker – so good, in fact, that in 2009 over

THE PERFECT CURE FOR A BLUEBOTTLE STING

a long lunch he convinced Sylvie that she should let me sail with him in the Sydney to Hobart Yacht Race, one of the toughest ocean races in the world. I wasn't a sailor or even a sportsman, and while I'd spent my life on boats around the harbour, I'd hardly ever been through the Sydney Heads and out to sea.

Belly told us he'd just bought a super-maxi sailbeat called *Rambler 100* and was putting a team together to race her.

Immediately Sylvie said: 'There's *no way* Larry's doing that. He's got no idea how to sail and he's never been to sea, he'd probably die out there.'

Always the diplomat, Belly could neither confirm nor deny that this would be the outcome.

After a glass of wine, he said it was all for charity, and the money raised would save lives.

After another glass of wine, he said it would be a great challenge for me personally, physically and emotionally.

After another glass of wine, he said it would be something I'd tell my grandchildren about.

There was another glass of wine, but I don't remember what he said after that. Four glasses is when my memory generally leaves the conversation and has a lie-down. It's also when I start agreeing to stupid shit.

Sylvie and I went home and spoke about it — for some reason that to this day I don't understand, she was slowly coming around to the idea. Maybe she wanted me to be a hero; maybe she wanted me to fall overboard so she could claim my life insurance.

Either way, Belly's powers of negotiation are *that* good.

We called Tia and Jye into my office and explained that Belly had just bought an amazing boat, and I might be joining the race team. It would be the experience of a lifetime.

So we all gathered around the computer, typed '*Rambler 100*' into the search bar and hit Enter.

The very first thing that came up was a picture of *Rambler 100* capsized in the Celtic Sea, with her crew being winched off her upturned hull by a helicopter rescue team. It wasn't just a little red flag, it was like I'd just walked into a flag shop, bought every red flag in the whole place and raised them all in front of my family.

To be honest, right at this moment, Belly's offer didn't look all that inviting.

Anyway, for some reason, I agreed to do it, with Sylvie's blessing. Maybe she was sick of me, and this was an easy way out.

Belly and I have had many wild and fantastic adventures together, but I've got to say there's no greater bonding experience than your mate holding on to you as you try to wee and vomit at the same time over the side of a yacht pounding through Bass Strait in angry five-metre seas in the dead of night.

We finished fourth. I jumped onto the dock in Hobart, kissed the ground and swore I'd never ever do anything that stupid again.

But Belly, the great negotiator, somehow convinced me to go again the following year. We got hammered that time: the conditions were horrendous; it was even too dangerous to wee or vomit over the side of the yacht, it was safer just to do it all in your bunk. Shame there were no bluebottles out there, I could've finally tested that theory without having to piss on Dobbo.

We finished second that year. It was thrilling, terrifying and bloody awesome.

I jumped onto the dock in Hobart, kissed the ground and swore I'd never do anything that stupid again.

The following year, Karl Stefanovic took my place on the crew and they won the race. I couldn't be beaten by Karl, it just wasn't right! I'd done years of prep, been involved in the campaign since the day the boat arrived in Australia, put my life on the line twice, placed fourth and second, and now Karl waltzes onto the dock on Boxing Day like Kim Kardashian arriving at the Met Gala, waves to all the cameras and his adoring fans, climbs aboard, goes downstairs, sleeps in his bunk for three days, then comes back up on deck just in time for the boat to cross the finish line in first place. I remember watching the end of the race on TV and feeling just a little bit sick as Karl – who's a great mate by the way – was waving at all the news cameras on the Derwent River as though he'd single-handedly just sailed this boat to victory. It was just so Karl and so wrong. And I knew he would never let me forget it. So I had to return for a *third* race in 2013, just to get that Stefanovic monkey off my back.

We came second that year, and Karl still merrily reminds me every time I see him that he's won more Sydney to Hobarts than I have.

I'm so glad I did those three races; I've never ever done anything more challenging in my life – apart from hosting *Celebrity Splash, that* was pretty scary. It taught me so much about inner toughness, resilience, focus and determination (*Celebrity Splash*, not the Sydney to Hobart). It also taught me not to drink too much at lunch with mates when they've got crazy ideas.

Belly continues to be a pillar of strength and a solid guiding light in my life. Would I risk my life and go to sea with him again? In a heartbeat, and I believe he would do the same for me.

And now when I go on buck's night–type affairs and I know things are going to get messy, I don't wear a clown wig and a mascara beard anymore – I just wear a Karl Stefanovic mask. It's a much better disguise.

Paul Hogan Made Me Spew But Saved My Life

1977

*H*oly crap! Here he is, in person, in the flesh.
Paul Hogan, the superstar, the legend, Australia's most famous film export, standing at his front door saying 'G'day' to me.

My childhood hero. The man who made me violently throw up everywhere.

The crew and I were in Los Angeles filming segments for *The Morning Show*. I'd been randomly stopping and interviewing Americans on Santa Monica Beach. My main question was: 'What do you know about Australia?'

It had been thirty years since Hogan's most famous movie came out, and still eight out of ten Americans we stopped said: '*Crocodile Dundee.*' By any marketing or PR measure, that is absolutely incredible.

It was pretty early in the morning as we pulled up to Hogan's house near famous Venice Beach. My producer Rebecca-lee Fenton asked if I was OK, as I seemed to be acting a bit strange. Truth was, I was nervous as hell. I'd idolised this guy forever.

When he answered the door he was smoking a cigarette; of course he was.

His thin blond hair was in its famously scruffy form. If you're not familiar, here's a modern reference for you to get your hair-bearings.

This was long before Boris Johnson's colourful Knightsbridge hairdresser of French–Belgian–Norwegian descent threw his arms in the air and, with a smile spreading across his heavily botoxed face, joyfully squealed to Boris: 'Darling, I'm going to do somezing soooo different with your hair, I'm going to make it look like you've juzz ztuck your head in a plane's propeller zen pulled it out and ztuck it in a Thermomix on scramble for twelve minutez. Borizzzz darling, let me do this style and we'll have zee whole vorld zaying, "What zeee actual farkzzz??" It vill be amaaarrrrrrrzzzzing!!'

Well, Paul Hogan was rocking that look forty years ago.

Today he was wearing a baggy pair of faded denim jeans. Not the modern cool type where you pay extra for them to be gangster-baggy and mindfully faded after being slapped with recycled kale stems. Nah, just old-man baggy because your bottom has drooped and sagged away into arse obscurity; and faded, well, just because they're old jeans.

(Note: this is exactly how my jeans are. Exactly.)

Hoges was a delight to interview. He was just him; I know that sounds weird, but so many celebrities aren't. A normal Aussie bloke, very humble, so likeable, totally not into the 'star' thing – and I was pretty much starstruck.

Should I tell him he once made me violently throw up, or not?

It started when I broke my leg skiing, but that's not even the best part of the story.

When I was about twelve, I went on a school excursion to Thredbo in the New South Wales snowfields. We'd been there for two days and it was time to come home.

Generally surfers make bad skiers. When you're on a surfboard, most of your weight sits over your *back foot* and you use the weight of your *upper body* to send power to the board. In skiing your weight needs to be distributed evenly through *both feet* and your power is more likely to come from your *lower body*. You can always tell a surfer on the ski fields: they're the one leaning into the mountain with their upper body and hoping and praying their skis will follow.

Gee, wouldn't it be good if one day someone invented a small surfboard-like thing you could use on the snow! It would be a cross between a surfboard and a ski; I would call it a boardski. Which is exactly what Sylvie says to me in her cute Polish accent when I'm telling her a long-winded story that's going nowhere: 'I'm boredski.'

There's only one thing more dangerous than a surfer trying to ski, and that's a man who's married to a Polish woman and putting 'ski' on the end of each word for cheap laughs. Because stupid Australians like me think if you just put 'ski' on the end of a word it sounds Polishski.

If you just smiled at that 'boredski' thing, then take it for granted Sylvie did not, and I'm probably in a bit of trouble, so let's move onski.

Plenty of skiers will tell you they've broken their legs on the last run of the day; it's that dangerous combo of tiredness, sludgy and patchy snow, and long afternoon shadows that make seeing the danger zones difficult. Add to that the fact I'm now running late for the bus home, and I'm screaming down that mountain with no skill, but I'm twelve, so I have two freshly descended balls full of bravado. All arse, no class.

I'm going too fast. I've seen people do those little jump turns to slow down or stop. I've been skiing for two days; sure, I can do this.

A little jump, turn the skis to the right, land in a sludgy patch, boot sinks into the soupy, Slurpee-esque mound, rest of body still moves down the mountain with amateurishly stupid, unstoppable force. Boot stuck in snow, foot stuck in boot. Neither tibia nor fibula prepared to play along and absorb such force.

SNAP!!!!!!!

My dilemma, apart from lying in the snow screaming with my ankle facing west and my calf muscle facing east, was that the bus was in the car park ready for the long drive home, most of the kids were already sitting on the bus and I was in more than a little bit of trouble halfway up the mountain.

Eventually the mountain rescue guys arrived, and they adjusted my leg so all my bones were kind of where they were supposed to be, albeit not connected. I was bundled into that cool sled and we zipped down the mountain and into the medical rooms.

The options were: either the bus goes, and I stay in the Thredbo doctor's office and they organise some sort of ambulance transfer home at a later stage; or they whip some quick, short-term, cast-style solution on my leg, spread me across the back row of the bus and get me straight home.

They called Dad at work. I was in a lot of pain, but not as much pain as Dad was in when they told him how much the ambulance transfer would cost if he chose that option to get me home. I imagine the proposed $250 bill made his decision easier. We didn't have much money, and if there'd been an Uber POOL option to do the six- to eight-hour trip home he probably would've tapped on that.

It was a *long, long, long* trip home. With every bump in the road my broken bones felt like two young teenage lovers who just couldn't stop grinding against each other. Except in this love story, we leave out the ecstasy bit and all we have is the agony bit.

Mum and Dad were waiting at the school, and with the help of the teachers they bundled me into the car and whipped me straight to hospital for a fancy fresh cast that went from my ankle to my thigh.

Once I was back home I was soon bored out of my mind. Like any twelve-year-old, I was super-active and couldn't sit still for five minutes, and now here I was, laid out on the couch for six weeks.

Every day I'd be left at home alone. Dad would go off to his salesman's job and Mum would go off to prison.

When we were still quite young, Mum, having successfully raised three little kids, became a bit restless at home, so she went off and studied social work. The study involved working as a prison counsellor. My adorable, tiny, five-foot-one mother, with her big blue eyes and surfer-blonde hair, working with criminals in jail! Mum could always see the good in people, and her time in prison – wait, let me try that again, her time *working* in prison – proved that beyond all reasonable doubt.

So I'd basically just lie around on my own all day. I didn't like reading books, and there was no internet, no PlayStation, no porn to google (of course I'm not suggesting for a single moment that your curious teenage sons are googling porn, not for a single moment would I suggest that, how dare I?). The highlight of my day was watching *The Mike Walsh Show* at midday on Channel Nine.

One day during the commercial break, a Winfield cigarette ad pops up, featuring Paul Hogan.

'G'day ...' he says, in even more yobbo-ish ocker than your most ockerish yobbo, as another bloke helps him onto the back of a wild brumby. ''Ang on to me Winfields for me, mate. They *are* the best smoke in Australia ... Any'ow, 'ava Winfield.' Then the orchestra cuts in with the Winfield theme tune.

I thought, 'OK. He's the coolest guy I've ever seen. Funny, famous, just bloody awesome. Maybe if I smoked, I could be like him.'

Anyone could buy cigarettes back then, even kids. In fact, I would often go to Jimmy's Milk Bar — where I'd developed my Surf Shake and pinnie addictions — to buy Dad his More cigarettes. They were long and skinny — I think Dad thought they made him look like Clint Eastwood in one of those old Western movies.

So when I hobbled in on my crutches and asked for three packets of Winfields, Jimmy didn't even blink. I told him they were for Dad; he wanted to try different ones from normal. Yep, it's true, I was even prepared to lie to be like Hoges.

I stuffed the three boxes in various pockets and hobbled back up the hill, and through the back door to the kitchen where I grabbed a packet of matches. Then I sat on the top step of the back stairs, laid my crutches down, opened the first pack and started choofing away.

I remember feeling pretty grown up and just a little bit naughty. I puffed away, patiently waiting to become funny and famous. Surely if I did what Hoges said, then one day soon we'd be friends?! So I waited for my new best mate Hoges to come up the stairs.

He never came up, but my breakfast came up, as did my dinner from the night before, as did a good sixty or seventy per cent of my stomach lining, as did what I reckoned were honey king prawns.

Now, we only had honey king prawns on Dad's birthday; that was in February and it was now August, so this was a mighty comprehensive regurgitation, I'm thinking Guinness World Record material.

'Wow! Isn't smoking just great!' I thought as I struggled to keep my eyeballs from popping out of my head. 'Wow, I can see why Dad loves this so much!' I reflected as I sprayed the side of the house, the back stairs and my cast with vomit. 'Wow! If only Paul Hogan could see me now!'

Now, the major problem with spewing on the back stairs with a leg in a thigh-high cast was I just didn't have the flexibility and nimbleness required to clean up. I couldn't get to the hose at the side of the house, and I couldn't run back and forth with buckets of water, so I was pretty screwed here.

When Mum and Dad got home, I had to fess up. All afternoon I'd tried to come up with stories like 'A guy broke into the house and threw up on the back steps after I threatened him with my crutches, then ran away leaving one and a half packets of cigarettes.'

I didn't end up telling Hoges that story when I met him, but if anything, I guess I have to thank him. That was the very best anti-smoking lesson I could've hoped for.

I never wanted to smoke, or ski, or eat honey king prawns again.

Thanks, Hoges.

The Mix Tape

1979

Kids today have got it SO easy when they want to tell someone they love them, or when they want to break up.

A quick text can be as simple as 'I LUUUUUURVE UUUUUUUU' with two big red heart emojis, and a breakup can be another quick text with a couple of words and two broken-heart emojis and a crying face.

But back in the day, it was complicated and challenging, and it could take a week or more to construct a thing we young lovers called The Mix Tape. It was how I let my early girlfriends know that I liked them, or wanted to like them more. Besides, why would I expose my real feelings or try to express my thoughts with poorly written notes and even poorlier handwriting when the Bee Gees, Cliff Richard or Air Supply could do the heavy lifting for me? I'm not sure whether it was clever or an emotional shortcut or a romantic combination of the two, but it was right.

THE MIX TAPE

Forget swiping left or right, young love back then was handing over a brightly hand-decorated cassette tape featuring ten songs that had been patiently waited for on the radio or television then manually recorded. They would be a smorgasbord of musical masterpieces that properly expressed the way you felt, or not-so-subtly signalled your intentions.

Once you put 'I Was Made for Lovin' You' by KISS on a mix tape, your intentions were clear. There was no way this could be misinterpreted as 'I really want to help your dad paint the garage', or 'I really want to go to church with your mum', or 'I'd really like to help your younger brother with his homework.' Oh, no no no. Once you included 'Kiss You All Over' by Exile there was no room for misunderstanding.

Dad had a Sony reel-to-reel eight-track recorder. A bit bigger than a case of beer and about as heavy. I'd get the big reel of recording tape, spool it through the hubs and bits and pieces, then thread it onto the empty reel, getting the tension just right. Then I'd set the microphone up on a pile of books next to the speaker and wait and wait and wait.

The idea was that whenever a good love song came on, I'd quickly hit the Play and Record buttons and record the song straight off the device. I would have this set up for weeks at a time, patiently waiting for the right songs to pop up on the radio or on the TV music shows *Sounds* or *Countdown*.

Some good soppy love songs were always a great choice, a victory of sorts, but it was a complete jackpot when a song with a suggestive title or lyrics came on. (Having said that, 'I'm in You' by Peter Frampton was a great song, but you'll be pleased to know I was never creepy enough or confident enough to include it on a mix tape.)

Getting a song that did the flirting for you or said what you would never be brave enough to say yourself was like winning the Love Lotto.

Imagine sitting next to the radio for hours on end, and then the DJ says: 'Here's Leo Sayer with "When I Need You"!' I'd jump up out of my beanbag and smash those buttons down as hard as I could. This was *the* perfect song for a mix tape.

There was no specific style or genre, anything that included a message of love would work. 'Lost Without Your Love' by Bread was also a bullseye. The Bee Gees gave great mix tape; 'How Deep Is Your Love' was a deadset cert.

It didn't always go to plan. I remember waiting a week or more to hear Exile's 'Kiss You All Over'. They finally played it, the reels on the Sony reel-to-reel were turning, then about halfway through Mum pokes her head round my bedroom door and yells: 'Dinner's ready!' Thanks, Mum.

I think the corniest mix tape I ever constructed included:

'Can't Smile Without You' by Barry Manilow
'Love Is in the Air' by John Paul Young
'Nobody Does It Better' by Carly Simon
'You're the One That I Want' by John Travolta and
    Olivia Newton-John
'I Was Made for Lovin' You' by KISS

Once I had all the songs that told my story and properly declared my feelings, I'd get my normal cassette recorder and set it up next to the big eight-track machine. I'd place the cassette recorder microphone in front of the eight-track, push Record and Play on the cassette machine then Play on the eight-track, and hope

Mum wouldn't walk in to tell me dinner was ready, because then I'd have to start all over again.

While the cassette was recording, I'd start decorating the case with little cartoon-style hearts and flowers, and infantile drawings of two stick figures holding hands. And of course, I'd also fill out the index page with all the lovey-dovey and suggestive titles.

It was time-consuming and frustrating and the tape was of dodgy quality, but it seriously added to the adorabilityness of Little Larry.

It took me a long time, but I eventually worked out it was easier to buy a girl a piece of jewellery.

Our Superyacht

1980

Siesta was about eight metres long, with an off-white steel hull that had rough patch marks where Dad had tried to repair some rusty bits, a badly varnished timber deck that had rough patch marks where Dad had tried to repair some rotting bits, and a cabin that looked like the original boat builder had finished the bottom bit and thought, 'Hang on a tick, maybe I should just build a shitty square plywood box and plonk it on top.' The cabin had probably originally been white but was now an out-of-date, left-out-of-the-fridge-on-a-hot-day custard colour. The cabin's Perspex windows were scratched, cracked and mouldy, and rusted either closed or halfway open, but whatever position they were in, they weren't moving without a crowbar. And, like the rest of the boat, the outside of the cabin had rough patch marks where Dad had tried to repair the rotting bits.

Dad and I had painted all the decks in a clear, non-slip paint. The manufacturer's recommendation was two coats, twenty-four hours apart, but Dad reasoned that if he did five coats, twelve hours apart, that should make the decks at least two and a half times safer.

One of Dad's clever boaty mates told him it'd be *even less* slippery if we sprinkled some sand in the wet paint. I didn't know whether taking a bag down to Bondi Beach and filling it with sand was illegal, but it sure felt like it. Every time a busload of international tourists ran down onto the beach, you would see them look around to make sure no one was watching, then fill up their pockets and handbags with sand. I kid you not. I thought it was absolutely ridiculous, but now this was me. I ran down to the beach with my empty school bag, looked around to check no one was watching, then filled it up.

In retrospect, I can completely understand why Dad sent me, because I was a kid and there was less chance I would go to prison for sand theft. He was a smart guy.

As Dad walked around the decks of *Siesta* with a roller applying the non-slip paint, I'd follow throwing in handfuls of sand, like a flower girl scattering rose petals in front of a bride as she walked down the aisle. The irony of Dad desperately wanting to make the decks safe while carrying a highly flammable tin of liquid in one hand and a cigarette in the other was lost on fifteen-year-old me. It's only now I look back and think, 'What the actual fuck??'

We wanted a smooth, consistent, non-slip finish, but we ended up with a surface that was blotchy and rough as guts. It not only looked completely shit but was also, once dry, like walking on a cheese grater.

Good news, though: it was now physically impossible to slip over, it was that non-slippery. But it could also shred the bottom of your feet, it was that non-slippery. Extra bonus: if Dad's cigarette *did* happen to ignite the highly flammable tin of liquid and blow us up, at least there'd be enough of our feet left in the cheese-grater-esque craters for the cops to positively identify us.

The non-slip surface was now also hyper-efficient in trapping, for eternity, any grime, food scraps, grease, fish guts or seagull shit that fell onto the sandpaper-like terrain. Within five minutes it was filthy, and no amount of scrubbing could clean it. One time the beetroot fell out of my hamburger and that stain was there for life and beyond.

In the cabin, though, we had carpet – *actual* carpet from a real carpet shop, not boat carpet from a boat shop. While that may sound super sexy and inviting, actually it was a dumb move. No one puts real carpet on an old open boat. It stank and held on to stains and crap as efficiently as the non-slip deck.

In so many old photos of Dad, he would have his shirt undone down to around his belly button and his thick chest hairs would be popping out all over the place like Austin Powers. So looking back, it probably shouldn't have surprised anyone that Dad went for a semi-shagpile. It was ridiculous, but kind of cool at the same time. When it rained, the shagpile would get soaking wet and then would take a week to dry. I don't think the underlay ever really dried out at all.

When you'd first get onto *Siesta* and force open the rattling old cabin door, she'd smell like mouldy carpet, diesel and a toilet that never flushed properly. That toilet smell was always pretty yuck. You know when you go into a public toilet and the cleaner was kidnapped a week to ten days ago by the husband of the woman the cleaner's having an affair with, and because the cleaner's flatmate was recently hospitalised with gonorrhoea no one has realised the cleaner's missing so no one else has come to clean the toilet? ... *That* smell.

You know that saying 'no expense spared'? Well, *Siesta* was built with simply 'no expense, at all'. *Siesta* cost Dad about $500. She was an absolute, one hundred per cent piece of shit, but to Dad and me she was our superyacht.

Hanging out with Dad on the boat on Sundays was awesome. It was Man Time. We'd leave Mum and my two sisters and go man-ing.

Siesta was moored at Rose Bay, about a hundred metres off the wharf, so we had to row out to her. Well, *I* had to row out to her; that was *my* job. At the wharf you'd pull one of the little rowboats out of the racks and drag it down the ramp, then row out to your boat.

It was like a very, very, very poor version of a gondola ride through Venice. There was Dad sitting in the back of this tiny dinghy, smoking his cigarette, proudly watching his fifteen-year-old son row him out to his superyacht.

The trip would only take a few minutes, then I'd bump the little boat up against *Siesta* and Dad would jump off with the rope. Cigarette in one hand, rope in the other. He'd tie the rowboat up, then every time, before anything else, he'd take all his clothes off down to his Speedos.

I've seen how billionaires stride around their superyachts in the south of France as if they own the world, with their hairy chests puffed out and their snobby noses in the air. Well, that was Dad on *Siesta*.

Despite the fact she was the shittiest boat on the harbour – the engine rarely worked, and it was covered in barnacles, rotting wood and rusty bits – when he stepped on that boat he became the king of his floating castle.

We never went anywhere, we just sat there on the mooring. There were no TVs, no mobiles, just AM radio, usually 2SM – endless repeats of The Beach Boys, Barry Manilow, the Bee Gees, Olivia Newton-John and John Paul Young. We'd sing along to the choruses we knew and hum the lyrics we didn't.

Dad was a good fisherman, and would always catch a fish when no one else was even getting a bite. As he was reeling in the fish, he could identify it even before he saw it. 'Oh, just a little flathead,' he'd say, long before the little flathead surfaced. 'This'll be a good bream,' he'd tell me as he pulled it in, and sure enough, up popped a good bream.

When the fish weren't biting, he'd polish the brass wheel. That's not a euphemism – he would *actually* get out the Brasso and a rag and polish *Siesta*'s brass steering wheel.

This wheel was his favourite thing on the boat. I think it was kind of a link to his dad, a reminder of how Grandpa Louis, an antique furniture restorer, could with a little bit of love turn something old and tarnished into something shiny and special. I don't think the wheel had any great value, but to Dad it was priceless.

Dad was never without a cigarette. It looked like it brought him great joy, but I wish I'd known then what I learnt later. I wish I'd been smart enough or strong enough to say, 'Hey, Dad, see this great time we're having? Well, those cigarettes are going to kill you and we won't be able to do this anymore. I love you and I can't imagine my life without you; you are my best friend in the whole world and I'm sitting here with a fishing rod in one hand, a can of Coke in the other, and we're singing and laughing and you're lighting up another cigarette. I would love you to take your grandkids fishing and have this kind of fun with *them*. But those cigarettes you've been smoking nonstop all day will mean you're probably never going to do that.'

God I miss him.

Now, the last thing Mum would say before we walked out the door to head for the boat was always: 'Have fun and don't eat any junk.' Not 'Don't blow yourselves up by smoking next to a tin of highly flammable paint' or 'Don't get arrested stealing sand from Bondi Beach', just 'Don't eat any junk.' And those words made this next bit even more exciting – *naughty* exciting.

At 11.30 on the dot, Dad would say, 'Pie time?' He'd give me a couple of bucks and I'd jump back into the dinghy, and as I started rowing away he'd always add, 'Don't forget the extra sauce, mate.' Every time.

I'd row back to the marina and go to the little shop upstairs. Those of you who live in Sydney may know The Boathouse restaurant in Rose Bay; it used to be Regatta, The Sailors Club before that, and for many years before that it was called Pier. Well, way back when, the front section of the restaurant was a milk bar, and that's where the Big Ben pie warmer was.

I'd get two Big Ben pies and two cans of Coke, and I'd ask for extra sauce and the lady would give the pies an extra squirt from the bottle and put them in a paper bag. By the time I got back to the boat, the extra sauce would be smudged all over the inside of the bag.

By then, Dad would be holding a glass filled with a generous nip of Southern Comfort. He'd open his Coke and pour it into the whisky, I'd clink his glass with my Coke can and then we'd have our Kings' Lunch. The pies would be the perfect temperature and ready to scoff, and Dad would have his extra sauce, which he had to wipe off the paper bag with his pie; it's what men do when they have to survive.

I've eaten lobster and caviar, I've drunk expensive champagnes and whiskies all over the world, but I simply cannot remember anything tasting as good as a pie and sauce and a Coke with my dad on a stinky broken boat with semi-shagpile carpet, floating in Rose Bay. It was like we were the wealthiest people in the world.

We didn't need anything else, we had it all. Those were the happiest days.

'Don't tell Mum,' Dad would say as we tucked into the pies, and we'd laugh. We were a couple of rebels breaking the rules; it was so wrong but it felt so right. This was our domain and we could do what we liked. We were men hunting and gathering to survive in the wilderness and we were strong and brave and fearless – except when Mum would randomly pop down from the house and we'd quickly have to hide the evidence.

We'd sing out loud to 2SM, and maybe we'd catch a fish, maybe we wouldn't, I couldn't have cared less. We slept over a few times; it was pretty uncomfortable. Dad would sleep on the one single bunk and I'd sleep on the bench seat, and we'd have farting competitions to try and get rid of the other smells.

I remember the day Dad got the phone call from the marina after a huge storm. *Siesta* had been blown off her mooring and they didn't know where she was.

We went down to the marina and the guys said there were a few boats that had broken away. We could see them up against the seawall but *Siesta* wasn't there.

A day or so later the water police found her sunk over the other side of Rose Bay, just off Milk Beach, about a kilometre from her mooring. She was in about four metres of water and lying on her side.

Dad was heartbroken. Our time together on the boat was over. The pies, the sauce, the Coke and Southern Comfort, the 2SM singalongs, the farting competitions, the non-slip deck, the old brass steering wheel …

Dad told the police he'd just go over and salvage the steering wheel; that was all he wanted from the boat. They told him he couldn't, because the case was now with the insurance company and the boat was no longer his property. He was really upset about that, and I could see how important the steering wheel was to him.

I thought, 'I'm going to fix this, I'm going to get Dad that stupid steering wheel.' So I got a hammer and a chisel out of the back shed and went down to Milk Beach with a mate. It was low tide and we could see the top of *Siesta* just under the water.

I knew this was illegal, but I didn't care. I'd already stolen golf balls from the golf green and sand from Bondi Beach, and got away with it, so I was a seasoned crim by this point.

Have you ever tried to hammer a chisel under water? Don't try it, it's like … impossible. My mate and I took turns going underwater, smashing the chisel into the steering column as hard as we could, but the old brass wheel, like everything else on the boat, was well and truly corroded in place.

It loosened a little bit, but wouldn't release. I wasn't giving up, though. Dad *had* to have that steering wheel as a reminder of our wonderful times on our superyacht. I *had* to get it. So we went back the next day.

I'm not sure how many times I held my breath, dived down, smashed the hammer, came back up, took another deep breath then went back down again. It must have been for hours and hours.

It was illegal and wrong, but that was what this boat had represented. We did everything we weren't supposed to on this boat. We ate pies, we drank Coke, we danced around singing Barry Manilow songs in Speedos, all of which is wrong and probably illegal – *especially* singing Barry Manilow songs in Speedos.

Then … finally! After hours and hours of trying, I got it!!! I couldn't get home fast enough.

Dad actually lost his breath when I surprised him with it. He cried and cuddled me tight. This meant even more to him than I'd known.

From that moment on, the brass wheel sat against a tree in his garden outside the sliding glass doors, in plain sight from his favourite lounge chair, and he would tell everyone the story about how his teenage son broke the law to steal it back for him.

Just after he died, we were all sitting in Mum and Dad's lounge room and I looked out into the garden and saw the steering wheel leaning up against the tree. I'd cried a lot that week, I thought I was all cried out, but I found a few more litres of tears in that moment.

I claimed the steering wheel for myself, deciding it probably didn't mean as much to Mum or my sisters. But to me it was a solid brass bond with my dad.

I took it to my house on the cliffs at Dover Heights and set it up on the balcony overlooking the ocean. That way I could see it from inside the house and Dad could see it from heaven.

It's been with me ever since. Every time we move house I find the perfect spot for it, as close to the water as I can get it, with the very best view.

When my wonderful niece Bianca married Eden at our house in 2018, I made reference to the wheel in my speech. I briefly told the story of our superyacht, and said that for me the brass wheel signified Grandpa Dave navigating us through all of life's storms. After the speeches, almost everyone moved outside to see the steering wheel, attached to the balcony overlooking the ocean. It was a lovely moment, a chance for all our family and friends to remember Grandpa Dave.

We have a little house on the river now; it's where I'm writing this. A real escape, only accessible by boat, as far away from TV studios as I can get. I love it. When we moved in, the very first thing I unpacked was the steering wheel. I've attached it to the balcony railing just outside the bedroom, which has breathtaking views straight up the river.

I'm looking at it now, as in right now, and I know if Dad were here he'd be thinking: 'What the hell are you doing trying to write a book? You've barely even read a book in your life, and you can't spell and don't know anything about punctuation!'

Well, Dad, *you* didn't know anything about laying carpet on a boat or applying non-slip paint to a deck, but you went ahead and you made it work.

Two things I know for sure: you'd be proud of me for even *attempting* to write a book, and wherever *Siesta* is resting on the bottom of the harbour, she's still got a beetroot stain in her non-slip paint.

How Did I Get Here?

1981

'Don't think about vaginas, stop thinking about vaginas, maybe if I stop trying to stop thinking about thinking about vaginas then I won't think about vaginas ...'

I remember thinking all this to myself as model and entrepreneur Lindy Rama-Ellis appeared on *The Morning Show* a couple of years ago to spruik her new vulva rejuvenation mask. (*What the ...?*)

I'm on live TV, I'm a man, this is dangerous territory. Say something, get judged. Say nothing, get judged. Sit on the fence, get judged.

I'm stuck between a rock and a potentially hard place.

'It's like a face mask, but for down there. Why shouldn't you give your vulva a treat?' Lindy says as confidently and as innocently as I would talking to my mates about a great pizza I had last night.

My tiny pea-brain is in utter turmoil. The left hemisphere of my man-brain, which apparently helps me with logic, comprehension and speech, is in a naked, greased-up Greco-Roman wrestling match with my right hemisphere, which takes care of my dad jokes, penis jokes, premature ejaculation jokes, inappropriate opportunities and general creativity.

You'll be hearing a *lot* from my right hemisphere in this book.

However, my left, boring-as-batshit hemisphere, with its snobby, analytical, logical, know-it-all attitude, is looking at the stories that have appeared so far in this book and has basically pulled out of the process. It doesn't want to be associated with the pages ahead; this attempt at a book is beneath it.

It has decided the fact I've used the word 'vagina' four times in the first paragraph of this story is just a cheap ploy by my right brain to get people who flick through this book in a bookstore to actually buy a copy, when my left brain knows full well that there's nothing very interesting past that page.

I'm not perverted or disgusting or pathetic – although that concept may be challenged in the chapters ahead – but I defy you NOT to think about something that someone is talking to you about. It's exactly what we're *supposed* to do when we're in a conversation, and exactly what *I'm* supposed to do when I'm interviewing someone.

So now I'm trying to stay engaged with the interview, but through no fault of my own I can't *un*think of vaginas, and Lindy Rama-Ellis keeps talking about them.

See how you're thinking about vaginas right now?? Well, that was me, but on live TV, struggling to stay on track and be a professional, mature, respectable broadcaster.

What the hell? I can't fool you – ten stories in and you already know me too well. I've *never ever ever* been a professional, mature, respectable broadcaster. *You* know it, *I* know it, all the network bosses know it, my co-host Kylie Gillies knows it, and now I'm pretty sure Lindy Rama-Ellis knows it too.

I was actually supremely proud of myself for staying almost on track and then the conversation turned to Gwyneth Paltrow's candle that's called This Smells Like My Vagina.

'OMG, YOU'VE GOTTA GO THERE, BOYFRIEND! YOU'VE GOT TO SAY SOMETHING INAPPROPRIATE! YOU HAVE TO! YOU CAN'T NOT! *SHE* STARTED IT!!!' screams my grubby right hemisphere.

'Stay the course, Larry! Be a mature, good, brave human being! Be a grown-up, Larry!' says the left side of my brain, which works overtime to keep me employed.

So, how did I get here? How did I get through forty years in the media game, only to find myself sitting on a morning-show couch on live TV, talking about masks for vulvas?

Well, back when I was sixteen and thought that Vulva was the off-yellow car owned by the old lady down the street, I was cheeky, naughty and seriously lacking in the attention and comprehension departments.

My school grades were very ordinary, perhaps *below* ordinary. The teachers reported that I was pleasant, but suggested over and over again that I needed to pay more attention, which I never did. (And I still don't, ask anyone. Except Lindy Rama-Ellis, because I was *really* paying attention during *that* chat.)

I was getting to the end of Year Eleven, and a few of my friends had already left school at the end of Year Ten. It was normal to leave at fifteen or sixteen and get an apprenticeship as a plumber, brickie, carpenter, sparkie or whatever got you out of school and out of trouble.

I didn't want to do any of those jobs, but I *did* want to leave school. The careers advisor had clearly put me in the 'Destined Not to Finish Year Twelve' file. He was a great guy, and we had plenty of good, supportive conversations about what I'd like to do if I left school now, like quite a few other boys did.

There were only *two* things I wanted to do.

One was to be a lifeguard. They were super-cool guys, got all the girls and got to surf before, during and after work.

There was this one lifeguard I used to hate so much, not because I actually hated him but because I was so damned jealous of him. He was a bloody legend on the beach. He was the epitome of the bronzed Aussie: six-foot-four, six-pack, blond hair, blue eyes, supremely fit, or as Dad used to say 'built like a brick shithouse'. He'd strut up and down the beach like a Marvel superhero, and every now and again he'd stop strutting, run down the beach, dive in the water and save a drowning tourist. Damn! I wanted to be like him. Luckily, when he married my sister Nicki and I had to stop hating him and start liking him, it wasn't all that difficult. Steve is one of the world's nicest guys and a great brother-in-law.

The other thing I wanted to be was a garbo. Seriously, I'm not joking. I had a surfing mate who was working as a garbo; he'd start at four in the morning and be finished by nine, and stay in the surf for the rest of the day. Compared with my apprentice mates he was getting good money and he had the ultimate surfer's lifestyle.

Recently my nephew Jake, a builder by trade, picked up some work as a garbo. He was living Uncle Lazza's dream life, finishing work early and hitting the surf … (That's some good thinking right there, Jakey.) As his truck drove past Mum's house in the early hours of the morning, she'd be sure to be standing on her balcony in her nightie, waving at Jake and yelling, 'I love you, I'm so proud of you!' – to the amusement of the other garbos on the back of the truck who, in concert, would all yell back, 'We love you too, Nanny Faye!'

I kid you not, I was a hop, skip and a jump away from pursuing garbology as a profession. Ironically, most of this book is about recycling my career, but my career could've actually *been* in recycling.

My parents were called in for an initial consultation with the headmaster and the careers advisor. Together they concluded that school wasn't for me, and if I could find a job it would be a good idea for me to get out of school and start my life in the big, wide world.

The word went out among our family that Little Larry was looking for a job, and not long after my seventeenth birthday, my Nanny Leah and Aunty Sabina called Mum at pretty much the same time to say there was a small ad in the (now-defunct) *Sun* newspaper: 'Copy boys required.' This was followed by the three most exciting words any young man could ever see in a job ad: 'NO EXPERIENCE NECESSARY.' Then, in small print down the bottom, the other three most exciting words any young man could ever see in a job ad: '$89 per week.' Yep, just over $2 an hour.

(I found my first payslip recently. It's hard to believe I earnt so little, but I was as happy as a little pig in a lot of shit.)

After a quick and successful interview, it was deemed that I had what it took to empty ashtrays, wash coffee cups, be abused by angry journalists and run papers around the building.

We got that message back to the school and started to wrap things up there.

As I was leaving for the last time, the deputy headmaster, whom I'd got to see a lot of when he was disciplining me over the years, said in his usual grumpy tone: 'Emdur, you'll never get anywhere without your Higher School Certificate.'

Well, turns out I *didnt* nead an educayshion and he coul'dnt have bean wrongerer, just tayke a look at me now! I'm an ortha!!!!!

Forty years later, and here I am on live TV on Australia's top-rating morning show, talking about masks for vulvas …

[Mic drop.]

Bad Boyfriend

1981

I'd like to take this opportunity to apologise to my girlfriends in my younger, dumber years.

I didn't realise it at the time, but looking back I reckon I was a shit boyfriend.

In those teen years, all I wanted to do was surf morning, noon and night, seven days a week, and when I wasn't surfing I was hanging out with my mates, talking about surfing, reading surfing magazines and watching surfing movies.

I was a good human being, but I just wasn't textbook boyfriend material. I don't think I had a lot to offer emotionally – I wasn't an overly engaged, lovey-dovey type. Words definitely weren't my thing; as you discovered earlier in this book, sending a girl a mix tape was probably the strongest yet saddest strategy in Larry the Loser's Love Lottery.

Mum was convinced that I was looking for a girl just like her. Never, NOT ONCE, did I bring home a hundred-and-fifty-five-centimetre blonde with huge blue eyes, but every time Mum was like: 'WOW, you're *really* trying to find someone like me, aren't you?!'

One friend I brought home to meet Mum was about a hundred and eighty centimetres tall and of Jamaican descent, with long, dark hair, piercing dark eyes and long legs.

After she left, Mum said: 'She's *exactly* like me, all your girlfriends are *exactly* like me! Don't feel like you *always* have to find girlfriends who look exactly like your mother, it's a bit strange …'

A few years ago, when Sylvie and I were moving house, I found a box of old photos and letters. This box had certainly done the rounds. It was stored in the attic of my bachelor pad for many years, then without looking through it I would've packed it into the truck for the move to our marital home, where it would've been dumped at the back of the under-stair storage area behind fifty other unopened boxes. After twenty years there, it would've been thrown onto the removalist truck for the next move and then straight into the garage in the new house for another five years.

Then, a few years ago, it was time for our major downsize from a five-bedroom family home to a two-bedroom couple's apartment, and it was time to look in these mouldy old boxes and see what was actually in them for the first time in thirty years.

Now, you young'uns reading this …

Hang on, I withdraw that, what a ridiculous proposition that any young'uns would be reading this book! Oh, yeah. I can just hear it in cafés all over Bondi now: young people drinking their double macchiatos on yak's milk, and eating their organic smashed avo on ancient Egyptian grain toast infused with San Pellegrino water and unripened ethically sourced kale sap, saying:

'I must go and grab a copy of that book by that old guy on TV, omg wtf he lols all over the place.'

'*Which* old guy on TV?'

'You know, the old balding dude, always with the dad jokes.'

'Kochie?'

'No, no, the other one …'

'Oh, Bert?'

'No, no, the other old one …'

'Tom Gleisner?'

'No, the other bald one, always banging on about stuff.'

'Oh, Tom *Gleeson* …'

'No, no, older than that, he's been around forever, he used to have hair but now he doesn't.'

'Alf on *Home and Away*?'

'No, no, it's like something like Barry, Barry Schmemder.'

But if you *are* a young'un and stuck on a six-month space mission, and you've completely run out of reading material, the internet is down, you've choreographed your next TikTok post, and you're sitting on the vacuum toilet and found this book that the other old astronaut packed in case you ran out of toilet paper … then let me explain how this relationship thing used to work.

Long before swiping and texting and sexting and dick pics … Actually, hang on a sec, we *did* have dick pics, but sending them to your girlfriend was a complex and dangerous procedure.

First you took the picture, then you'd have to go down to the one-hour photo shop and hand over the roll of film without looking suss.

The shop attendant, inevitably a young girl, would ask which quality paper you'd like your pics printed on. I think I usually went for glossy. I always thought if I was going to send a picture of my dick to my girlfriend it should be on glossy paper, like the picture of the Queen in the headmaster's office. Yes, I wanted it to look *that* important. I'm not sure if my penis deserved the glossy paper – I mean no one has ever referred to my penis as 'your majesty' – but that's what it got.

The girl would say, 'OK, here's your receipt, I'll see you in an hour.'

As you turned to leave, you knew what was about to happen in the back room of that photo shop. You see, unlike when you use your iPhone nowadays, you couldn't scroll through the pics on your film camera and delete the bad ones, then choose the best ones and edit them in any way, shape or form. You would never know what they looked like till you got them back from the shop.

Exciting times. Depending on the raunchiness of the photos, that one-hour wait could seem like a lifetime.

So now the young girl has put my film into the machine and the dick pics that I want to send to my girlfriend are coming out the other side. How stupid were we back then???

'Geeeez, I hope they were good shots,' I'd mumble to myself while I counted down the minutes. Of course I hoped they were good shots for the sake of my girlfriend, but I *really really* hoped they were good shots for the sake of the shop attendant.

Because I'm about to go back and collect the pics and she now knows more about me than just about anyone else.

'Is the lighting good? Are the angles good? Or is she laughing at the pics as they come out?'

Two critical rules for picking up freshly minted dick pics: *never* look the attendant in the eye, and *never never* check the photos at the counter.

Sometimes, after printing normal family or holiday snaps, if you weren't happy with them you could ask for a reprint. But can you imagine doing that with a dick pic?

You open the envelope, you take out the bundle of pics, you flick through, you're unhappy with one, you show it to the girl and protest: 'Look, I'm really not happy with the exposure on this one, can you lighten it up a bit?' as the dear old lady behind you in the queue jumps in and says, 'Yes, I agree, the exposure on that penis isn't quite right,' before she suggests she do you a favour and flick through the other photos to give you a second opinion.

NO WAY. Just grab the pack, keep your head down and run.

Anyway … before texts and dating apps, there were also things called love letters. Some people were good at these; I was not.

So, as I was packing up the house for our latest move, I was in the garage surrounded by a hundred packing boxes. In the pile was a curious oldish, smallish box; its corners were crushed and the sticky tape that was meant to be sticking the top of the box down had long retired from its one job of sticking. Curiosity got the better of me and I opened the box. It was full of photos and love letters from an old girlfriend. I stopped packing and sat down to read through these handwritten letters.

They were really powerful, heartfelt, and *very* special. Tanya, my girlfriend at the time, had poured her heart out, and must've spent hours and hours composing these wonderful letters.

And back in the day I think I probably just chucked them in this box without even reading them and went for a surf.

I started crying when I read them. I was now a fifty-three-year-old man, reading letters that had been written thirty-seven years earlier, and I was sitting in my garage crying.

I wasn't crying because the letters were sad; they were really beautiful and full of joy. I was crying because I realised how much of a fuckwit I must've been back then. I don't think I ever wrote her a letter back, and sitting there at that moment, I felt an enormously heavy sense of guilt. I phoned another old friend to get Tanya's current number, and called and called with no response. I left a message, and about an hour later she called back. She was overseas with her husband and the line was dodgy.

I explained that I'd just found a box of her beautiful love letters and I'd read them all and they were very special. I told her I wanted to say sorry for being such a fuckwit, and felt really upset that I'd had nothing to give her back, no response after she'd poured her heart out to me in handwritten page after handwritten page after handwritten page.

Her reaction was as beautiful as her letters. 'Laz, we were young, young boys never understand love.'

I just kept saying sorry, over and over again.

We *were* very young, and our relationship involved all those important first steps. I think your first serious girlfriend or boyfriend will always have a special place in your heart.

A note for people looking for scandal: Sylvie knows Tanya well, we're all very grown up now, and it's all good.

But hopefully she's lost those pics, he writes with a nervous smile.

The Bondi Spectator

1982

'What the hell are you doing trying to write a book? You've barely even read a book in your life, you can't spell and you don't know anything about punctuation!'

That was my sister Nicki's response when I told her I was writing this book, and she's write on both counts (or is it right?). Funny ... it feels exactly like something my dad would have said.

When I was seventeen and writing little articles for the local paper, I would call Nicki and ask her to check my spelling or punctuation, and whether I should write it this way or that way. She is smart, I am stupid, end of story – or start of this one, but you know what I mean.

So how the hell did I get to be a journalist, a reporter, a TV host? Well, to pull off this great fraud I had to cheat and lie like a fraudulent, lying cheater.

As you'll remember, I started my life in the media as a copy boy at *The Sun*. The job of a copy boy was pretty ordinary. I'd often get called upon to empty overflowing ashtrays from journos' desks. Yep, smoking in the office was allowed, and common. In fact, as deadlines crept closer, stress levels rose and the plumes of cigarette smoke around the office thickened, as did the yelling and swearing. I'd be replacing coffee cups and racing down to the little sandwich shop at Central train station to get bacon and egg rolls for all the journos. It really was a glamour job.

When a journo had finished smashing a story out on his or her typewriter, they would yell out 'COPY!!!', then one of us copy boys or girls would have to race over to the desk, grab the typed story and pass it on to the editor or the printers.

Most copy boys and girls had joined the company at the bottom of the food chain, with the intention of one day getting a journalistic cadetship and moving up the ranks. It was a common and accepted pathway. But that wasn't on my radar at all.

Remember, I was 'encouraged' to leave school because I couldn't read or write, so the thought of becoming a journalist had never crossed my mind. I was surrounded by bright, ambitious, focused young would-be journos, whom I really liked, admired and respected, but I definitely wasn't aiming that high myself.

The morning shifts and afternoon shifts were hectic – you'd be racing around the whole time. It was a thankless job. We were just little dung beetles in the journalistic jungle.

But I *loved* the overnight shift. Essentially the job was to monitor police, fire and ambulance radios, and if you heard a callout to some sort of big job, you would find the nearest journo and photographer and dispatch them to the scene.

I'd sit at a huge desk in the Police Rounds room, in front of a wall of different-coloured panels that indicated different regions and different emergency services. The panels were actually audio speakers for these emergency service radios. On the desk were rows and rows of volume dials, colour-coded to match the speaker panels on the wall. It was a bit like being on the flight deck of the starship *Enterprise*.

The night shift was really exciting – especially when something big was going down.

You'd listen to the fire brigade HQ call out some trucks to reports of smoke, you'd turn up that speaker and wait, then within minutes you might hear the fire officer arriving at the scene and saying, 'Rubbish bin fire', so you'd turn that speaker down and relax.

But sometimes you hit the jackpot and you'd hear him yell back to HQ: 'Code RED RED RED!!!' This meant the situation was out of control and more crews were urgently needed. Code red was a no-brainer; you'd immediately find a photographer and journo and shoot them out there.

It was similar with the police radios. If the original callout sounded interesting, you'd turn up that particular speaker and sit there like a fisherman waiting for a nibble on his bait. Sometimes we could go for a few nights without a single police-round story; other times it could be all hell breaking loose – a huge car accident in one part of town, a possible shooting in another, an out-of-control factory fire somewhere else.

I'm not going to lie, those were exhilarating nights in the news game.

The overnight shift worked perfectly for me. I'd catch the train into Central and walk the short distance to the John Fairfax

Building, which was where the University of Technology is now on Broadway in Sydney. At the end of my shift, I'd catch the 6.15 am train back to Bondi Junction then the 380 bus home, grab my board and head to the beach. I'd surf for a few hours, come in, run up and grab a fried-egg sandwich and pineapple juice for breakfast from Vallis's Milk Bar, fall asleep on the sand for an hour or so, then head back into the surf for a few more hours. I'd have lunch about 3 pm then sleep till about eight then get up, and go to work like a real man, or at least a real boy-man. And repeat. I was living my dream life.

I was still at home but I didn't see my parents or sisters too much. When I came home from surfing, they'd still be at work or school, then I'd go to sleep, and I might see them all briefly as I grabbed some leftovers from dinner before I left for work at about 9 pm.

The overnight crews were great; we always had fun together. This was the shift where young journos were bled on tough stories – at least, that was what we were always told, but looking back, I realise it was because the older journos didn't want to work overnight. Dddddeeeerrrr!!!!!

I was happily sitting in the Police Rounds starship *Enterprise* room about two o'clock one morning when one of the young journalists came in and said, 'You live in Bondi, don't you?'

'Yeah.'

He handed me a freshly printed copy of that morning's *Sydney Morning Herald*, which shared its offices with *The Sun*. It featured a big story on crime in Bondi. He suggested I rewrite it and submit it to my local newspaper, because that was what the young copy boys and girls would do for extra experience.

It was a quiet night in Police Rounds, and back then there was no real way of mindlessly killing hours and hours like you would today on Insta or Twitter or by googling porn (I don't why that keeps coming up). I was bored enough to try to be a journalist. So I looked at this article and started to rewrite it – or, to be more accurate, *steal* it.

Same quotes from cops and authorities, same stats, pretty much same everything.

My local paper was *The Bondi Spectator*, a thin weekly rag that mainly carried council stories, local sports results and lots of ads. I'd seen it on my doorstep every week of my life but I'd never really paid attention to it.

As the slow shift continued, I finished rewriting (stealing) the article, then typed it out on one of the old *Sun* typewriters. I called it 'The Bondi Crime Plague'.

Then I typed a letter to the *Spectator* editor. Something like:

Dear Editor,
My name is Larry Emdur and I'm interested in journalism.
Would you be kind enough to look over this article and give me some feedback?
Thank you.

It was a Monday morning. I knew where the *Spectator* office was, because we used to ride our skateboards a lot around Bondi Junction. So on the way home I jumped off the 6.15 train, ran up to the *Spectator* office and slid 'The Bondi Crime Plague' story with the intro letter under the front door.

And went for a surf.

I didn't hear back, but that didn't bother me. To be honest I didn't really expect to – this was, after all, a poorly written crime story that fell off the back of a truck and was rebirthed in the middle of the night, like a stolen car with a few big bits taken out and replaced with other bits, so its owner wouldn't recognise it.

Then on the Thursday Mum came in and woke me up at about 5 pm with a *Spectator* in her hand.

'*Is this you?*'

On page 3 of *The Bondi Spectator*, in big black bold headline print, I read:

THE BONDI CRIME PLAGUE
BY LARRY EDMUR

I was in total shock. This was *unbelievable!* Apart from the fact they'd spelt my name wrong, this was the greatest moment of my life.

The *Spectator* definitely didn't have a crime reporter, and this story filled an important gap. I didn't really want to meet or speak to the editor – I was a kid with long hair, pimples, a squeaky voice and a permanently sunburnt nose – so I just decided not to call him or anything. But I was *very* excited.

The next night I searched through the *Sydney Morning Herald* and *Sun* archives for other stories about Bondi. I found one and stole it – or, as the good folk at Disney would say, 'reimagined it' – and slipped it under the office door on my way home in the morning.

The paper came out the following Thursday, and this time I was on the front page!

My well-developed ego was through the roof. There was no denying it, I had magical hands! First my incredible 'downward-facing with purpose' thumbs had won me the marching trophy at

Rose Bay Public School, and now my two forefingers had typed me onto the front page of *The Bondi Spectator*. I was famous – well, that's what Grandpa Louis told me as he unwrapped his fish and chips which had been parcelled in my front page. I'm a kid who can't read or write, and now I'm on the front page of the paper??!! And this time they'd even spelt my name write (or was it right?).

'Holy shit,' I thought, 'I hope my deputy headmaster, who told me "Emdur, you'll never get anywhere without your Higher School Certificate", gets to see *this*!'

Although if he did, he probably would've quickly put my front page in his budgie cage and taken great joy watching his budgies shit on my story.

I never wanted to meet or speak to the *Spectator* editor, I never asked for money or a job, but each week I'd slip another story under the door. My stories regularly ran on the front page, or right up the front of the paper.

Who *was* this phantom columnist who, under the cover of darkness, would slip stories under the *Spectator* office door? Was he a cop who wanted to leak stories? Was he a retired journo just trying to stay busy? Was he a teenage mutant turtle living in the sewers below Bondi Junction who just wanted people in the bustling metropolis above to know the real facts???

No one had ever heard *of* him or *from* him. Was that even his real name or was it Barry Schmemder using Larry Emdur as a catchy pseudonym?

This went on for the better part of a year. It was a good relationship, in that there was no relationship, so it worked really well.

All the little local papers were delivered to the Fairfax offices, and the journos would scour them for potential stories for the

Herald or the *Sun*. There was a good chance that, any day now, a journo would be reading a Larry Emdur story in the *Spectator* that I'd stolen from him or her in the first place.

Awkward ...

I waited for an angry phone call, but none came. Bottom line, I got away with it. That's another crime to add to my rap sheet.

By now I had a thick green scrapbook full of stories, many of them on the front page. Now I could *actually* call myself a journalist, as opposed to a naughty boy stealing stories from *other* journalists.

Let the lying, cheating hunger games of my life begin ...

PART II

A CHEAP WATCH AND A SHINY SUIT

AUSTRALIA'S YOUNGEST NEWSREADER

1980s–1990s

'Be nice to everyone.'

Dave Emdur

The Moment

1983

I had no qualifications, had left school young after failing most subjects, and was (still am) terrible at spelling, grammar and punctuation ... but now I had a scrapbook of clippings from *The Bondi Spectator*, so when I applied for reporters' jobs I could make it look like I was a real journo!

Smoke and mirrors. Smoke and mirrors.

I decided TV might be easier than newspapers, because no one saw your writing. As long as you could deliver your words on TV, no one would ever have to know you couldn't spell or your apostrophes were in the wro'ng plac'e (or worse, werent there at all). Using that scrapbook as a calling card to prove beyond all reasonable doubt that I was fully qualified (*OMG, I'm going to hell!*), I actually got a little bit of work here and there with a couple of freelance TV production companies.

I did everything from holding the microphone for interviews to carrying the tripod and even washing the cars. But I got to see proper news crews and TV reporters in action, and I liked what I saw.

The reporters were cool and kind of famous. They would fly to jobs in choppers, and the crews would park their news cruisers wherever the hell they wanted.

It looked exciting and glamorous, and I was a dreamer who had always wanted the exciting and glamorous job, like the front counter position at Dairy Queen or the pizza spinner at Nino's. But I was ordinary ... And lazy ... And stupid ... Still, this news reporter thing looked particularly awesome! I had to get in on this act.

After about six months of freelance jobs, I wrote to all the networks.

I got a letter back from Channel Nine saying, 'Sorry, there are no junior positions available at the moment.' I remember thinking, 'OK, so what about *senior* positions? I mean, I *was* the Senior Crime Reporter for *The Bondi Spectator* for almost a year. Really, applying for a news reporter's job is probably a waste of my valuable time. I should just skip the news and go straight onto *60 Minutes* ...'

A cocky kid having a crack, knowing he was way out of his depth but just putting it out there for shits and giggles. I believed I would make a good journalist. In a war zone, I could duck and weave – just ask Diana Strum from the Rose Bay Public School bell pole incident. I could also survive any potentially explosive situation, like I did when Dad was smoking while carrying four-litre tins of highly flammable boat deck paint. Yep, I'd be good at this.

The letter back from SBS was the most interesting. Words to the effect of 'Thank you for your application, but unfortunately you don't fit our ethnic criteria.' Can you imagine the uproar that sort of letter would cause today?!

Then I got a letter from Cliff Neville, one of the bosses at Channel Seven News. He asked me to come in for a meeting. I took my thick green scrapbook along to prove that I was a journalist.

He was a really nice guy, and it was a very casual chat. He finished the meeting by saying, 'We have nothing at the moment, but let's stay in touch.'

I was too young to know that probably meant 'We'll never talk again.'

While I waited for my brilliant career to take off, I bought a cheap backpack and a Eurail pass and went backpacking around Europe for the rest of 1983.

I returned with even more chutzpah than when I'd left. It was December 1983 and I'd just turned nineteen.

In the week leading up to Christmas, I rang Cliff Neville and asked if there was anything I could do around the newsroom. I basically offered myself as a dogsbody work-experience kid. Maybe I could just hang around, go out on the road with the crews and, you know, just see how it all works. I knew most people would be off on holidays and, like any organisation, they'd be short-staffed.

Cliff agreed. He told me I could start on Christmas Eve. I was thrilled!

I rummaged through Dad's wardrobe for something appropriate. I found a fawn flecked jacket, and a blue business shirt which Mum ironed for me. I had a skinny leather tie that I'd bought at Paddington Markets a couple of years earlier to wear to a debutante ball. Yes, that's how cool I was: a thin leather tie. Rock on! (Confession: it only cost $2.50 so there was a big chance it wasn't real leather.)

I did the first-day-of-work-experience thing and arrived an hour early.

The Chief of Staff was in the process of sending a camera crew to the Wayside Chapel in Kings Cross and told me to tag along.

The Wayside Chapel is famous to most Sydneysiders. It does incredibly important work, offering meals, support and services to the homeless. Its founder, the Reverend Ted Noffs, was an absolute saint, and this Christmas Eve lunch was a really big event for the Kings Cross community.

We walked through the front door. The place was crowded and full of good cheer. I was dressed like a reporter, but I wasn't, I was the work-experience kid wearing his dad's jacket and a cheap leather tie he bought to match his debutante ball partner's shoes …

I immediately spotted Ricky May, an entertainment superstar. He was hard to miss.

Ricky May was a big man with a bigger voice and an even bigger heart. He was one of those rare characters who loved everyone, and everyone loved him back. A New Zealander who had found success here, he was a huge star in the 1980s in every sense of the word. He was Mr Variety, a must-have guest on any morning, midday or tonight show, an all-singing, all-dancing, all-jazz-hands legend.

And now we'd somehow made eye contact and he was heading my way!

These were my first moments of work experience, so I wasn't at all offended when, for some reason I will never ever understand, he bounced up to me and said: 'You look like you don't know what you're doing.'

Said with his famous huge smile and booming voice, it wasn't insulting at all. In fact, I laughed back and said, 'I have no idea.'

And this is the moment my life changed forever.

This is THE MOMENT.

This day could've so easily gone absolutely nowhere. A poorly dressed, beady-eyed, big-toothed kid dressed in an oversized jacket and shirt, carrying a tripod for a TV crew. I could've simply hung around the newsroom for a week like so many other work-experience kids then drifted off, never to be heard of again.

'OK,' said Ricky, 'just grab your camera guy and follow me around. I'll tell you when to film stuff.'

I told the cameraman what Ricky May had said, and he was like: 'OK.'

We followed Ricky as he weaved his way through the hall serving big lunches to hungry and homeless men, rough-looking men, men who couldn't afford food and were sleeping on the streets around Kings Cross. Men who were openly reduced to tears, tears that were rolling down dirty faces and into unkempt beards, at the love, warmth and generosity being served up along with the food.

I got pretty caught up in this moment. I think I cried watching them. I was young, and it was powerful and confronting and highly emotional.

One elderly man, scruffily dressed with rough, messy hair and just a few teeth left, grabbed a Santa hat off the table and started singing to Ricky: 'O, come let us adore him, O, come let us adore him …'

He was aiming that squarely at Ricky, not the other bloke the song is usually about. Everyone joined in. It was beautiful.

I was glad I was there and got to witness this, but it occurred to me I was probably one of the only people who *wanted* to be there. If all the attendees had had a choice, I was sure they would rather have been with loved ones. It's the happiest time of the year for many, but the saddest and loneliest time of the year for others.

Ricky was moving through the crowd, a man-mountain of love. He'd sing up close to the camera then put his big, loving arms around some of the men, and they'd join him in a rousing rendition of a Christmas carol.

It was clear that these people, in their day-to-day lives, didn't have much joy. I'll never forget the smiles – big genuine smiles, many through missing teeth – or the laughter. Maybe away from here, these men didn't smile or laugh that much at all.

I remember people singing loudly, badly but fabulously, at the very tops of their voices. They felt safe here, this was their big party – and as a huge bonus for me, it was, I'd go on to learn, great television.

It was a fabulous story, we couldn't miss; it was all there happening in front of us for the camera. I interviewed some of the homeless men, and some cried as they explained how important this day was for them, and how wonderful Ricky was. I interviewed Ricky too, and asked what this day meant to him. He just let fly. He was a born performer and his answer was big and loud and emotional and perfect.

The instructions from the Chief of Staff as we headed out on this job had just been to get some nice pictures for the newsreader to read over at the end of the news. But as we wrapped up, the cameraman suggested I do a piece to camera just for fun, just for the experience of doing it.

So I stood in front of the camera at the back of the room and said something generic. Like: 'A very special day with a very special guest. Move over, Santa Claus, today it was *Ricky May* spreading love and joy and hope,' followed by the words I'd only dreamt of saying one day: 'Larry Emdur reporting for Seven Nightly News.'

This bit definitely wasn't meant to be going anywhere. But as I sat with the editor back in the newsroom edit suite to watch how he put everything together, he said, 'This is really good stuff. It's a whole story, not just pictures for the end of the news.'

He went out and had a chat to the News Director, who agreed to let him try to put my story together.

Everything you'd need for a whole package was there: wonderful interviews with Ricky May and Ted Noffs, happy and often emotional interviews with the homeless men.

It ended up being a beautiful story: the perfect balance of heart and soul, tears of joy and tears of sadness. And Ricky May had done it all. He had virtually taken me by the hand, and made sure the cameraman and I were in the right place at the right time. And through absolutely no doing of mine, it had morphed into a magical Christmas news story.

We finished editing it quite late – there was no hurry, as it was destined for the end of the news bulletin – but somewhere in the process a news producer had come into the edit suite to check on the progress and decided it had to go up the *top* of the news. He asked if I'd done a standup (a piece to camera), and I said yes, the cameraman had got me to do one just for fun.

The editor showed it to him and he said great, put it in.

Wait – what?! I came in this morning to look around and help carry the tripod, and now *I'm about to appear on the primetime news* with a standup I did just for fun?!?!

I called Mum urgently. 'Mum, can't talk, I'm going to be on the news tonight, call Nanny Leah and Grandpa Louis, call Nanny Minnie!'

The story went to air at the top of the bulletin, and it looked like a *real* news story, done by a *real* reporter.

WOW! What a day. *How the hell did that just happen?*

I would get to see Ricky May many more times, at many more events over the years, and we'd always talk about this.

But wait, there's more!

Because that story had magically gone so smoothly, the Chief of Staff asked if I wanted to come back tomorrow, Christmas Day, to do *another* report!

I jumped at the chance – but I knew Dad only had one summer jacket, so I realised I might be in a spot of bother in the old wardrobe department.

Mum and Dad and my sisters were *so* excited when I got home. I had to tell them all about the day and what had happened, then I had to call Nanny Leah and Grandpa Louis and tell *them*, then Nanny Minnie. They had all seen it, of course, and no one could really believe it had just happened.

We dug deep into Dad's wardrobe, frantically trying to piece together an ensemble worthy of the Seven Nightly News. He wasn't much of a suit and jacket kind of guy, but finally we found a dark, winter-weight jacket at the back of his wardrobe. It smelt a bit musty, so Mum saturated it in Fabulon ironing spray to give it a slighter fresher odour and hung it on the clothesline to air out overnight.

I left home around dawn on Christmas morning, and the whole way to the studio I was practising saying: 'Larry Emdur, Seven Nightly News.' I must've said it a hundred times, in a hundred different ways.

I arrived there very early. I'd got *so* lucky yesterday with that Ricky May story. What would today bring?

'That was a good yarn yesterday, Larry!' said the Chief of Staff. 'Take a crew and head down to Bondi Beach and do a story on how Australians spend Christmas.'

'Oh, my God!' I thought. 'That's where I live, that's where I grew up! I know where all the different nationality groups gather. I know *exactly* how Aussies spend Christmas at Bondi!'

This was an incredible opportunity.

'Have a go at that,' the Chief of Staff went on, 'and make sure the cameraman gets lots of pictures, in case we don't want to use *you*, just the pictures.'

'Fuck you! Fuck that! I'm embedding myself so deeply into this story you'll have *no choice* but to use me!' I thought to myself as I turned to leave.

It was a great story. Once again, it just happened. I made it like an SBS documentary, showing how all the different ethnic groups celebrate along the beach. (See, SBS, I *can* tell ethnically diverse stories.) It was fun and colourful, I looked comfortable and at home – because I was! – it went to air and I had just landed myself a news reporter's job on Seven Nightly News.

Thank you, Ricky May! If the magic that happened that day hadn't happened, I could still be the world's oldest golf-ball thief!

If This Van's A-Rockin' ...
Circa 1984

Having sex in the back of a panel van was always awkward, fun and interesting. It always seemed super sneaky and super naughty.

It could be next to the pub, outside the shopping centre, on the street in front of your family's house. It could be in the middle of the day in the car park at the beach, with hundreds of people walking right by without having a clue what was happening inside.

You had to master the art of quiet sex, not crazy, screamy, yelly sex.

A mate and his girlfriend were famous around the beach for their loud sex. It was like a *Fifty Shades of Grey* broadcast. It was the same every time. He'd be in the surf with a few of us, she'd be sunbaking on the beach with her girlfriends. At the end of his surf, he'd paddle into the beach, walk past her, then she'd walk with him to the panel van.

We'd all paddle in and go with her girlfriends to the vicinity of the panel van and listen to them having sex. One time her friends had timed their purchase of fish and chips perfectly, so it was like dinner and a show.

He was a bit older than the rest of us, and he used to say that it was the perfect storm of horny.

He's out paddling around in the surf, which essentially means he's grinding his penis against his surfboard for an hour or so, and she's on the warm sand, rubbing suntan oil into herself. He's thinking about her, she's thinking about him. Sex in the panel van, he would say, was the natural conclusion to this story.

Her girlfriends used to say she'd boastfully invite them to come and stand around the van and listen, and he would say the same to us, so I guess they were a bit exhibitionist and proud of their behaviour. They wanted to share the love with their friends, which I'm sure you'll agree is a very generous and noble thing to do. You gotta look after your friends.

When they got going, they were like the beans inside the maracas during Peter Allen's solo in 'I Go to Rio'. Bouncing off the walls, screaming, shouting, feet against the window. He's yelling, she's yelling, she's whooping, he's whooping.

If this van's a-rockin', don't bother knockin'.

Now, remember this is in the middle of a summer Sunday, parked on the main promenade at the world's most famous beach. It was a real show. We'd watch people walk past, everyone would look and we'd death-stare back as if to say, 'What *you* looking at? We're all having a private moment here!'

We'd look at them like you look at those young kids who sneak into a movie halfway through and you know they haven't paid. The rest of Bondi didn't have tickets to this show, *we* did, and we were very protective, like the bouncers at Archie's Nightclub in Bondi Junction. It was like our little group was invited to an exclusive show, and no one else was allowed to enjoy it.

Panel-van sex was proper flat-bed sex, not like that super-awkward sitting-up-straight-in-the-front-seat-of-a-car-at-the-drive-in-with-hands-everywhere-under-a-towel kind of sex.

Now, when I say 'proper flat-bed sex', I need to let you know it wasn't *classy* proper flat-bed sex, it was probably a bit frantic and feral. We were eighteen, nineteen, twenty.

This was a bed in a van, usually with shagpile carpet lining the ceiling and surfing posters on the walls. If that doesn't scream romance, I don't know what does.

Everyone was complicit and consenting. Nothing forced, no pressure. But it was a particularly prominent part of surfie culture.

My favourite car was my Mini Moke, an especially cool kind of surf buggy. It was yellow and I could fit three mates in it, plus a whole bunch of boards across the roll bars. The Mini Moke was great for cruising the beaches but terrible for sex. The total opposite of the panel van. It was low, it was completely open, the seats didn't recline at all and the side panels were the same level as the seats. So not only was there no more flat-bed sex, but there weren't even any more hand jobs.

But it was a fantastic surf buggy, and that was important to me.

It only weighed about four hundred kilos, so my mates and I would pull up alongside the tiniest of parking spots and the four of us would lift the front end into the tight spot, then go around the back and lift the rear end in. Sometimes, if there wasn't a big enough gap, I'd just park it rear-to-kerb in between two properly parked cars. These were cheeky days.

We could park it anywhere – except outside the Astra Hotel at South Bondi, where the bikie gangs would've picked it up and crushed it like a Coke can.

The ongoing joke with the infamous Bondi Astra was you'd only go there to score drugs or get into a fight. It drew a certain class of clientele, and unfortunately there were regular newsworthy brawls between bikie gangs and Maori groups that had also moved into Bondi.

Bondi had become as famous for these as it was for the beach, so when the Astra shut down in the early '80s, there was a real sense that Bondi was changing for the better. Growing up. A couple of nicer restaurants opened up, the nightlife calmed down – less aggro, fewer police sirens. There was now a slightly more sophisticated, yuppie vibe. You'd see nicer cars starting to park near the beach and along Campbell Parade. I even saw a guy in a polo shirt with the collar up. Yep, this signalled a monumental change.

The first mobile phones were also making their way into the nice cars of rich people.

Looking back, I realise those first phones were ridiculous. The battery was like a small briefcase. The whole thing weighed about fifteen kilos and could only store a handful of numbers. No camera, no internet, no googling, no emailing. Just a phone, a really *huge* phone.

And it cost more than $4000. It became an instantly recognisable status symbol of the rich and famous. You could even wire it to your car, so that if you were away from the car and you got a call, the horn would start honking and the headlights would start flashing.

This was a particularly funny period at Bondi Beach. We'd all be out surfing and car horns would be honking and lights flashing all over the place, and with each new honk someone else would get out of the surf to run up and answer their phone. Wankers.

All of a sudden there was an influx of people in expensive cars, driving around talking on their phones. It seemed so pretentious, yet so aspirational. I would look at these people and think, 'You absolute tosser, but hot damn, I want to be just like you.'

My mates and I would be driving around in my Mini Moke, which had cost me $200 — so, twenty times less than the phone the guy in the Porsche at the traffic lights next to us is talking on.

We'd all be staring at him on his phone, bloody wanker. He'd look down at us, bloody losers. The lights would turn green, he'd buzz off doing zero to a hundred in 3.8 seconds, I'd grind my clutch and force the gearstick into first and we'd try to catch him doing zero to thirty in thirty seconds.

We were young and stupid, we were taking the piss. *We* were going for a surf, *he* was probably going back to his penthouse apartment to eat oysters and lobsters and drink champagne with his model girlfriend who'd just got back from a *Vogue* cover shoot in the Bahamas. Then they were probably going to have a dip in the spa on his balcony overlooking the beach, before making sweet, sweet love on a mattress that didn't sag in the middle, then cooling down in a shower that worked and drying off with nice soft towels that couldn't walk themselves to the laundry like mine. But *we* were going for a surf, so technically *we* were the winners.

I know people like to make confessions in books like this, so here's mine.

(Now, please note, I have a fear of going to jail, so hopefully this doesn't end up with me doin' hard time in the clink. I think I'd be popular in jail, though – not just because I'm adorable, but also I always thought if ended up in prison I could host little game shows after dinner and give away cigarettes and magazines.

Most of the guys would like me, and the superintendent would like me too because I'm lifting morale, but of course there's always a Bubba, the cellmate whose hands are the size of baseball mitts and whose fingers are as thick as Chiko Rolls. His aunty missed out on winning a fridge on *The Price Is Right* years ago and now I'm locked in a cell with him, he's angry and horny – or, as we call it in prison, *horngry* – and the rest is history – or, as we call it in prison, *horngrystory*.

So you can see why I have a fear of going to prison.)

That said, here's my confession, which hopefully doesn't lead to some retrospective charges being laid.

The guy at a particular Bondi corner store was a dick. Best comparison: the Soup Nazi on *Seinfeld*. He was rude, he was nasty, but there weren't too many convenience stores then, so if you wanted a Sunnyboy Glug or a can of Fanta or a packet of Twisties after a surf, this was one of the only places to go.

We'd parked the Moke badly outside his shop and were just sitting all over it – on the hood, on the mudguards … You could do that with a Moke, the whole thing was like one big uncomfortable lounge and sitting all over it was the cool thing to do.

A guy pulled up in his fancy car on his fancy phone. His roof was down, he was talking loudly, and after a minute or so he got out, walked into the store and grabbed some stuff, then jumped back into his car, got back on the phone and drove off, zero to a hundred in 3.8 seconds.

At that moment I noticed the red payphone outside. For reference, they were about the same size as a carton of beer, and they sat on a white stand. You'd need to put coins in to make a call.

Wait – what?! A phone with a cable, outside a shop, in which you'd have to put coins and then use a round disc to rotary-dial the numbers? Bloody hell, has this book turned into *Back to the Future 10*???

So I stole it. I sent the boys in to distract the Soup Nazi and I stole the payphone. I just picked it up off the stand and raced back to the Moke.

I thought it would be really funny, and a good way to take the piss out of the wankers driving around on their phones.

So this bright-red payphone sat in the middle of the two front seats of my bright-yellow Mini Moke, and when we pulled up next to a wanker on their phone, or a car full of girls, we'd pick up the phone and start talking loudly in a posh accent.

Remember, the Moke was all open and low, so this was highly visible.

We thought we were hysterical. And, looking back, I think we successfully out-wankered the wankers.

The Moke was a perfect summer car, but winter was a whole new story. It had a terrible rotten canopy and busted side panels, and the clear vinyl rear-view panel – what would be a rear window in most cars – was ripped in several places. Everything flapped and leaked, and the windscreen wipers were useless – in fact, I'd had to replace one with a chopstick and a sliced-up dish sponge.

Once you were going more than forty ks, every panel starting flapping in a different direction. If it was raining, water would be pouring in from every joint and seam in the canopy, and over the chopstick and the dish sponge, which were gaffer-taped to the stump of broken windscreen wiper that no longer worked …

For some reason I also had constant headaches. I regularly had a sore neck from surfing for hours and hours at a time, but these headaches were different. I went back to the doctor several times and he couldn't work out why.

I was driving around the beaches one day and a police car drove up behind me and hit the siren.

Luckily I was past my red-payphone-as-a-mobile phase by then, so why were they pulling me over?

Had the insurance company dobbed me in for stealing the brass wheel from Dad's sunken boat? Had the guy from the North Bondi golf course supplied them with a photo-fit sketch of two boys in the bushes grabbing strangers' balls? Had the lifeguards dobbed me in for stealing sand? Had the water police dobbed me in for singing Barry Manilow songs on the back of *Siesta* wearing Speedos?

I'd been running from the law for at least a decade, and now my time had finally come. I was going to have a terrible time in prison — I was adorable and spunky, and when I told the other inmates I was in the clink for grabbing strange men's balls I was going to be *very* popular, and not in a good way …

So I indicated and pulled over — oh, yeah, I forgot to mention that the indicator stick was another chopstick taped onto the stump of the broken indicator with electrical tape.

The cop was a reasonable guy. All he said was: 'Mate, you want to get that checked.'

'What?' I asked, alarmed.

He said, 'Your exhaust fumes, all that black smoke. It looks like it's coming straight up into the flapping window panel at the back.'

The car was so clunky and noisy – the engine sounded like a drunk sewing machine at its first rave party and all the roof and window flaps would be flapping loudly – I hadn't noticed all the exhaust fumes pouring in and swirling round.

My headaches and numb lips after a long drive? The early stages of carbon monoxide poisoning, according to the doctor at my next visit.

It was still one of my favourite cars, but I reluctantly swapped it for a case of beer. Only recently a mate sent me a link to one for sale online, exactly the same as my old beast, for $51,000.

$51,000???

I should've asked for a better brand of beer.

News Overnight

1984

I'm going to start this story by setting the record straight. A historical correction, if you will. For years and years, when stories have been written about me, it's been reported that I became Australia's youngest newsreader at the age of seventeen.

It may shock you to learn that the media can get things wrong ... Well, this statement isn't actually true.

So I just want to lay out the facts here once and for all, so you'll be able to see where it all went wrong.

As you've already learnt, I started at Seven Nightly News when I was nineteen. I loved being a reporter; I was covering everything from general news, crime, animal stories, celebrity interviews, even politics. At one stage, the network decided it wanted to be the first to say it broadcast news 'twenty-four hours a day'.

Of course, this meant they had to run news during the night. Not major bulletins, just lengthy updates on the hour, every hour.

No one in the newsroom wanted to do the overnights – but remember where this all started for me? Working overnight as a copy boy so I could surf all day.

I couldn't read an autocue, and I certainly didn't look, sound or present like a newsreader, but this new opportunity was mutually beneficial: *I* got to work overnight and surf all day and *the network* got to say, 'News twenty-four hours a day.'

In 1988, when I moved to Channel Ten to work as a roving reporter on *Good Morning Australia* with Kerri-Anne Kennerley and Tim Webster, they sent out a press release about me that began:

> Larry Emdur started working in the media at seventeen and became Australia's youngest newsreader.

Now, both of those facts are true *independently*, but when fused together, they're *not*.

This opening line got picked up by all the major newspapers and magazines, and you can see how it easily morphed into my becoming a newsreader at seventeen. I *did* start at *The Sun* aged seventeen, and I *did* become Australia's youngest newsreader, but they just happened a few years apart.

There was no internet back then, and by the time the information had appeared in all the major publications in one form or another, it was impossible to put that genie back in the bottle. From there on in, every time someone wrote a story about me, they'd refer back to the *last* story written about me, and so it went on.

I've tried many times in interviews to put the true version out there, only to see the original incorrect mishmash of facts used in the final story. So to be completely honest I've just kind of given up and played along with it. But writing my own book is a great opportunity to finally set the record straight.

It's also a great opportunity to tell you about how I totally and completely screwed up the very first *News Overnight* broadcast.

It was scheduled for 2 am, at the end of the American *Today* show, which was running on Channel Seven from midnight. Pretty simple, really: Bryant Gumbel and Jane Pauley would sign off on *Today*, the new flashy Seven News promo would play, boasting 'News twenty-four hours a day', then I would read the headlines and weather from a desk at the back of the newsroom.

Everything was ready to go. I'd had two hundred coffees to make sure I was in tiptop shape. Not those fancy coffee capsules that make you look like George Clooney if you drink them, oh no no no, it was International Roast only in the Channel Seven tearoom back then. You'd open the industrial-size tin, use the spoon that everyone else had been using all day, scoop a generous serving of coffee powder into a mug – maybe properly washed, maybe not – and hope for the best.

I was bouncing off the walls: a combination of nerves, excitement and probably the equivalent of the entire industrial-size tin of International Roast coursing through my veins.

The camera and lighting were all preset on the news desk. There were a few other people around doing other jobs, but the news desk was mine, ALL MINE!!! It was just little high-school drop-out loser Lazza on his own at the news desk. What could possibly go wrong?

It was up to me to keep the twenty-four-hour news dream alive. There was a small knob under the desk, and while this appears to be an amazing opportunity to do a penis joke, I'm just going to move on, because I'm telling you a story about being a newsreader, and newsreaders don't do penis jokes.

Anyhow ... it was now about 1.50 am, and I was sitting at my desk running through the scripts. I was planning to walk across the newsroom and sit down at the news desk at about 1.55, then set up my notes, calm my nerves and prepare to engage that mystical third testicle a young man must engage when he's trying to talk like a grown-up newsreader.

Then at about 1.51 one of the editors screamed: 'Laz, we're on, something's wrong with the *Today* feed! We're on, NOW!! *Run run run!!!*'

My desk and the news desk were at opposite ends of the newsroom. I leapt up and started racing like a crazy man.

'*Hurry, hurry,* YOU'RE ON!!!' the editor was yelling.

How can I be ON? I'm nowhere near ON. In fact I'm still twenty or thirty metres away from being ON. I'm running like Tiger Woods being chased by his golf-club-swinging ex-wife, jumping over desks, sidestepping wastepaper bins ...

I get within striking distance of the desk. I can see the *News Overnight* intro is just about to finish. Nice one, guys, run the intro before the newsreader is even there.

I can see the intro coming to an end and on comes a shot of the empty chair.

I'm close enough, I can make this jump, I can do this, because, as I always used to say, 'Two hundred cups of International Roast gives you wings!', before you-know-who came and stole that saying from me.

The shot of the empty chair is live on air. I launch myself, take a flying jump and stick the landing perfectly. If this were an Olympic chair-jumping event it would be tens from all the judges.

Even those pesky, notoriously tough judges from Liechtenstein would've thought this landing was something very special.

The only slight, slight, minuscule problem is that the chair is on wheels.

So the opening shot of the much-anticipated launch of Seven's *News Overnight* is a silly young guy jumping into a chair, that then violently rolls off the set, while screaming:

'SHHHHHHIIIITTTTTTTTTT!!!!'

Like a cartoon character slipping on a banana peel, I was gone.

Welcome to *News Overnight*, everybody.

The Watch

1985

It was my twenty-first birthday. Some of my work colleagues took me out for drinks and presented me with a beautiful new suit. They'd all chipped in for this special birthday present. It was a fancy suit – well, fanc*er* than what I'd been wearing up to that point.

I was a reporter on TV, but I had a terrible wardrobe. I had a network clothing allowance these days, but I'd sneakily concluded that if I borrowed Dad's clothes for work, I could use it to buy surfboards instead. Clothes weren't important to me, surfboards were.

I think buying me the suit was like a fashion intervention. I was wearing Dad's double-breasted, wide-lapelled jacket and triple-pleated slacks that day, and I saw my friends look me up and down as they handed over the gift.

Maybe I dressed like an old man, but I had a carport full of the best surfboards in Bondi, so technically I was the winner.

My new suit was grey and shiny – not classy-expensive shiny but cheap-synthetic shiny. But all my socks were black, and everyone knows only losers wear black socks with a grey suit. It's highly unlikely any man wearing a grey suit with black socks has ever managed to convince a woman to sleep with him. Like a guy wearing socks with Crocs, you know he's not getting any sex anytime soon.

I got home late that night and went straight to bed. Next morning, I set off on the Great Grey Sock Hunt.

My sock drawer was a dark and dangerous place; I would never let Mum or those guys from *CSI* with the blue lights within a mile of it. I desperately rummaged around but couldn't find anything suitable. Sure, there were some white socks that had accidentally been washed with black socks, but they were smudgy, blotchy grey, not that special 'shiny TV suit' shade of grey.

So, next stop: *Dad's* sock drawer. Mum and Dad had already left for work. I moved all Dad's white, black and blue socks around – and then I saw them, curled up in the back corner: a pair of lonely, lost, unloved grey socks.

This was a huge fashion victory. A grey suit and grey socks! Could this day get any better??

Well, given you're only a few hundred words into this story and nothing's really happened yet, you can take it for granted this day got a *whole* lot better. Because the socks were actually hiding an even greater treasure, something that would change my life forever.

A dusty old wristwatch.

It looked cheap, plain and pretty unimpressive, which was how my last girlfriend had described me. The inner part of the face was blotchy and off-white; perhaps it had once been shiny white but not now. The gold-coloured hands had tiny green segments that glowed in the dark. The band was red, black and grey striped, one of those really cheap ones you used to buy in a barber shop.

It might have been ordinary, but it did the job, which was exactly how my current girlfriend described me. I thought it was beautiful.

I picked it up and turned it over. Inscribed on the back was 'To David from Mother, 8/2/56'.

Dad was into his modern, flashy watches, so I couldn't picture this antique-looking thing on his tanned, hairy wrist.

I phoned him at his office and told him I'd just found a curious old watch. He said he hadn't seen it or even thought about it in many, many years, and couldn't have found it if he'd wanted to.

Then came the moment I'll never forget. He said: 'That was my twenty-first birthday present.'

Neither of us spoke for the next few seconds as we came to terms with the very strange coincidence in front of us.

'Wait, wait, hang on,' I said, 'you got this watch for your twenty-first birthday, you'd completely forgotten it even existed, and then I find it at the back of your sock drawer the day after *my* twenty-first birthday?'

Was this an incredible coincidence, or – as I would ask myself hundreds of times over the ensuing decades – had I somehow been divinely guided here to find this?

I immediately asked if I could have it, and Dad said yes, of course, as long as I looked after it. I put it on and thought, 'WOW, this is *really special*.'

THE WATCH

I gently wound the crown and the thin second hand started moving around the face. It worked! Having spent years and years lost in the darkest, loneliest corner of a stinky sock drawer, it just jumped up out of a twenty-year multi-cog coma and got straight back to work.

From then on I wore it every day and night. It wasn't waterproof, so I would take it off for a shower, but it was the first thing I put back on, even before my clothes. Every morning, I religiously wound it twenty-one times.

For the next twenty-five years, it became my most valuable and important possession. It held a beautiful magic, a constant spiritual connection with my dad. A bit like the way that old brass wheel on our superyacht had been a spiritual link between my dad and *his* dad. Neither the watch nor the brass steering wheel were at all valuable, but they were both absolutely priceless. I've had cars, motorbikes, boats and fancy clothes, and I could have happily lived without any of them, but I could never have lived without this watch.

When I went on surf trips to Bali, I would leave it in the hotel safe. On assignments and photo shoots it was safely with me in my pocket. Once I was running very late for a flight. About halfway to the airport I realised I'd forgotten the watch, so I asked the taxi driver to turn around and take me home. I knew this would mean missing the plane, but there was no way in the world I was travelling without it.

Every time I saw my Nanny Leah I would hold out my left arm and show her I was still wearing the watch she gave her son for his twenty-first. She had the most beautiful smiling eyes, and seeing the watch would always make the smile in her eyes even bigger. Towards the end of her days, just the action of showing her the watch would make those eyes fill with tears.

Just before a big event — a public appearance, a business negotiation, even at our wedding as Sylvie walked down the aisle — anytime I needed to calm my heart and mind I would hold my right hand over the watch on my left wrist and take a deep, deep breath. This would always centre me and give me strength.

On every single episode of every TV show I've ever hosted, just before the doors opened up for me to run out I would cup my right hand over the watch and draw on its power.

I'll never forget the first time I got to fill in for Daryl Somers and host *Hey Hey It's Saturday*. It was 1994 and *Hey Hey* was the biggest show on TV. This would be the most important night in my career so far, and I was desperate to nail it. It was going to be two hours of craziness and chaos and I was absolutely shitting myself.

The producers had sent me a huge pile of notes the day before, including the show rundown, information on the segments and guests, and suggested gags from the writers. I pored over these and made a million scribbly notes on them, using a thousand Post-it notes and five different-coloured highlighter pens, till I had it all worked out page by page. I was confident I had everything I needed in this comprehensive stack of loose-leaf papers to get me through these crucial two hours.

About three minutes to showtime, I was standing backstage. I had my massive wad of pages in my hands and was waiting for the floor manager to take them over and set them up on the host desk before I ran out.

Red Symons, the show's resident larrikin and shit-stirrer, walked over to wish me luck. He looked at the pile of papers and asked, 'What's all that?'

'That's all my notes for the show,' I said.

He leant over, ripped the bundle out of my hand, declared, 'You won't be needing those!' and threw them into the air.

I watched my precious notes rain down all over the backstage area.

'One minute, Larry,' said the floor manager as Red walked off laughing.

With my plans for the show completely scuttled, my head was spinning, my heart was pounding, I felt totally discombobulated, and in thirty seconds I had to bounce through those doors and begin the most important role of my life.

I only had time for one thing. Right hand over the watch on my left wrist and breathe. 'Calm, peace, focus ... OK, OPEN THOSE DOORS, LET'S FUCKING DO THIS!'

The show went really well. The litmus test for this is whether you get invited back to do it again. And, yes, I did; however, according to an old TV theory that could've also meant that a regular host wanted a shit host as a replacement so the regular host would look really good. Gotta love TV.

When I was at Dad's bedside in his final days, I would take his hand and place it on the watch, then put mine on top of his. He'd smile, because this was our magical thing, our bond, our connection. He knew the watch would always be his but always be mine and always be ours.

As he was slipping away from us, I asked the nurse if I could put the watch on his wrist, but she said he couldn't have any jewellery on. And then I realised that he'd probably want *me* to have it, that of the two of us, *I* was the one who would need the power, the strength, the magic to get me through the horrible hours ahead.

I tried not to cry as I wound the watch on the morning of Dad's funeral. This watch had always brought me strength, not made me sad.

For maybe a minute, I held it to my ear and listened to the hypnotic ticktock. I imagined the tiny cogs pushing the bigger cogs. I wound it as slowly as I possibly could, feeling every single click of the winder. With each twist of the crown came another tear. Twenty-one winds, exactly twenty-one winds.

The watch that had, over the years, told me it was time to run out onto the TV set, time to marry Sylvie, time to pick the kids up from school, was now telling me it was time to go and bury my dad, my best friend.

I held Mum tight as they lowered Dad's coffin into the ground, but at one point I took my right hand off her shoulder and gently placed it on the watch to calm my broken heart. There was no amount of magic this watch could produce that could heal my pain, but I hoped it would at least bring me peace.

It worked. It's always worked.

Sylvie has always wanted to buy me a really beautiful watch, a cool, modern watch. For years she'd remind me on my birthday, and every year I'd say no thanks. Every birthday, same conversation. We never fought about it, but at one point I did ask her to stop asking me. She didn't understand what my watch meant to me, and maybe never will.

Around 3 pm on 29 April 1994, our first child, Jye, was born. I was delirious with joy and pure, pure adoration for our new baby boy, and in awe of Sylvie and the miracle she had just performed. As the two of them rested, I collapsed into a chair and instinctively cupped my right hand over the watch and held it tight.

THE WATCH

Then I looked at the watch and burst into tears. Not happy tears, not sad tears, but sort of confused tears. Jye was less than an hour old, and there I was asking myself:

'Do I have to give my son this watch on *his* twenty-first birthday?

'Twenty-one years from today, do I have to give him this watch so it can protect him like it's protected me? So it can bring him joy and luck and strength when he needs them most? It's calmed me down during my most anxious and stressful moments, it's my most sacred and precious possession, and I'm not sure I can live without it.'

I hadn't slept in days, and I was tired and emotional for sure, but I sat there trying to work out how many more times I'd get to wind it before Jye turned twenty-one. It was a bizarre thing to think about an hour after my son was born, and it even feels weird writing this.

On every birthday of Jye's, once he was old enough to understand, I'd talk to him about this cheap watch, so he came to fully understand its importance. We had literally hundreds of conversations about it over the years, and he'd tease me about how I had to hand it over on his twenty-first, hand over the magic, pass it down the line.

Then, as his twenty-first birthday drew close, he told me that he knew what the watch meant to me and couldn't imagine me without it. He didn't have the mystical connection that I had to it, so in all honesty he didn't expect me to give it to him.

That was a huge relief to me. I'd been struggling with this for twenty-one years.

The day of his birthday arrived. It was 9 pm and the house was full of drunk twenty-one-year-olds, the music was thumping and the party was going off. The time had come for Dad to make that embarrassing Dad speech before leaving the kids to raid the cellar, vomit in the pool and destroy the house.

I eventually got the rowdy bunch quiet and started my speech.

'OK, everyone, Jye asked me not to say this, but I can't believe this handsome young man standing in front of us used to be swimming around in my balls!' Huge laugh from his friends.

I can't really remember exactly what I said next, it's all a blur, but I remember looking at Jye and thinking, 'He needs the watch, he needs Grandpa to watch over him, he needs the power and strength and spiritual connection that come with this cheap old watch.'

So, after a few more silly dad jokes, I stopped and said, 'There's something else I've got to do, and I want to do it in front of all of you so you understand the importance of it.'

I looked down at the watch, put my right hand over it, paused and took the biggest breath I've ever taken.

I glanced towards the back of the room, where Robbie, my oldest mate, was standing. He knew what this watch meant to me, he understood the magic and he knew it was always with me. He could see what was about to happen.

He's a big tough guy, but I could see the tears were welling up. Then I looked over at Jye, who also realised where this was going.

I told an abbreviated version of the watch story, then took it off, called Jye over and handed it to him in front of all his friends. He cried, I cried, and many of his friends were tearing up too.

Can you believe I'd been struggling with what would happen at this moment from the day Jye was born? And now it had been done, it felt right.

We were still crying when Robbie raced straight over to us, ripped his very expensive watch off his wrist and offered it to me. It was a breathtakingly beautiful gesture from one of the most generous guys I've ever met. I declined – which, once I'd googled the price of his watch the next day, I realised had been a big mistake!

Jye, like his grandfather, is into flashy, sexy watches, and my special watch is not a watch he'd wear every day. So we have come to an arrangement whereby I look after it for him, and get to wear it on special occasions when I need the magic. I wore it when I auditioned for *The Chase Australia* and when I filmed the first episodes. I recently wore it to my niece Maddie and her special man Todd's wedding because I knew she would have wanted her grandfather there. I of course had to wear it for my first photo shoot as an author – you can see it on the back cover of this book. And here's the funny thing, I know Jye will wear it to my funeral.

I know he'll understand what it means to wear the watch on that day. I know he'll wind it slowly in the morning, exactly twenty-one times.

He'll know it will always be Grandpa's, it will always be mine, it will always be his, it will always be ours.

Toga, Toga, Passion Pop, Toga!

1985

On the day of my twenty-first birthday, I'd had drinks with my workmates, but I wanted a party. I *needed* a party. I wanted it to be EPIC. And my friends (who had questionable taste) also wanted it to be EPIC.

I wanted noise complaints from kilometres away, I wanted everyone to be drunk and dancing, I wanted people having sex in the bushes and throwing up in the bushes, preferably at the same time. I wanted it to be so wild and out of control the police would shut us down – although actually, that was never going to happen because I'd invited all my mates from the Bondi and Waverley police stations.

I wanted it to be SOOOO EPIC that if I got round to writing

a book about my life over three decades later, there would be BIG stories about this party still circulating.

It was in the back courtyard of the Bondi Pavilion. All my surfer mates were there, all my TV workmates and bosses were there, all the Bondi lifeguards were there, it was a toga party and it was heaving.

In anticipation that it would go all night, many of us had brought our surfboards along and left them at the back of the basketball courts, so we could just drink and dance all night then jump en masse into the water for a birthday surf at first light.

We were primed for a BIIIIG night.

A year earlier I was drunk in the Greek islands, which I believe is how every great story starts, and I was arrested for arranging a huge toga party – which sounds innocent enough, right? Late in the afternoon a bunch of us started running up and down the beach, telling everyone there was a toga party that night in the town square. Word spread faster than a cold sore on a Contiki tour (and that's *incredibly* fast!). We never anticipated literally *every* backpacker on the island would go back to their accommodation, rip the sheets off the beds and turn them into togas. At some point the hotels and hostels realised that all their single sheets had been stolen, the police arrived in the town square and asked who'd organised this, and a lot of people pointed at me. I was in a shitload of trouble, but for that moment I was a hero of the people. I felt like Donald Trump at a Trump rally!

I wanted my twenty-first to be *that* loose.

And it was.

It was like a scene out of some sorority movie – *Porky's* meets *Animal House* meets *American Pie* meets *Puberty Blues*. There were tables of beer and punch and ouzo, and cheap cheap wine and cheap cheap cheap champagne.

I mean, I said 'champagne' to impress you, so you'd be like: 'WOW, wasn't Little Lazza fancy, supplying his twenty-first birthday guests with champagne!' But now that I think it through, I reckon it was more likely Passion Pop.

For those of you who don't know what Passion Pop is, it's described on the Dan Murphy's website as 'soft, approachable passionfruit sweetness, it's a crowd pleaser'. Which also perfectly describes me at my twenty-first. I was sweet and bubbly and very very cheap, and I was passioning and popping all over the place.

It was a hot summer's night and there were three hundred people in togas, with body bits bouncing around everywhere. Some togas were able to contain the various body parts, but other guests just hadn't properly worked out the critical height–weight–bounce ratio, then added the PPE, or Passion Pop Effect.

If you hadn't scientifically calculated the bounce ratio and the correct quantity of Passion Pop, if your toga knots weren't tied properly or your toga was tied too high or too low, then you were going to spend the entire night on the dance floor just trying to keep your bits from bouncing out.

The cynical readers among you will now have reached the sad conclusion that young Emdur had decreed he wanted a toga party knowing full well that body parts would be flipping and flopping and struggling to stay contained.

But, in my defence, I didn't invent togas, I didn't invent boobs and I didn't invent Passion Pop, I simply put them all together on the same dance floor at the same time.

My friends drank early and quickly, just in case we ran out of ouzo or Passion Pop. I think this is a fairly typical twenty-first scenario.

Getting completely into the Roman spirit of the event, Mum had spent hours writing out Latin-esque nametags for everyone to stick on their togas.

I was Lazarus, and I don't remember anyone else's but I *absolutely* remember Mum's and Dad's. Dad's nametag boldly screamed in thick black Artline 'Lazarus Spermus Injectus'. And Mum's was 'Lazarus Spermus Receptus'.

(After writing those names, the Spellcheck on my laptop has just thrown its hands in the air and screamed: 'That's it, I can't do this anymore! I'm out! I quit!!!')

Mum and Dad and the rest of the 'adults' were gathered in the designated back corner, out of the way of my drunk, inappropriate friends, until after the speeches, when they were supposed to leave.

It's the unwritten law of twenty-firsts.

Among them was my gorgeous Nanny Minnie, my biggest fan. She was super proud of all her kids and grandkids, but she got *lots* of mileage out of having a grandson who was on TV.

Some years after this, when I was hosting *The Price Is Right*, a woman came up to me and said, 'Your grandmother is *so* proud of you.'

I responded, 'Oh, you know my Nanny Minnie?'

She replied, 'No, no, I don't *know* her, I was on a bus with her the other day.'

I said, 'Oh, no, I'm sorry you had to sit through that, she loves talking about her grandkids, that must've been a long ride sitting next to her.'

She laughed and said, 'Ha ha, no, I wasn't sitting *next to* her, *she* was up the front of the bus and *I* was down the back.'

The vision of Nanny Minnie announcing to a crowded bus that she was Larry Emdur's grandmother, and it was nearly 5.30 so everyone should go home now and watch *The Price Is Right*, was not only horrifying but also totally believable.

Nanny Minnie wasn't wearing a toga that night, and I don't think she was drinking ouzo or Passion Pop, but everyone else was, and it was nearly time for the speeches.

The DJ got everyone's attention and called everyone over in front of the stage for the drunken shemozzle that would be the speech section of the evening.

Mum and Dad were first up.

All my friends absolutely *loved* my mum and dad. Our house was a sort of surfer HQ, and there were always a few guys and girls hanging out there on their way home from the beach, or on their way *to* the beach – sleeping on the lounge-room floor overnight so we could surf early, or because we came home late. Mum would always feed and hydrate them and Dad would always just be one of the guys. So when Mum and Dad got up to make their speech, they got a *huge* whooooping and hollering from the crowd.

Dad was a very funny guy and always made great speeches. I can't remember much of this one but it would've been classic Davo. I remember a joke about how I wasn't wearing underwear under my toga, and another one about how the music was so loud that someone had complained to the police, but that didn't matter because most of them were here. At which point the gaggle of local cops held up their beers and yelled out, 'Woohoooo!' and 'Yeeaahhhhhh!'

Then *I* stumbled up onto the stage, now particularly conscious of my lack-of-underwear situation and the fact I was wearing a short toga while standing on a stage with people below me looking up. I was *hyper*-conscious of Nanny Minnie, whom Mum had shuffled to the very front of the stage so she didn't miss any of the speeches.

At this moment I wished I'd paid more attention to Pythagoras' Theorem at school. I had a serious angle problem going on here. Now, we know that C-squared = A-squared + B-squared, but if I got *this* angle wrong then Nanny Minnie in the front row was about to see my D-squared.

I started my speech: classic pissed twenty-one-year-old surfer-boy stuff, totally inappropriate by today's standards.

At one point I noticed a slight commotion among some friends in front of the stage, then one of them took something out of a bag and threw it up to me.

At first I thought it was a soccer ball, which might have been a decent present.

But no.

It was a sex-doll head.

Blonde flowing hair, big blue come-hither eyes that rolled back into a rubbery, plasticky face. I don't remember the nose as being overly special, probably because my eyes were drawn straight to the mouth. It was moulded wide open with big bright-red lips.

It being just a head told me two things: firstly, it could be easily and conveniently stored in an upright position on any flat surface, and secondly, my friends had been too stingy to buy the whole body.

Everyone was laughing loudly as I held my friends' gift up high, being very careful not to flash myself to Nanny Minnie in the front row.

There was a lot that was unsexy about this moulded, rubbery, plasticky thing, but the unsexiest bit of all was the cord coming out of the neck and running into a small plastic box. It was the vibrating control for the head.

And the best way to further describe this is with three simple words.

Low–medium–high.

I wasn't very bright, but my guess was penis goes in mouth, you choose your favourite vibration intensity, then eyes roll back in head (the doll's and yours).

My friends meant well; it was a great present *in 1985* – or was it? – but fortunately it was one I would never need to use.

After walking around the stage with it and making sure everyone had seen it and laughed (*at* me, not *with* me), I went to throw it at my dad, who was standing right next to Nanny Minnie. But guess who caught it?!

There were some VERY awkward scenes that night, but this moment was without doubt the most awkward. The visual magnificence of when my grandma Nanny Minnie met my sex doll with a vibrating head will forever be the defining image of my twenty-first. And that's saying a lot, because I think I saw plenty of things I wasn't meant to see that night. It's what happens when Passion Pop and togas collide.

Candy – seriously, what else would my twenty-one-year-old self have called the doll? – spent the rest of her years on the TV unit in the lounge room of my bachelor pad, wearing a North Bondi Surf Club cap and Ray-Bans with a huge Cuban cigar.

Our relationship remained platonic, I swear, but not surprisingly, when Sylvie moved in, Candy was the first thing to go.

It was a sad farewell. I lovingly placed Candy on the very top of the garbage bin, facing upwards, in the faint hope that a lonely garbo would decide to give her a happy home. She deserved that – but if not, I feel as though she'd still have those bright-red lips and big blue eyes and odd, rubbery, plasticky complexion even under three decades of landfill.

I like to imagine that in a thousand years' time, Candy will be the only thing the *Mad Max*–type scavengers, perhaps looking for an ill-advised twenty-first present for *their* mates, will find intact (oh, *and* my KFC foamie surfboard).

Death Knocks and Dingoes

1986

'Fuck off, you little weasel! Get the fuck away from my house! How about I kill someone in *your* family then ask you how *you* feel?!'

This was what a grieving father once yelled at me on his front doorstep at 6 am. His son had been killed in a terrible accident the night before, and I had been sent out to do The Death Knock.

It's the most horrible job you'll ever do, and back in the day it was always assigned to the junior reporters because, quite simply, none of the senior journos wanted to do it anymore.

I was the junior guy stuck in that cold, grey slab of my career where I wanted to impress and I couldn't say no to the boss.

You'd get a call in the middle of the night and the overnight Chief of Staff would brief you on the situation: a young boy run over by a train, someone's husband or father killed in a car accident, someone's mother killed in a house fire. It was always a horrible call to receive.

Then the Chief of Staff would give you the address of the next of kin and tell you to get out there and try to get an interview before any of the other channels.

Sometimes you'd arrive with a camera crew, other times you'd go on your own to see if they wanted to talk before you called in the troops.

I was never a tough, hard-nosed journo; I envied those guys, and still do. I never had the inner grit, intestinal fortitude or smarts to do what they do. I was the happy-go-lucky kid. I had slightly more ambition than I did working at Dairy Queen, but I still wasn't that super-focused, super-intense type.

If there was one lesson my dad taught me right from the get-go, it was: '*Be nice to everyone.*'

Being nice to people is nice; it makes *them* feel good and it makes *me* feel good. It's free, most of the time it's simple to do, and I love it that the word 'nice' has somehow made it into the generic press description of Larry Emdur.

One of my favourite magazine covers says (next to a picture of me sitting casually on a stool) 'TV's Mr Nice Guy'. I remember seeing that magazine for the first time and being really chuffed that the lesson Dad had always drilled into me had really paid off.

Dad had long since passed away, but I knew he would have been particularly proud of that cover.

(As a test of Dad's Proud-o-Meter, it's worth noting that he was extremely proud of the cover that screamed 'Larry Emdur in Bizarre Love Triangle with Penthouse Pet'. He'd show the laminated copy of that one to all of his friends and say things like 'That's my boy!' That said, I know he would've been just as proud of the 'Mr Nice Guy' one.)

Back at Seven Nightly News, I think I was nice enough, but you needed to be so much more than that to be a successful reporter. I was relatively innocent and kind of immature, and at the same time I was caring and compassionate. So The Death Knock was the worst assignment I could ever have been sent on.

Oddly enough, some people didn't mind speaking to me, didn't mind telling their story; maybe it was cathartic, but I think more often than not they were still in shock. Remember, this was usually at 6 or 7 am after a tragic overnight death.

I'd knock on the door, gently at first. When I did this, I saw so many sleepless, sad, bloodshot eyes that had been crying all night. I remember women answering their doors still in their nighties, dishevelled and heartbroken; I remember men opening their doors smelling of alcohol. Some wanted me to 'fuck off and die'; others invited me in for a cup of tea.

I was young, I had no way of dealing with this properly. I'd sit and listen to their stories, all the while looking for an opportunity to say: 'Would you be prepared to talk about this on the news? Maybe if you speak out, the council or the government will be forced to put speed humps on that road, put a fence on either side of that railway line, lower the speed limit around that kids' playground, or simply put up a stop sign.' This chat wasn't really about consoling them, it was about getting a grab for the evening news.

I always left feeling physically sick and emotionally inadequate. But if I got the interview for the news, at least the boss would be happy. What a wonderful victory ... NOT.

On one particular occasion, I had been working overnight in the newsroom. There was a Death Knock to do but I was about to go home. All the other journos, all much more senior than I was, had said no to it, and I knew the Chief of Staff was making his way around to me. I didn't want to do it, he *knew* I didn't want to do it, but he yelled: 'Call a fucking cab and get out there NOW!!!'

This Death Knock would be the start of the end of my career as a serious news reporter.

The address the Chief of Staff gave me was about an hour's drive from the newsroom. I called the taxi company and they told me it would be a forty-five-minute wait. I thought that might get me off the hook, but when I told the Chief of Staff, he threw his car keys at me and said, 'Take my car and meet the crew out there, and fucken hurry up.'

I'd been working overnight, so I hadn't slept, and now I was *really* pissed off. So I get in his fancy car and start driving out of the car park, my blood boiling. I hate this day, I hate Death Knocks, I'm fuming.

As I drive out of the TV station, I ever-so-gently start to apply the handbrake, then the car slows so I accelerate a bit more; more handbrake, more acceleration. I was going to vent my anger by wrecking his car. I could feel his fancy car fighting against itself.

I accelerate more and more, until I've brought the handbrake almost to its locked position. I can smell shit burning and hear weird noises, but I just keep on accelerating, and I've got an hour's driving to go. I was so angry at my situation I wanted to blow up his car.

It ended up being the best drive of my life!

Two great things happened: firstly the grieving family wasn't home, so I didn't have to confront them; and secondly, because of my overenthusiastic and constant application of the handbrake while accelerating, as well as the constant putting the gear into reverse while the car was still moving forward, the boss's car kind of blew up. Oooooopppppps – sorry, not sorry.

I never wanted to do another Death Knock. More and more after this, drawing on my dad's philosophy, I threw my hand up for the lighter stories, the positive stories, the stories that would make viewers happy. I was always smiling, always trying to be nice, and fortunately, over time this became my thing.

I remember the day my career took a complete 180-degree turn from which it would never, *could* never turn back.

Because I was in a working newsroom, gathering news, sometimes there'd still be serious stuff to do, even if it wasn't my thing. Not with this face – have you *seen* this face?

I had a nervous smile, still do. Not a Luna Park smile, just a little nervous one where the corners of my mouth curl upwards, and little bits of my big teeth punch through and give the impression that I'm smiling, even if I'm not. You can still witness it every day on TV. I still get nervous on *The Morning Show* and *The Chase Australia*, but fortunately smiling mostly works on those shows.

On this particular day, reports started coming into the newsroom that there had been a head-on car accident with multiple fatalities on the Pacific Highway just north of Sydney. It was late in the afternoon, and I was in the editing suite working on a story for that evening's news.

The Chief of Staff buzzed in and told me to run up to the chopper pad; a pilot and camera crew were there waiting for me. We were to fly to the accident and report on it.

The newsroom was a well-oiled machine, and these live crosses were pretty standard. The Chief of Staff would gather any available information and feed it to you over the radio in the chopper, you'd gather as much information as you could when you landed, then you'd go live into the news.

It was a quick flight and we landed just off the side of the road near the crash site. Because the traffic was backed up for kilometres on either side, the emergency vehicles were struggling to get through, so we were among the first people on the ground, meaning the police hadn't set up their usual operational perimeter, which would typically keep us well back from such a scene. We were just freely walking around the devastation, and it was horrible. I'll never forget the sight of the bodies still trapped in the wreckage.

As more and more emergency services arrived, we moved further away. We set up for the live cross a fair way back from the crash itself, to capture a wider view of the chaotic scene. I was nervous for sure, and also completely rattled, having just seen multiple dead bodies close up and several people in agony trapped in cars.

I'd only done a few live crosses into the six o'clock news by this point, and they'd been light, fun, fluffy reports, in which a bit of a smile was completely fine. Even if it was a nervous 'Shit, I'm live on the news' smile, at least it had appeared at a time when I was *meant* to be smiling.

I delivered the information efficiently enough, but at the time it was all a blur. When I viewed the footage afterwards, though, the stupid corners of my stupid mouth had stupidly curled up and my stupid big fat white teeth had popped through.

'Why the *fuck* were you smiling during your live cross?' the Chief of Staff yelled across the newsroom when I walked back in. 'Get in here!' he ordered, pointing towards his office door.

I tried the 'I always smile when I'm nervous' line, but it didn't seem to calm him down much.

'Look,' he said – and I will never forget these words, mainly because they were so true – 'with that stupid smile –' yes, I was nervous right then and actually smiling at him as he yelled! 'you're never going to be a solid news reporter, mate, you'll either sell Amway or become a game-show host bimbo.'

From there on in, I would mainly be covering light and fluffy stories: the new baby penguin at the zoo, the man who grew a zucchini that looked like Jesus, the research that said chocolate improved your sex life …

Now, many a budding young reporter would have considered this a huge demotion, a setback on an oft-dreamt-of career path that would one day lead to *60 Minutes*. But I loved it! I was having the *best* time. I could find my own stories – the crazier and zanier the better – I could have fun writing them, and I was always smiling. I *owned* it.

Most of my stories would be right at the end of the news, after the weather. They'd be promoted throughout the rest of the bulletin, in the hope of keeping the audience there till the end. So, as light and fluffy as they were, strategically they were a pretty important part of the mix.

'Coming up later, the poodle that thinks it's a kangaroo.'

'Coming up later, Taronga Zoo's newest baby arrives, with a face only a mother could love.'

'Coming up later, the animal-shelter worker teaching rescue dogs to sing the national anthem.'

So you're sticking around, yeah? There's no way you're leaving the news till that zany story comes on.

That last story of the night was also important because it gave the newsreader an opportunity to smile when they said goodnight, which was always a nice, warm, friendly way to end the news. Still is today.

Because I did a lot of animal stories, back in the day I became known as 'The Dog Reporter'. Once again, for any other ambitious young journo this would have been an insult, but *I* wanted to be the best dog reporter in the country and tell the lightest, fluffiest stories with a huge smile on my face. I wanted to deliver positive, fun, warm stories that would give the audience some levity after the heaviness of the rest of the nightly news. Like Dad always taught me, I tried to be nice to everyone, and worked hard to make people smile.

The term Dog Reporter stuck. I'd turn up to an animal-related story and automatically introduce myself as The Dog Reporter and that would always get a smile from the person we were interviewing.

Well, almost always.

It was 3 February 1986, and the massive news came through that police had found Azaria Chamberlain's matinée jacket at Ayers Rock (Uluru). Azaria's mother, Lindy, had always maintained that a dingo took her baby and that Azaria had been wearing a matinée jacket at the time. Prosecutors had always dismissed this claim because police had never found the matinée jacket, so this new find was monumental.

The newsroom had secured an interview with Azaria's father, Michael Chamberlain, who was living on the New South Wales Central Coast. The larger story was being compiled by one of the senior reporters, but I was the one who had to jump in the chopper and fly up to interview Michael.

This wasn't a 'chase him down' kind of interview; on the contrary, he was very eager to talk to us, because the discovery of the matinée jacket would essentially prove his and Lindy's innocence in the disappearance of their baby daughter.

The crew and I landed on his property, and once the rotor wound down we jumped out of the chopper and started to set up. We waited about ten minutes, then Michael started walking towards us. He came up to me and we shook hands.

He said, 'I don't think I've seen you before.' He was used to seeing the senior Walkley Award–winning journalists who would've always covered this, one of the most baffling crime stories in Australia's history.

'No,' I said, 'we haven't met, Michael, I'm The Dog Reporter.'

'I beg your pardon?' Michael cocked his head and looked at me oddly.

The cameraman cleared his throat very loudly and obviously.

I hadn't clicked, and continued, 'I'm The Dog Reporter, I usually just do dog stories.'

Michael's face buckled; the cameraman groaned.

It took me a few seconds to unpack what had just happened. And then began the greatest round of embarrassed apologies ever delivered.

Turns out introducing yourself as 'The Dog Reporter' to a man whose baby was taken by a dingo is not the greatest way to build rapport. Who knew?!

Awkward interview done, back to the chopper, then a flight at top speed back to the safety of my light and fluffy *actual* dog reports.

Hairy Nipples and Her Majesty

1988

'What are you, some sort of freak or somethin'?'

Said the befuddled lady sitting next to me.

It was 1988, and I was sitting among a row of ladies in a ladies' hair salon. I was the only guy there, I was wearing a rubber cap with little holes, and tufts of my hair had been pulled through the holes with some sort of crochet needle. Yep, I was having my hair streaked.

I felt stupid, and I looked stupid.

I'd been coming here for a few years now. It was the hairdresser in Epping where nearby Channel Seven would send its on-air 'talent' for all our follicle fabulousness.

It was during a simple trim that I'd mentioned to the hairdresser, as a bit of a joke, that I was sad my natural blond surfie streaks were fading away. I wasn't spending as much time outdoors these days, and my sun-bleached bob was turning a bland office-worker brown.

I'd gone from Cool Blond Bondi Surfer Sam in beach mode to Boring Brown-Haired Brian in Accounting. I was losing my hair mojo.

It wasn't a really important conversation, the one next to me was *much* more important. The lady was telling her hairdresser that, all of a sudden, she was getting a lot more hair on her nipples.

I should *not* have been there to hear that.

The hairdresser and I laughed about it – *my* dilemma, *not* the other woman's hairy nipples.

Her solution? Streaks – that's streaks in my hair, *not* on the other woman's hairy nipples.

Put some sort of poison at various random intervals through your hair, and wait for the timer to ding and let you know your hair is fully cooked.

I'm like, yeah, sure, why not? I want to keep looking like a surfer, what could go wrong?

There was a *lot* wrong with that look, but it was the 1980s, a time when some men had blond streaks in their hair and thought it was coooooool.

The year 1988 was a big one in my career: my orangey, greeny hair and I made the move from Seven News to *Good Morning Australia* on Channel Ten. My silly smiling news reports had been noticed by someone at Channel 10, and they reached out to me to see if I wanted to come over and do light-hearted features on morning TV. 'Just have fun, do fun stories' was the brief.

I couldn't get over there fast enough. It was a perfect move for me, and it suited me right down to my imitation leather shoes.

Even when I moved to Ten, I kept going back to the Seven hair salon in Epping. There's a slim chance I put a haircut or two on the Channel Seven account, but that's OK, because years later, when I was back at Channel Seven, I may or may not have found a couple of old Channel Ten Cabcharge vouchers, and may or may not have used them to get home from the pub. So you can see how the TV universe balances out, yeah?

Long before Elton John stole the words, those of us in the TV biz would call that 'the *Circle of Life*'.

At Channel Ten I wasn't just reporting on *GMA*. That year, 1988, I also went to Seoul to report on the Olympics. I was doing non-sport stories of interest, called 'colour pieces', and they would scatter them throughout the broadcast. It was great fun. Mum has a photo of me in my Olympic outfit – I think for years she told her friends I went there as part of the swim team, not the broadcast team.

That year I was also part of a global broadcast team covering the opening of World Expo 88 in Brisbane.

Sure, it was a bit part, but it was a *big* bit part. I was young, and it was really an older, more experienced broadcaster's job. I knew this because a drunk, grumpy executive said to me after the briefing the night before: 'You should never send a boy to do a man's job.'

It's about 8 am on 30 April 1988, and I'm on the Brisbane River on a small police boat, with my camera crew and a couple of young cops.

We were positioned just off the Royal Yacht *Britannia*, the Queen's floating palace. It was an incredible ship: 126 metres long, with 270 permanent crew members including a platoon of Royal Marines, and a two-car garage for the Duke's Range Rovers.

Our police boat formed part of *Britannia*'s security flotilla, so no one was closer than we were.

Britannia was spectacular – but she was no *Siesta*. She probably didn't have mouldy semi-shagpile carpets, cracked windows that didn't open, toilets that didn't flush and engines that didn't work, but I'll bet the non-slip deck on *Siesta* was much more non-slippery than the decks on *Britannia*, so by that measure alone *Siesta* was clearly the safer craft.

And I'll bet there was nothing being prepared in the Executive Galley by the gaggle of international-award-winning royal chefs that tasted anywhere near as good as a pie and sauce and a can of Coke gulped down while fishing off the back of *Siesta*.

On paper my role was pretty straightforward. This is how it was supposed to work.

The Queen would appear at the door at the top of the ship's gangway, probably stop and wave, then walk down the gangway and onto the Royal Barge to gently cruise down the river to the fancy welcoming area, where she would officially open Expo 88.

We were the crew who would capture that gangway moment. It would be the first time in the coverage when we'd all get to see the Queen.

The plan was that when the Queen appeared, the main broadcasters would throw to me with something like: 'And here she is now! Channel Ten's Larry Emdur is right there. Larry, what a special moment! How's she looking?' Too easy, right?

But the whole thing *didn't* go to plan. The Queen was running late – not Mariah Carey diva late, just late enough that Channel

HAIRY NIPPLES AND HER MAJESTY

Ten had moved on from the scheduled live cross to me and continued around the ground with other reporters.

After a while we were led to believe the Queen would do the short trip by road instead of the planned barge cruise, so we were effectively stood down.

My cameraman locked his shot off on the doorway at the top of the gangway, from which Queen Elizabeth was meant to appear. I had a communications earpiece, through which I could hear the director and the program going live to air. But because we were no longer needed, I took this out.

Now, when you're on a police boat on the Brisbane River in 1988 at the start of Expo, being 'stood down' means relaxing and looking in the opposite direction at all the bikini-clad girls on the fancy boats going past.

There's no real way to sugar-coat what happened next. I can't really blame anybody else, which of course is precisely what we usually do in television.

The *Britannia* was behind us, the bikini-clad girls on the nice boats were in front us. We were looking the wrong way, but the camera was looking the *right* way.

Suddenly the Queen emerged from the door atop the gangway. We had no idea, but the broadcast had cut to the live footage from our camera.

The commentator announces: 'And here it is, the moment we've all been waiting for: Her Majesty, Queen Elizabeth II, emerges from the Royal Yacht *Britannia*. Larry Emdur is right there. Larry, how is she looking today?'

At that exact moment, as THE WORLD – yes, it was a live international broadcast – was looking at a close-up of Queen

Elizabeth II, THE WORLD heard one of my bikini-besotted crew yelling:

'*PHWAAAAAAAAW! Check out the boobs on THAT!!!*'

For everyone around the world who heard it, it would've looked and sounded like this.

[Shot: close-up of Queen.]
Commentator: Larry, how is she looking?
Answer: PHWAAAAAAAAW! Check out the boobs on THAT!!!

Just another in a long, long line of Larry Emdur career lowpoints.

And that, my friends, is *exactly* why you never send a boy to do a man's job.

But at least – and this is the *only* saving grace in that entire live global broadcast – my hair looked fabulous.

Yoko Oh No

1988

(Warning: if you are a Beatles fan, you may find this chapter distressing.)

Growing up as a surfer dude in the 1970s and dancing at the disco to 'Play that Funky Music', fuelled by Southern Comfort and Coke, always convinced me I was a great dancer, like a *really* great dancer.

I was always slow to hit the dance floor. I was more like that creepy guy watching from the bar and sort of swaying, out of time. The more Southern Comfort I had, the more I would sway and the sexier I thought my swaying had become.

Sometimes, though, I would drink my Southern Comfort and Cokes extra fast and get to a level of swaying confidence sooner.

Then I'd turn that creepy bar-swaying into some kind of Magic Mike dance-floor action.

My legs would kind of stay in one spot while my upper body and arms flapped around, usually four to eight beats behind the music. I was a sad and pitiful sight, but it was how surfers danced. None of us wanted to put any real effort in, that would be soooo uncool. Bloody hell, I mean, the guys who could actually dance looked like total wankers. So for me, dorky drunk dancing was the law of the floor.

More than thirty years later, it would be this exact dancing style that earnt me some of the lowest scores and most scathing judges' comments ever handed out on *Dancing with the Stars*.

I knew when I signed up to do the show that I couldn't dance. I still had mental dancing reflux from my days at Archie's Nightclub in Bondi Junction.

If you want some sort of visual reference for how I used to dance in the '70s, just google my jive on *Dancing with the Stars* to 'Wake Me Up Before You Go-Go'. If you couldn't be bothered doing that, or you're on a limited data plan and saving what's left for something more important, then let me just describe it to you.

Picture a newborn giraffe trying to take its first steps after a double hip replacement, with twenty Southern Comfort and Cokes under its belt, on a plastic floor covered in baby oil in a southerly buster. Sexy, right?

In my head I thought I looked like Michael Jackson, but to everyone else I was more like Brian Ferry in 'Let's Stick Together': kind of whacked, with arthritic knees and elbows swaying in different directions. Or maybe I was more like that inflatable dancing tube guy they put outside car yards for the end-of-financial-year sales.

Speaking of 'Wake Me Up Before You Go-Go' … I was still hanging out on the dance floor in the Wham era, wearing tight denim jeans, probably acid-washed, along with some sort of fluoro shirt, tucked in, and probably white Dunlop Volleys. Only maybe probably, but yeah probably.

But the best thing that ever happened to my disco days was the hypercolour T-shirt of the early '90s. It would magically change colours when your body heated up.

The only problem was it would change colours *in the places where your body heated up*, typically under your sweaty armpits and around your waistline where it was tucked into your jeans. So the novelty shirt that looked cool coming into the disco was now highlighting your gross sweaty bits.

Originally I thought it would be another tool in my mission to meet girls, but turned out it just made me a bigger tool. It was meant to be a conversation starter: 'Hey, look, have you seen these hypercolour T-shirts? They change colour!' But sadly, to demonstrate the wonders of the technology, you had to point out *where* the colours had changed.

So the pick-up would turn into a piss-off pretty quickly. And yes, you're right, with a solid nightclub game like that I would usually leave the disco alone.

If I'd had too many drinks I would walk home. On a warm night I wouldn't get all the way, I'd just lie down on the beach and sleep till the sun came up. I loved doing that. It never felt dangerous, it just felt right.

When the sun rose I'd just kick off my acid-washed jeans and hypercolour T-shirt and jump into the surf in my undies. Mum always said jumping into the surf would cure anything. Whenever I had a cold or flu, even when I got a stubborn pimple, Mum would push me out the door towards the beach, and sure enough, more often than not, the salt water would have a reasonable healing effect.

It also worked for a hangover, so falling into the water after a huge night was a great way to start the day.

Other nights I'd make it all the way home, singing for the whole three kilometres from Archie's to my bed. After singing the Eagles' 'Hotel California' about five times, I'd swap to 'California Girls' by the Beach Boys. Sometimes I'd stop to throw up, then start walking and singing again.

Of all the music I danced to, listened to or sang along to, the Beatles never featured, *ever*. I've never liked their music, and it had no place on the flashing disco floors of Bondi's beachside clubs, or in the back of our shagpile-carpeted panel vans.

But over a couple of chaotic days in 1988, I was forced to become an instant Beatles superfan, and it was a huge challenge.

Basia Bonkowski, one of the great entertainment reporters of the late 1980s, was on *Good Morning Australia* with me at the time. I was doing the fun feature stories and she was interviewing all the big stars as they arrived in Australia. Occasionally she'd even get to go and interview a superstar overseas.

On this occasion she was due to fly out to New York to interview Yoko Ono, but the day before the flight she strained her back badly. The *GMA* boss called me in and told me to race home and pack, as I would be flying to New York in twelve hours' time to interview Yoko Ono. I think the interview was about the release of a new documentary about John Lennon, but it could've been about her launching a new teabag – I didn't care, I was going to New York, New York.

My first thought was: 'I really don't like the Beatles' music and I've got nowhere to go with this interview.' But it was a big deal for *GMA* and I was the only one who could drop everything and jump on a plane at a moment's notice.

I raced home and threw a suit into a bag and the next morning I headed off to the airport.

I knew nothing about the Beatles, so I popped into the bookstore at the airport and asked the shop assistant if they had anything at all on them. Well, I was in luck: a book called *The Lives of John Lennon* had just been released! I was thrilled that I'd happened upon such an up-to-date book to use for my research.

I was a terrible reader with a very short attention span: traits I'm still famous – infamous – for today. But I got comfy on the plane and ordered a long black coffee with three sugars to wake myself right up and begin my research.

The book wasn't at all flattering to John Lennon: it delved into his drug use and schizophrenia, framed him as an anti-Semite and spoke about his rumoured homosexuality and long-running affair with Beatles manager Brian Epstein.

I ordered another long black coffee with three sugars as the plane headed across the Pacific to LA. I was highlighting all the interesting details with a pen, then folding down the corners of the pages that had something useful on them.

I was right into this! With every page I was learning more and more about John Lennon, Yoko Ono and the Beatles, and by the fifth chapter I felt like an expert.

Another coffee; I wasn't going to sleep. I'd promised the boss I would do a great interview with Yoko, and now I was going in so well prepared I felt great.

I didn't sleep, I kept highlighting and corner-folding, and with each new juicy bit of info I would frame another question in my head and feel bolder and more confident.

Finally we landed.

'*What do you mean you've lost my luggage???* I only had one bag and one suit, and I need them for an interview tomorrow in New York, please, please help me!' I pleaded with the lady behind the desk at LA airport.

'Calm down, sir, someone has made a mistake, I'm sorry, it happens.'

'But I'm going to interview Yoko Ono, and I need my suit, otherwise I only have these clothes I'm wearing!'

Jeans, a T-shirt and a fake leather jacket from Bali.

'Please leave me the details of your hotel in New York, and as soon as we locate your luggage, we'll send it on,' she promised as she pointed me towards my connecting flight.

I arrived in New York late and got a cab to the scummy hotel I was booked into. I explained to the front desk that the airline had lost my luggage and I urgently needed it for a big interview the next day, so could they please bring it up as soon as it arrived.

I went up to my room. I was furious and desperate and really hungry. I called for room service but the concierge said, 'Sorry, room service finished at eleven pm.'

'Mate, it's five past eleven, are you serious? I can't get a sandwich or a pizza or *anything*?'

My Bondi-boy attitude was no match for the grumpy New York concierge begrudgingly working the night shift in a shit hotel, and he just kind of shut me down: 'Nothing I can do for you.'

I slammed the phone down and headed for the lifts. I was tired, hungry, luggageless and really pissed off.

The hotel wasn't in a nice area. It was freezing cold and pouring rain outside. I stormed over to the concierge and asked where I could get something to eat. He told me there was a pizza joint about two minutes down the road, so I headed for the revolving door.

'Sir, sir, don't go out wearing that jacket, you'll get stuck for that!'

'I'll what?'

'You'll get stuck for the jacket.'

At last I picked up what he was putting down and said, 'Mate, this jacket cost me $30 in Bali, it's not even leather.'

He said, 'Please, sir, don't wear that jacket out there!'

'Oh, for fuck's sake!' I muttered angrily as I ripped the jacket off and threw it at him. 'Mind this for me please.' I stormed out as quickly as you can through a revolving door. I would've liked my exit to be more dramatic, more aggressive, but the revolving door kind of pumped the brakes on the whole *Bold and Beautiful*–esque dramatic departure.

It's maybe five degrees outside, still raining heavily, and I'm walking with purpose and a serious NYC attitude down a back street in a wet T-shirt, looking for some shitty pizza joint. I get my pepperoni pizza slice and storm back to the hotel, soaking wet, frozen to the bone, and with no sign of my luggage.

I was hating today soooo much, but at least I was well researched for my big interview tomorrow, even if I had to do it in my Bondi T-shirt and jeans.

I hung them over the radiator and tried to sleep, but of course with the equivalent of fifty coffees in my system that was never going to happen.

I was meeting the crew at 10 am in the foyer of the Central Plaza Hotel, where Yoko lived. I started calling the airline at 6 am, trying to find my suit, but of course they'd seen no sign of it. My jeans and T-shirt were now dry, but they sort of stank of twenty-five hours of travel, and of course my deodorant, toothbrush, toothpaste and fresh undies were all in my lost suitcase.

I raced around the corner to a convenience store and bought the essentials. There was a clothes store across the road that opened at 9 am, so I waited outside then quickly bought a cheap jacket and an even cheaper shirt.

Remember I'm the king of the mix-'n'-match ensembles. I'm the guy who wore a fake leather tie with a flecked jacket on primetime news and made it look good(ish). In my NYC hotel mirror at least, the shit new jacket and crap new shirt went perfectly with my jeans (that I'd been wearing since I left Sydney) and scrappy shoes. It was a seamless fusion of New York chic meets $29.99 daggy jeans from Just Jeans.

Not long after ten, we were all set up for the interview in the lounge area of Yoko's enormous apartment. The door swung open and a small scrum of her entourage bowled in, with a diminutive Yoko somewhere in the middle.

I was jetlagged and sleepless but I had *miles* of great questions from the book. So I felt pretty confident and was looking forward to this great chat. The interview was to go for ten minutes, and Yoko's publicist told me she'd start waving at me around the eight-minute mark, at which point I would be expected to start winding up the interview.

Yoko sat down and seemed very condescending towards and nonplussed by this uncomfortable-looking kid. She was used to being interviewed by the big guns, the top reporters, not the juniors. In fact, she said something to the effect of: 'They sent *you* all the way from Australia?'

OK, the cameras are rolling and I have the green light to start the biggest, most important interview of my career so far.

'Yoko Ono, welcome to *Good Morning Australia*,' I began.

'Thank you,' she replied with a half-smile.

'So, if we can start with this book *The Lives of John Lennon* …'

Now, I need you to keep in mind that my whole interview revolved around this book. I wasn't a Beatles fan and I kind of had nothing else.

Yoko stayed silent, but her eyes were screaming at me. I'll never forget those cold, steely pupils as they zoomed in on me. You know in those shark documentaries where just before the great white attacks it hyper-focuses, then a protective layer unfurls over its eyes?

She angrily pivoted towards her publicist, then back to me.

'I don't answer questions about that book. It's all rubbish, it's all fantasy, I'm not talking about it.'

You know that feeling you get in high-stress life-or-death situations where your liver, kidneys and heart all curl up and hide in your small intestines and your testicles dive back into your body because they think they're about to be chewed off by a hungry wild boar with four rows of teeth?

'UMMMMM …' I looked down at my scribble pad, which held nothing but pages and pages of questions about the book. 'Ummmmmmmmm … I … ummmmmmm … is there anything in the book you'd like to comment on?'

'No, absolutely not. I told you, I don't talk about that book.'

Well, I had nothing, AB-SO-LUTE-LY nothing, and there were nine minutes and thirty seconds to go.

I was a nice enough kid, but I wasn't a tough investigative reporter by any means, and I had just turned to custard before her very eyes.

I started furiously flicking through the pages to find a question that I could frame without referring to the book.

Finally I fell back on the most clichéd question of all time.

'So ... ummmmmmm ... have you ever been to Australia?'

'Oh, I have some great Australian friends, they're *so* friendly!'

'Oh, really? Is that a different sort of friendly from your American friends?'

'Well, in America so many people have different agendas, even your friends.'

OK, we were off and running, we were riffing. We were way off course but it was actually going swimmingly, we were hitting some great notes.

I think I asked what her favourite Beatles song was. I remember asking about the Beatles' success and if John Lennon had written a song about a chocolate bar melting on the street whether it would've gone to number one. She laughed and agreed it probably would have.

We were chatting, she was smiling, in essence I think she felt really sorry for me and something just clicked in her and she decided to play along, even help me out.

At the eight-minute mark the publicist came up behind Yoko and started with the international sign for 'wind it up'. I glanced up at her and nodded to acknowledge that I understood the signal, but Yoko turned to the publicist and said, 'No, no, leave us alone, we're having a nice time!'

We ducked in and out of personal stuff: favourite New York restaurants; her son, Sean; how her hotel room was better than mine; Australia; how I lost my luggage and just bought this jacket ... We ended up talking for about thirty minutes and it was a truly lovely chat.

It only ended because she had another interview commitment, otherwise I reckon we would've gone on for much longer.

I stood up to thank her. I was very grateful. This could've been a disaster, but she'd actually been very generous. She gave me a hug and said, 'I enjoyed that – well, most of it.' She was smiling: a nice turnaround from thirty minutes earlier, when it had looked like she wanted to skin me alive.

As we were leaving, we saw another Australian TV crew in the hallway waiting to set up. They were from Channel Nine's *A Current Affair* and were about to do a satellite interview with Jana Wendt back in Australia – so maybe the interview *was* about the doco, as it's unlikely Jana would've been doing one about the launch of a teabag.

Back in the day it was always really shitty doing a story for *GMA* that Jana Wendt was also doing on *ACA*. Jana was the best in the business, and no matter which way you sliced or diced your interview, it was never going to be as perfect and polished as Jana's.

That said, I was confident that what we had in the can was good TV, 'cause Yoko and I had literally been chewing the fat and talking shit for thirty minutes. It was no Jana Wendt interview, that was for sure, but it was a warm, friendly, often clumsy and clunky, sometimes funny chat. It revealed a much kinder, softer side to Yoko that people hadn't seen before.

I got back to the hotel, where of course my luggage had now arrived, a few hours too late. The first thing I did was pick up *The Lives of John Lennon* from the bedside table and chuck it into the bin as hard as I could.

I don't think I initially told the boss about the monumental fuck-up at the start of the interview, but I remember she was rapt with the result, because instead of the one feature interview we'd planned, we ended up promoting a week's worth of Yoko Ono interviews, which was huge for *Good Morning Australia*.

So I survived this horror show with my dignity and my cheap imitation leather jacket from Bali intact.

And I still don't like the Beatles' music.

A few years ago we interviewed Yoko on *The Morning Show*. You'll be please to know that, tempted though I was, I didn't mention the book.

'MUM! It's Jason Bloody Donovan!!!'

1988

Life was good. In spite of the fiasco concerning Her Majesty, I was still a reporter on Channel Ten. I was travelling around the country and the world on fun assignments, I was earning good money, but I was still living at home.

My bedroom was under the staircase at the front of the house. It had that distinctive mouldy badly-built-Bondi-house aroma. My window, which didn't lock, opened directly onto the carport and rattled in the wind.

Really, not much had changed since my sisters and I shared a tiny bedroom and sunroom in our previous house on Hastings Parade. But at least now Nicki, Martine and I had our own rooms – if you could call mine a 'room'. It was what a real estate agent would today describe as a 'generous study nook'. Let's just go ahead and call it 'cosy'.

Instead of a desk and a chair, this 'study nook' had a single bed and a pine chest of drawers. Now, I know what you're thinking, and you're right! I rarely brought girls home.

But instead of taking my parents to The Hague for what was clearly a breach of United Nations Bedroom Standards, I actually *loved* living there.

This is how it would work. I would wake up, and without even sitting up I'd lean over and pick my boardshorts up off the floor next to the bed, slip them on, stand up on the bed, slide open the window, slip my right leg out and onto the ground then climb out, grab a surfboard from the carport and run down to the beach a few hundred metres away. Even if I was busting for a morning wee, I wouldn't waste time going to the toilet, because I'd be in the surf in two minutes and I knew I could do it in there. Just like when I was seven in the kiddies' pool at North Bondi.

(Don't judge me, and don't pretend *you* haven't done it. You can *say* you haven't done a wee in the water at the beach, but no one believes you. *I* don't believe you and I don't even know you.)

Sometimes this was at 5 am, sometimes 6 am, depending on what time I was starting work. Sometimes I'd surf for an hour, sometimes fifteen minutes, and sometimes if I was *really* pressed for time I'd just catch two waves and run home again. Every single day, rain, hail or shine, summer or freezing winter, big waves, little waves, no waves, bluebottles, lightning. Ever since I'd made that pact with Dobbo aged twelve, it was how I had to start my day.

Occasionally the network would ask me to host various events away from TV. Was it because I was a fabulous, engaging, funny host or because I was easy, available, inexperienced, eager to impress the bosses and dirt cheap? You decide.

Neighbours was the biggest show on TV, and its two young leads, Scott – Jason Donovan – and Charlene – Kylie Minogue – were massive stars all over the world. I'd been asked to host a series of events at Westfield shopping centres around Sydney, where Jason Donovan and Kylie Minogue and other *Neighbours* stars would appear.

Kylie and Jason had recently released a duet, 'Especially for You', and it was at the top of the charts in Australia, New Zealand, France, Finland and Switzerland, and number one in the UK, Ireland, Greece and Belgium. They were so hot right then.

The scenes at the Westfield centres were absolutely crazy: thousands and thousands of screaming fans, hanging over the balconies overlooking the central stage. On the news, they compared these overwhelmingly hysterical scenes to when the Beatles came to Australia. It actually felt unsafe at one stage as thousands of young fans surged forward to get closer to their idols.

At the first event, there were just a few police present, and they were completely overwhelmed by the craziness. The next event, the police operation had escalated to a level similar to that used for a visiting American president; there were ambulances parked outside and teams of riot squad police.

It was off the charts, an unbelievable vibe and just a little bit scary, such was Jason's and Kylie's star power.

I didn't get that close to them in the makeshift marquee behind the stage. They were surrounded and protected by an entourage of publicists, make-up artists and security guards. It was quite the scene, and in fact my instructions backstage would've been something like: 'Stay out of the friggin' way.'

From an MC perspective, I remember thinking, 'This is kind of cool.'

But then the sad – no, devastating – reality would kick in. And the little voice in my head that calls me a wanker when I overstep the mark whispered: 'Larry, these fans aren't screaming for *you*, they're not looking at *you* lovingly, they're not begging *you* to sign their forearms or *TV Week* covers. In fact, if anything, you're just annoying them: you're in the way, *you're* what's standing between them and Kylie and Jason.' If I could have harnessed the crowd's collective thoughts, I'm sure they would've been: 'Shut The ***k Up And Just Bring Them Out Already!'

But I had a job to do, Channel Ten had given me a Cabcharge voucher to get out here, and in the '80s that meant I had a blood pact with the network.

So I was obliged to do the best job possible to rev up the crowd, to build anticipation. I was *so* good at bringing them right to the edge and then pulling them back, and they hated me for it.

'Who's ready to see Kylieeeeeeeee and Jaaaaaaaaason????!!!!'

Deafening screams and foot-stomping so violent the whole building shook.

'Are youuuuuuuuuuuu readyyyyyyyyyyyyyyyyyy??????'

'YESSSSSSSSSSSSSSSS!!!!!!' they screamed, with the verve of Mel Gibson's army during the great *Braveheart* charge.

'OK, well, before they come out, let me tell you about the ten per cent off sale at Katies on the second floor.'

'BOOOOOOOOOOOOOOOOOOOOOOO!!!!!!!!'

Eventually, I'd get the thumbs-up from the PR boss, then I'd introduce the *Neighbours* stars and interview them onstage. It was *such* a hoot. The energy was incredible, they were all great fun, and the crowd of course couldn't get enough of them.

At one Saturday morning event, like a small metal ball in the pinball machine at Jimmy's Milk Bar, I kept bouncing around Jason Donovan's entourage backstage until I got close enough to him to say hi. He was a surfer, and we made a quick connection talking about different surfboards and favourite surf spots.

I can read people pretty well. I have to make small talk all the time, I know what it looks like, sounds like and feels like. And I have to say, at that moment I felt Jason was *really* happy to talk about anything but *Neighbours* and the song and his relationship with Kylie. They were all he ever got asked about. This was a little break when he could just chat about something he actually loved: surfing.

He was up from Melbourne and staying in a hotel, so I said, 'If you ever want to go for a surf in Sydney, give me a yell. I live at Bondi and I've got a carport full of boards.'

He immediately said, 'Great! I'll come round tomorrow, and we'll go for a surf!'

Not gonna lie, this took me by surprise! He was one of the biggest TV stars in Australia and the UK, he had a number-one hit around the world, and I was a silly little morning-TV reporter whose parents kept him under the stairs.

But I felt the need to play this moment pretty cool, so my response was something like: 'Yeah, that'd be great, man.'

Here's my graphic example of the great divide between us. By the time his stretch limo had dropped him back at his presidential suite in the hotel for his two-dozen oysters and French champagne, I'd still be standing in the taxi queue at Westfield, being harassed by Cathy and her three teenage daughters, who were here at 4 am, after leaving home at 2.15 am and catching two trains and a bus, but they still couldn't get close to the stage and this was somehow my fault.

There are ten people in front of me in the taxi queue, and the taxis are coming at a rate of one every two minutes, so I have another twenty minutes of being abused by Cathy and her daughters. I may or may not have given them my Channel Ten Cabcharge voucher to pay for their cab back to the train station. (I can't openly admit to this crime in case the Channel Ten Accounts Department is still forensically auditing Cabcharge vouchers from the '80s. I do feel, however, that I have a legal buffer, inasmuch as I'm withholding my emotional distress case against them from when they made me host *Celebrity Dog School*.)

Anyway, you know me, Mr Nice Guy, blah blah blah, especially when it involves other people's money and/or Cabcharge vouchers. You can call it hush money if you like. Not as in 'I broke the law and here's a blank Cabcharge voucher to stay quiet', but as in 'Cathy, please hush, please *shut up*!'

I remember heading home thinking: 'I wonder if Cathy did the right thing and used her Channel Ten Cabcharge voucher for the ten-minute trip to the train station, or if she decided to use it to take her girls to the Gold Coast instead.'

It didn't really matter to me, though, because JASON DONOVAN was coming to my house tomorrow!!! And if the scenes at Westfield were anything to go by, I was going to need a bigger house and possibly some riot-squad police.

We were never a soapie-watching family – wait, let me rephrase that. Not one person in my house had ever watched a single frame of *Neighbours*. Mum was never into glossy magazines, so probably hadn't noticed that Jason and Kylie had been on the cover of every single magazine in every single newsagent for every single week of the past year.

Brighton Boulevard is your typical Bondi street: very narrow, almost impossible to park in. It's one-way now, but back in the '80s it was still two-way. It was that clunky system where if someone was driving *down* the street and someone was driving *up* the street, one of them would have to surrender and find a gap to pull into to let the oncoming car go past.

On warm beach days, our street would be this angry traffic jam full of anxiety and sweaty arses in Speedos sticking to hot vinyl car seats, as beachgoers with no air conditioning battled for the prized parking spot like seagulls fighting over a chip at the beach.

It was no place for a massive stretch limousine. And 20 Brighton Boulevard was probably no place for Jason Donovan the superstar.

I'd told Mum and Dad that a mate from Melbourne was coming over for a surf. I didn't say who because I thought it would be a fun surprise for them.

I was in the carport grabbing a couple of boards down from the rafters, which doubled as board storage racks, when the stretch limo pulled up. It completely blocked the narrow street. The chauffeur emerged, put on his hat and opened the back door, and Jason jumped out.

Thinking back, I reckon he got out in slow motion. I reckon he flicked his gorgeous hair back, also possibly in slow motion like in a Pantene commercial, and maybe I imagined it but I seem to remember hearing the song 'Dream Weaver' playing in my head as he walked towards me.

He was a superstar, getting out of a superstar car driven by a chauffeur wearing a hat. This was truly a surreal moment.

Jason was excited for a surf, so I suggested he tell the driver to head off and come back in a couple of hours. But the driver just said, 'No, I'll wait,' and drove up onto the footpath.

'Yep,' Jason explained, 'it's mine for the day, he'll just wait there.'

Wait? What?! Such superstar power!!! So when you're a limo driver for Jason Donovan you've got special rules, like diplomatic immunity or something??? This is awesome!!! One day *I* want to be a superstar and have my chauffeur arrogantly drive up onto someone's front lawn and keep the air conditioning running for *me* for three or four hours. *Damn, I want to be famous too!!!!!!*

Yep, that's how Channel Ten used to treat its most valuable stars: a stretch limo on call anytime, anywhere, for anything. I felt like a sad loser as I remembered how much trouble I'd got into when one of my Channel Ten Cabcharge vouchers came in about $6 over normal. (Luckily they never knew about the one I'd given to Cathy and her three teenage daughters ... until now.)

I could see my narrow, overcrowded street buckling under the weight of stardom, and I was proud to be a part of it. If standing outside my house all day with Jason Donovan as people walked past had been an option, I would've taken it.

At first they probably would have been a bit pissed off that they had to sidestep the limo that was parked on the footpath, then they would've realised it was Jason Donovan, but what do you do then? There were no phone cameras for selfies, and you were on your way to the beach, so you wouldn't have had a pen and paper for an autograph. So sucked in, losers, he's mine, piss off!

'OK, so I don't have a photo, but I'm definitely going to write about it in my book thirty or so years from now,' I may have thought at the time.

I said to Jason, 'Let's just pop inside and I'll grab some towels, then we'll head off.' We walked down the side passage; I was going at normal speed but I distinctly remember Jason still seemed to be moving in slow motion as 'Dream Weaver' played in the background.

The door was open and we walked in and found Mum and Dad in the lounge room. They were used to my friends dropping around to go for a surf, but they'd never watched *Neighbours* – what could possibly go wrong????

'Mum, Dad, this is Jason, he's just up from Melbourne.'

Anybody else in Australia would've screamed, passed out, wetted themselves, or an inglorious combination of all three.

Dad just jumped up out of his chair and said, 'G'day, mate, nice to meet you' and shook Jason's hand, and that was him done and dusted.

Then it was Mum's turn. 'Hi, Jason, I've got lots of family in Melbourne, where do you live down there?'

Maybe I nervously smiled, maybe I died. I can't really remember. Jason was happily leaning into the awkwardness and just going with it. Bless.

Then Mum came in like a wrecking ball, an alien from another solar system who knew diddly-squat about planet Earth.

Mum: 'And what work do you do in Melbourne, Jason?'

At this moment I utterly regretted inviting Jason over. I even regretted the initial decision all those years ago to work in television that had led me to this moment. An average human male ejaculation involves about five hundred million sperm. Why was *I* the winning one, why did it have to be *me* who was conceived and born? WHY?? WHY??? WHY?????

Jason smiled a big smile at Mum and said, 'I work in TV.'

Mum: 'Oh, that's lovely! A reporter like Larry?'

'No, no, I'm an actor,' Jason politely responded.

Mum: 'Oh, how lovely! Are you working on anything at the moment, Jason? Would I see you on any show?'

I *had* to jump in. '*MUM! It's Jason bloody Donovan! From Neighbours!!!*'

It probably still didn't make that much sense to Mum, but she could tell from the sheer panic in my voice that there was some sort of game happening here and she should probably play along.

The *Neighbours* conversation was mercifully short. We gently looped back around to Melbourne and Mum's family and where they lived. It was a bridge, a bridge too far, but it somehow got us through the next few minutes.

Jason was a lovely guy and he was very pleasant to Mum and Dad. He actually said afterwards that he enjoyed these normal conversations with normal people about normal families; he simply didn't get to have those anymore.

We had a great surf, before he jumped back into his limo with sandy feet. OMG, when you're *that* famous you can jump into a limo with sandy feet?! Can you even *imagine* that??!!

Lesson for the future: make sure parents are properly briefed on all famous visitors, move out of home, or hire different parents from a casting agency for any future celebrity drop-ins.

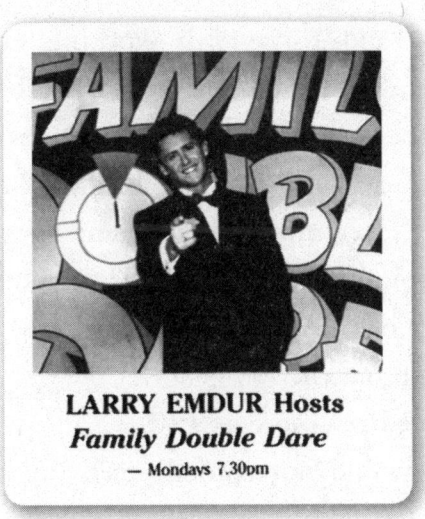

LARRY EMDUR Hosts
Family Double Dare
— Mondays 7.30pm

'How Many Fs Appear in the Word "Dolphin"?'

1989

It was my big break.

An American TV executive named Bob Shanks had been brought in to save Channel Ten, which was dying in the ratings. His solution was to turn it into The Game Show Network! How very American, and how very *un*-Australian.

There would be a game show on every night of the week. At the network meeting he was like Oprah giving away cars. He would point to different network hosts and yell: 'You get a game show! And YOU get a game show!! And YOOOUUUUUUUU get a game show!!!'

Everyone got a game show to host, and when they ran out of hosts, they picked me.

It was 1989, and I was still working on *Good Morning Australia*. I had no real aspirations to be a TV host; in fact, I was very happy as the ever-smiling *GMA* reporter chasing all the fun stories.

Anyway, they asked me to audition, and I got the job, possibly because I was completely adorable and incredibly talented, but more than likely because I was still amazingly cheap, naïve and ever so slightly up myself.

I couldn't have been more excited.

The show I would now proudly call my own was named *Family Double Dare*. It was announced that *Family Double Dare* would spearhead the beginning of the new-look Channel Ten, and would be launched on a Monday night at 7.30. *I'm going primetime, baby!*

It was an enormous amount of pressure, but I was young and dumb, and my main thought was that maybe this show would make me famous and then I'd get free clothes and stuff, like other famous people did. Yep, the needle on the Wank-o-Meter was starting to shift. I never cared about clothes before, but now my, until recently, underactive fame gland was getting a little tickle. Maybe one day I'd be *so* famous my limo driver would be able to park on someone's footpath while I went for a surf for a few hours, then I'd get back in the limo with sandy feet, just like Jason Donovan!

Family Double Dare was the grown-up primetime version of *Double Dare*, a popular afternoon kids' game show. Basically, two families would compete against each other, and the losing family in each round would have sixty litres of pink custard poured over them. I know what you're thinking – you miss that sort of TV, right?

For the launch episode of my very first game show, I thought I'd splurge and hire the Presidential Suite of the Intercontinental Hotel in Sydney. Just so my family and closest friends could eat, drink and adore me on a couple of big screens.

It was a pretty big deal for me: stepping up from Dog Reporter to primetime custard chucker. The launch had received a *huge* publicity push, so without even seeing the show you got the impression it was going to be a big deal.

'What can I bring?' Mum asked over the phone three days before. (I'd finally decided it was easier to move out of home than hire fake parents in case Jason Donovan came back to visit, so I was now living in Wairoa Avenue, above what is now the famous Raw Bar, just round the corner from Mum and Dad's.)

'Nothing, Mum, it's my treat, I've got it all worked out, just be there.'

'OK. I love you, I'm so proud of you!'

Then, two days before, Mum says, 'I've thought about it, I think I'll just bring some fresh sandwiches.'

'Mum, I've organised everything, it's all catered. There'll be *plenty* of lovely food.'

'But shouldn't I bring some sandwiches just in case they run out?'

'Bye, Mum.'

'Bye, darling, I love you, I'm so proud of you!'

The day of the launch party, Mum rings and says, 'I've just been up to the fruit shop and I'm going to make a lovely fruit platter for the party.'

'Mum, honestly, there'll be more food than we can all eat, and it's really nice food I've organised. Please don't make or bring anything. Just come and enjoy.'

The sight of Mum walking through the doors of the Presidential Suite with a platter of her mashed mayonnaise egg sandwiches, then trying to find room for it on the fully catered table of oysters, prawns and smoked salmon, was classic. That's Mum, classic.

Then the fateful hour of 7.30 arrived and it was time for us all to crowd round the big TVs and watch the launch episode.

I hadn't seen the finished product, but within a minute I could tell it was SHIT. It was even shittier and tackier than I'd remembered it being during the actual recording.

My family and friends were all very polite and tried really hard to fake enthusiasm, and about halfway through the second segment, when I just wanted everyone to leave so I could shrivel up into a ball and eat all Mum's egg sandwiches in the hope I could asphyxiate myself in the inevitable post-egg-sambo-fart-storm, I caught Mum's eye across the room.

She mouthed the words, 'I love you, I'm so proud of you!'

How could she be proud of me? This show was completely embarrassing and bloody horrible. Maybe what she meant was she was proud of me for organising sufficient catering.

Now, I want to be totally honest with you in this story (unlike so many other stories in this book – please refer to the WARNING at the front). Recording the actual show was all such a blur – a crazy combo of nerves, excitement and custard. But here's how I remember it.

There was a mum, a dad and two kids in red tracksuits on one side of the studio, up against a mum, a dad and two kids in *blue* tracksuits on the *opposite* side of the studio.

I bounced out wearing a tuxedo with white sneakers. (I told the wardrobe lady I thought the white sneakers looked really silly. She agreed, wholeheartedly, but said I had to wear sneakers for safety because sixty litres of custard on the floor would be pretty dangerous. I remember thinking, 'Not as dangerous as this show is going to be to my career.')

My newly acquired game-show host role required me to engage both my testicles to achieve a lower, more authoritative, more professional, primetime voice, instead of just the one testicle required for my normal high-range, Fran Drescher–esque reporting voice.

Deep breath, smile, engage second testicle, and here comes the question that will lead to the show being axed by the end of the night …

'How many Fs appear in the word "dolphin"?'

Red Tracksuit Mum smashes the buzzer, while her kids look up at her with great pride. This is going perfectly – there's drama, there's family love and support, there are educational *and* entertaining questions. All the planets and testicles are perfectly aligned, and if this goes well I'll be getting free clothes and stuff in no time.

'Yes, Maria? Your answer is …?'

'Larry, TWO! There are TWO Fs in "dolphin"!!!'

The show was axed straight after that episode went to air – no more to be made ever. The two remaining episodes we'd made on that first recording night played out and then the whole thing died a highly celebrated death.

On a positive note, it earnt me an award for Worst Television Show Ever, so that's a sweet one to put on the shelf next to my marching trophy from Rose Bay Public School.

It remains one of the shortest show runs in Australian TV history. But I'm eternally grateful for my shot at that show, because it pushed me out of reporting and gave me a break into game-show hosting, which became my absolute Career Happy Place.

As for that stupid, stupid answer, well, I got kicked out of school when I was seventeen and even *I* know there's only ONE F in 'dolfin' …

No More Mr Nice Guy

1989

In 1989, my younger sister, Martine, decided to head off on a huge twelve-month adventure round Europe. It was her first big trip away.

Martine is the baby of the family and this was a massive deal for us all, especially Mum and Dad. It was long before the internet, Facebook and WhatsApp, so when someone went away, they *really* went away. There were no daily catch-ups on social media, or five texts a day to say you were OK.

The airport farewells were always going to be highly emotional. Mum was crying in the car on the way. Dad was being brave, but Martine was his little baby girl.

After an hour of anxiety-building farewells in the food court, the time had come for Martine to head off through those huge departure doors. My baby sister, loaded up with the obligatory

Tim Tams, Vegemite and travellers' guide, heading off into the Big Mean World on her own!

Mum was a complete mess, Dad was now sobbing, and so were Nicki and I. We were all in a huddle: a blubbering, sniffling, sobbing sponge of Emdurs. No one wanted to talk, we just needed to soak up this moment.

Suddenly I felt a tap on my shoulder. With tears rolling down my face and my arm around my inconsolable mother, I awkwardly turned around.

It was a friendly looking middle-aged lady, holding a camera. She said she watched me on *Good Morning Australia*.

'I was just wondering if I could have a quick photo with you?'

I was dumbstruck. Couldn't she see what was going on here? Talk about bad timing.

I said, 'I'm sorry, I just need to be with my family for a moment.' I said it very calmly and politely; I've never been angry with a member of the public who's asked for a photo or an autograph, or just wanted a chat.

Then I turned back to rejoin the monumental family moment.

Maybe five years later I was sitting next to a nice lady on a plane. We'd talked for a while and then she said: 'Do you get annoyed at people recognising you and wanting a piece of you all the time?'

I laughed and responded, 'Nooo, it doesn't happen that much.'

She continued: 'Because a friend said her aunty said she asked you for a photo at the international airport a few years ago, and you really got the shits with her.'

Now, I told you that I'm known in the media as 'Mr Nice Guy'. But I don't want to paint a picture of myself waking up every morning with a huge smile on my face, jumping out of bed and walking straight to the mirror, giving myself a big smile and saying, 'You're going to be nice today!' one hundred times, before putting on a smiley-face T-shirt and spending the rest of the day waving and smiling at all the people I meet.

I'm not *that* nice, and of course people will have stories about times when I *haven't* been nice.

My entire professional existence is based on people watching me on TV, so if someone wants to say hi in the street or get a selfie with me, 9.9 times out of ten that's no problem at all.

It's strange, but I find people rarely consider the circumstances around a momentary lapse in niceness.

Only a few times – *only* a few – people have approached me with stories of how I was unpleasant to their cousin, or their former workmate, or their long-lost pen-friend. If people tell me stories about how I was un-nice, I always urge them to flip things around and have a quick look at the *other* side of the story. Consider a wider view for just a tick. What was happening for me at that moment? Farewelling Martine at the airport is the classic example.

When a sentence starts with 'A friend said her aunty said …' or 'My cousin's brother-in-law said …' or 'My workmate's ex-girlfriend said …' or 'The guy at the chicken shop said …' then I know the Pub Story Morph has already well and truly kicked in.

You know the Pub Story Morph? Let's play – it's fun …

1992, one drunk guy in a pub to another drunk guy: 'I saw that Larry Emdur in a kebab joint in Kings Cross at two am last week. It was so funny, this guy asked him for a photo, and as the guy's girlfriend was taking the photo she threw up on the doorstep of the brothel next door.'

1993, after being told by a few more drunk guys at a few more pubs over the ensuing twelve months: 'A mate of mine saw that Larry Emdur guy passed out, and he threw up all over himself in the brothel above the kebab joint in Kings Cross.'

1994: 'My mate says he saw Larry Emdur throwing up on a prostitute in the kebab joint in Kings Cross, then the prostitute slapped him with her kebab. I think he said it was a beef kebab, but he wasn't sure.'

1995: 'Apparently Larry Emdur owns that brothel above the kebab joint in Kings Cross where everyone keeps throwing up.'

I can count the number of times I've said no to a photo or an autograph on one hand. So I knew *exactly* which occasion the lady on the plane was talking about. I told her the full story, and she completely understood – but there's no putting that genie back in its bottle. For years and years, that woman from the airport had to be telling people about her encounter with Larry Emdur, and how he isn't the nice guy you see on TV, he's a rude arsehole in real life and he refused to do a photo with me.

It's common for TV networks to include a 'public decency' clause in their contracts. Essentially it means you can't give anyone a reason to complain about you, or bring the network into disrepute. It has a wide scope; the bit about 'bringing the network into disrepute' could mean almost anything at all. It's really just a wordy legal way of saying you need to be a nice person, a good human.

I was brought up that way anyway, thanks to Dad's philosophy. I hate arguments, I hate abuse, I hate fighting. To the frustration of those who've tried to argue with me over the years, I usually just go quiet and withdraw. And in spite of what you may have read on Wikipedia about what I do to my friends when they get a bluebottle sting, the closest I've come to anything kinky is the sex-doll head in my bachelor pad. May she rest in landfill.

The first time I remember seeing a public decency clause was in my contract for *The Main Event*, a big show on Channel Seven on Sunday nights, up against Nine's flagship current-affairs juggernaut *60 Minutes*. When I was a young reporter, I always dreamt of being on *60 Minutes* on Sunday nights at 7 pm; now I was going to be on Sunday nights at 7.30, just surrounded by cheerleaders with pompoms instead of soldiers with rocket launchers. Oh well, close enough.

It was the fantastical brainchild of soccer legend Craig Johnston. A brave but brilliant programming idea to put a silly, fluffy piece of light entertainment up against the hard-nosed, award-winning, serious journalism of *60 Minutes*.

Craig always dreamt big and never followed the norm, and that was what made him so brilliant and exciting to be around. He wanted to create a game show in a stadium-style setting that felt like a major sporting event. It was big thinking for the time.

Craig was a genius in many ways, and spending time with him was always eye-opening. He was forever thinking about new things and making old things better. He is one of the coolest dudes I've ever met; he had a big Harley and long hair, and he is a deadset legend and a wonderful guy.

I'd been out of work for a while, after being hosed out of Channel Ten like sixty litres of pink custard from the studio floor.

Hosting *The Main Event* meant a return to the network where it had all started for me. It was 1990, I was twenty-six, I had great hair and big white teeth, I was young and fresh and cheap. They bought me double-breasted suits and fancy ties. My Wank-o-Meter was starting to zing.

The voiceover man with the huge voice would introduce me, the huge doors would whip open and the little guy with the huge smile would bounce out with more effervescence than six Beroccas in a can of Fanta. I was surrounded by gorgeous cheerleaders with pompoms, I was in a very happy place, and as an added bonus I was about to become famous-ish!

Two teams of three celebrities would play for families at home. The families would all be sitting on their lounges, and at the end of the show we'd drive a Subaru up the winning family's driveway. It was truly interactive, really innovative TV for its time, and it was a lot of fun to host.

The show worked: the first Channel Seven show ever to beat *60 Minutes* in the ratings. I was loving this time; the press about the show was all positive, and I was having a blast.

You'll read a lot about me hosting shit shows in this book; I wear them as badges of honour, and they're very much a part of my story. But this was a good one, this was a *great* one. My first really big game show, and we were winning the ratings in the most coveted timeslot on TV.

So with the signing of the *Main Event* contract I became aware of the need to be a nice bloke. When my new manager explained the public decency clause to me by saying you basically shouldn't go to the pub, get really pissed and start abusing the family with small children at the next table, I'm like, OK, I can easily *not* do that.

Do the right thing, and don't get pissed and abuse families with young children – OK, Laz, you got this.

So in my late twenties, when all my friends were having huge nights out, breaking some rules and being silly, I was usually (but not always) the boring guy who left early to keep himself and his network squeaky-clean.

All my friends knew this was the way it was. In fact we'd sometimes get to a point in the night when my mates would look at me and say, 'See ya, Laz.' That was my cue that things were ramping up and my public decency clause was about to be tested. I'd bail out.

Now, this is important, and it may shock you – NOT …

I'm not a saint by any means. If anything, I probably put the *ain't* into the word *saint*. I think I'm a pretty nice guy, but have I been in the wrong place at the wrong time? YES! Did I say things to girls in nightclubs thirty or forty years ago that today would be considered inappropriate? YES! Over four decades in the entertainment business, have I said stupid things in the pub with my mates, and on the sets of TV shows with other members of the cast and crew who were *also* saying stupid things? One zillion per cent (plus GST) I have!!!

But there'll be people reading this going: 'Hang on a sec, Lazza! What about that time in the car park of that pub up the coast?', or 'My third cousin's ex-girlfriend said you stared at her boobs in a club in 1989', or 'I remember seeing Lazza and all the *Price Is Right* models absolutely smashed in a nightclub at four in the morning.'

Yes, there are plenty of those stories, and lots of them are true, BUT … remember how we just played the Pub Story Morph? There are many stories that follow me and haunt me, like what happened at the airport in 1989, where the truth has somehow got lost in translation.

One time years ago, Sylvie was upset about something and I was getting the silent treatment. I kept asking what was wrong and eventually she told me. The conversation went something like this.

> Sylvie: You didn't tell me you took one of the *Price Is Right* models out for dinner!
> Me: What do you mean?
> Sylvie: You went to that Japanese restaurant in Melbourne with her. You didn't think I'd find out?
> Me: No, I never did that – who told you?
> Sylvie: A guy I know from Ansett was at another table and saw you there with her.
> Me: Rubbish – when?
> Sylvie: Last month.
> Me: I told you that I took the whole crew there.
> Sylvie: He said it was only you and her.

Sylvie worked for Ansett for many years, and there were thousands of Ansett flight attendants all over Australia. So I just took it for granted that everywhere I went, socially or professionally, there would be someone who knew Sylvie, or at least someone who knew someone who knew Sylvie.

I *was* at the Japanese restaurant that night; I'd taken the *Price Is Right* cast out for an end-of-season thank-you dinner. There were ten of us, but this person had reported that he'd only seen me and one girl, quietly sitting together at a table for two.

I'd paid for the dinner myself; I even showed Sylvie the credit-card receipt: $1800 – ten $140 banquet options plus wines.

Now, this little story in no ways absolves me of all my sins – and in my life there have been many – but whenever I hear rumours or gossip about other people on TV, I remember the

Pub Story Morph, and allow for the possibility that someone said something to someone who told someone else in a noisy pub, who got drunk and told someone else, who then told their grandmother, who then told a friend in her nursing home, who then told her son on his next visit, who then told his mate at the pub, who then went home and told his wife, who told her hairdresser, who told everyone else.

But on the flipside, and while I'm making a few confessions, the following story is *very* true.

I've been to a few strip clubs in my life – not many, it isn't really my thing, and once the recognition factor kicks in, it's definitely not the right place for me to be. Mostly when I've gone out with my friends on a buck's night or something, I've bailed out before the inevitable twists and turns.

Over twenty years ago, I arrived in LA to take part in a screenwriters' course. I had a great idea for a feature film and I wanted to try and write it myself. Screenwriting is quite technical, so I found the best course in the world and headed off with stars in my eyes and Oscar speeches already written in my head.

You know that feeling you get right at the start of a trip that it's all just gonna be shithouse? I got to my hotel late at night; it had been a horror flight with plenty of delays, then there'd been the classic LA shit traffic. I was smashed, I checked in and my room was bloody horrible.

The heavy old blinds were all closed. I walked over and pulled them open, and there it was.

A blinding pink-and-purple sign, two storeys tall, pulsating with the words LIVE NUDE. It was flashing, LIVE NUDE LIVE NUDE.

It was directly outside my hotel window, and in my worn-down state I felt like it was a sign from above. I convinced myself that I'd been really really well behaved for most of my career, and this was divine payment for following my public decency clause to the letter.

This was a heavenly gift.

OK, now, let me try to justify this. I was smashed, my defences were down, I wasn't thinking straight, I just wanted to blow off some steam, I'm a sex addict. Actually, that last one isn't true, but it's a very popular excuse in Hollywood for just about anything.

'Movie star **IR* **A***T**** was caught shoplifting at Starbucks in Santa Monica today. His attorney claims his sex addiction made him steal the baguette.'

LIVE NUDE LIVE NUDE LIVE NUDE. I couldn't ignore it if I wanted to. I collapsed on the couch and stared at the sign as it hypnotised me with waves of subliminal messaging.

I could hear voices … 'Come hither, weary traveller' … 'Relax into the heaving bosom of Los Angeles' … 'Welcome to LA, where your public decency clause matters not' … 'No one will know you're here' … 'No one will ever know about this unless you're stupid enough to write about it in a book and tell everyone, but you would never do that, why would you do that? That would be so very very stupid, just take the story to the grave like every other travelling businessman' … 'Come on down, Larry … Stand up, brush your teeth, grab some cash, you'll need it … Come on over LIVE NUDE LIVE NUDE.'

The usher was kind enough to give me a seat right beside the runway where the young ladies would be performing their 'dances'.

I felt a bit too close and a bit uncomfortable, like that lonely loser in a strip joint on his own – you know the type?

I ordered a double bourbon and Coke to try and relax a bit. I know it sounds prudish, but I was feeling a bit weird. My right brain, which, as I mentioned earlier, looks after inappropriate stuff and makes crude jokes out of thin air, was like, 'Yo, chill little man, nobody knows you, drink your drink and enjoy the hospitality of these very talented dancers.' I'd left the sensible left part of my brain in the bar fridge back in the hotel room, because I knew it wouldn't want to be a part of this.

There was only one other guy there, and he was seated directly opposite me. One of the young ladies was playing up to him and he was generously putting dollar bills in various parts of what was left of her outfit.

He looked like he was having a nice time; she was really paying him a lot of attention and was maybe even considering a life outside of this place with him …

Then he ran out of dollar bills and she quickly turned her attention to me. I'd seen what that guy was doing with his dollar bills, so I grabbed a couple and put them in her bikini strap …

With that the guy, the only other guy in this whole stupid joint, leans over and yells out at the top of his voice:

'*Is the price right, Lazza, or what?!*'

I sculled my drink, left the bar, sat in my room watching the flashing neon sign and cried myself to sleep.

Don't Drink and Bid ... Or Do

1992

My very very first paid job, even before I started stealing golf balls with Robbie, was as a paper boy. I was around ten, and I think I got about $2 for the morning's work, paid in ten- and twenty-cent coins.

This was all happening at the North Bondi bus terminus. The newsagent has only recently closed down; it used to be next to Roper's Seaside Chemist, which is next to the laundromat on the corner. Jimmy's Milk Bar was once a couple of doors up.

Being a paperboy was easy and kind of fun. I'd get there at about 6.45 am on a Sunday, all the yellow barrows would be lined up out the front, and the newsagent guy would give me a handwritten piece of paper listing how many *Sun-Herald*s and *Sunday Telegraph*s I'd need and the address each one was to be delivered to.

I'd load them into one of the yellow steel barrows with their rusty corners and wonky wheels, throw in about a dozen more copies of each newspaper for random street sales, grab my whistle and my free can of Coke, and head off.

My paper round was Ben Buckler, three streets that zigzag through the peninsular pocket at the northernmost end of Bondi Beach. It's the area immediately above the North Bondi kiddies' pool, where my sisters and I used to play.

It's currently one of the best-publicised and most crazily priced property hotspots in Australia.

But back then, it was just where we lived, and there was nothing fancy or special about it at all. Sure, we were right on the beach, but the houses and apartments were actually pretty crappy.

There are three main streets along Ben Buckler, and they are where I would spend most of my early life: Hastings Parade, where I grew up at number 161; Brighton Boulevard, where we moved into number 20 when I was thirteen; and Ramsgate Avenue, where I moved when I was twenty-eight.

When I moved out of home aged twenty-four, I bounced around a few little apartments on Brighton Boulevard, Ramsgate Avenue, Wairoa Avenue, and the main road of Bondi, Campbell Parade, but I was never more than a few hundred metres from Mum and Dad or my beloved Bondi Beach. In fact, my first bachelor pad was so close that Mum would walk around the corner to drop off dinner and pick up my washing. Very sad, very true.

All I had to do as a paperboy was drop the assigned paper onto the doorstep of the matching address, and in between these drops, as I pushed my barrow along the street, I'd blow my whistle and anyone else who wanted to buy a paper would come out, usually in their pyjamas or nighties.

It was a close community back then; everybody knew everybody and everyone was nice. Except one time when I started to get a bit tricky on the whistle, and went from a quick two-pitched sharp-rising blast to using all of the air in my lungs to get more of a song thing going on. I thought people would appreciate it, but it was seven o'clock on a Sunday morning and I got lots of 'Shut up!'s and 'Oy!'s.

As I rolled past our house, number 161, Mum would come to the front door and wave to me. I could see the pride in her eyes. Her little boy was *something*, he was delivering vital news to the masses. Was this a sign of greater things to come??

She would put her hand on her heart, wave with the other and mouth the words, 'I love you, I'm so proud of you!' as if I were a doctor saving a life, or an astronaut going to the moon.

But I was a kid pushing a rusty steel barrow for $2 and a free can of Coke.

There was one building at the end of Ramsgate Avenue, a four-storey block of flats right on the tip of Ben Buckler. The guy at the very top would order both the *Sun-Herald* and the *Sunday Telegraph,* and I would have to park my barrow and run all the way up the four flights of stairs.

One morning, the front door was open and I could see right through.

It was an incredible view straight over the beach, like nothing I'd ever seen before. I was mesmerised as I dropped the papers on the doorstep.

We lived just one street further back from the beach, but this unit on the end of Ben Buckler was something else. I didn't know what Bondi Beach would look like from a helicopter, but maybe it would look like this.

As I grew up, I'd spend more and more time in the park at the end of Ben Buckler, which was literally underneath this apartment block with the incredible top-floor unit. This park was where my mates and I would go for some underage drinking. It was the scene of a few clumsy, late-night rolls in the grass with girlfriends, and later, after I got my licence, I'd take my girlfriends to watch the submarine races in the car park, which also used to be directly below this unit block.

That's code for messing around in the car. It's also code for what boys did when they couldn't afford to take their girlfriends to the drive-in.

You'd get a Hawaiian pizza from Nino's and a bottle of Coke from Vallis's Milk Bar and go and park in this car park with twenty other young couples in cars, usually all with P-plates, usually all doing the same thing.

It was kind of the naughty end of the beach. Sure, we could've parked on the promenade, but there were lots of people around and it was well lit, so if by chance the date progressed from pizza and pashing to pizza and groping, you wanted to be in the dark car park up on the point … watching the submarine races. There were panel vans and P-plates and pizza boxes as far as the eye could see, but oddly enough not a submarine in sight.

A lot of my teenage years happened in the shadow of this apartment building on the point. You could see the block from everywhere in the surf, and I would look at it all the time and remember its spectacular view. It just stuck with me.

Fast-forward to 1992. As usual, I was in the surf – this time at South Bondi, a kilometre away from the Ben Buckler unit block at the opposite end of the beach.

I was just waiting for a wave when I glanced across the beach, looking aimlessly at nothing.

Then I noticed a big white sign hanging over the balcony of that top-floor unit. I remember that exact moment now, clear as if it happened yesterday.

I remember thinking: 'NO WAY!!!!'

I caught the next wave in and ran, carrying my surfboard, the whole kilometre to North Bondi, then hopped like a frog around the North Bondi rocks, eventually ending up in the park under the unit block.

Sure enough, it was a FOR SALE sign.

Honestly, my heart skipped a beat. I'd had a weird fascination with this old apartment for coming up to twenty years, and who knew, perhaps now it could be mine ...

I raced back to my apartment to call the agent.

He was a young guy named John McGrath, the slick new kid on the Sydney property scene. We'd spoken before about a couple of apartments, but this was different, this was something *really* special.

He told me it was one of the best apartments he'd ever seen in Bondi, it had views like no other apartment, and the owners were looking for a price in the high $100,000s.

Now, a quick reality check. In 1992 you could buy virtually any apartment you wanted in Bondi for $100,000–$150,000. All the apartments on Campbell Parade looking straight over the beach were around $100,000 (plus), and now sell for $4 or $5 million. If you went back a street or two you could buy a unit that is now $3 or $4 million for $60,000 or $80,000.

So when he told me they wanted close to $200,000, it was actually a ridiculous price for Bondi, keeping in mind that no one back then had any idea how ridiculous the Bondi property market would become.

I was obsessed. I went to every inspection. The unit itself was pretty ordinary – a rundown kitchen and bathroom, windows that rattled and leaked in the rain – but that view was out of this world. The unit took up the whole top floor. (Well, actually, half of it was a massive deck that was common property, but as John happily pointed out, no one else ever used it.)

Every time I walked up the stairs to the inspections I remembered doing the same thing as a ten-year-old. The building looked exactly the same, even *smelt* exactly the same. It was that Old Bondi smell: a combination of the cooking smells of residents of a variety of nationalities.

Auction day was fast approaching, and I was in constant contact with John McGrath. I kept asking him if I could buy the apartment pre-auction; he kept saying no, it's the hottest property in Bondi, they're definitely going to auction.

I'd spoken to the bank; interest rates back then were a whopping seventeen per cent, but because I didn't have much of a history with them I could only get a loan with a rate of NINETEEN FUCKING PER CENT!!!

Didn't matter, I didn't care, I *had* to have this unit. I was hosting *The Main Event* and lots of corporate gigs, there was a bit of money floating around, and I'd been obsessed with this unit forever.

The auction was on a Saturday morning. I was nervous but determined.

My old mate Dobbo and I decided we'd just have a normal morning then go the auction. So we had a surf then sat on the beach at North Bondi, about two hundred metres from the apartment.

Except on this day we thought it would be a good idea to drink a bottle of Wild Turkey to help calm my nerves.

(My connection to Wild Turkey had started in 1990, when I'd just auditioned for *The Main Event* and was summoned to the office of legendary TV executive Lyle McCabe. Here's the sexy bit of the story. Lyle's office was a beautiful big boat – apparently having a fax machine on your boat made it an 'office' in the eyes of the tax department: genius! The boat was called *Wild Turkey*, and of course as soon as you got on board his wonderful assistant Helena would offer you a Wild Turkey bourbon. It just felt SO right.)

It was now coming up to auction time, and I was drunk, drunk and brave, drunk and brave and stupid, drunk and brave and stupid with a blank cheque. What a fabulous combo.

Dobbo and I had planned to have a few drinks on the sand then go home, get changed and head up to the auction, but now we were just a little bit pissed and running a little bit late, and so, wearing wet boardshorts and no shirt, I raced across the road to my current apartment and grabbed the blank cheque, and we ran up to the end of Ben Buckler for the auction.

Bare feet covered in sand, wet boardshorts, no shirt, towel over shoulder, pissed, blank cheque.

This was Bondi gangster shit.

The red Ferrari parked illegally across the entrance to the apartment block was sending out a strong message. Whoever it was, was being a dickhead and wanted everyone to know that 'the money' was here.

I got to the top of the stairs and John McGrath came over to me, looked me up and down, and laughed. He said, 'Mate, that guy over there in the fancy suit is buying up everything around Bondi, he's got heaps of cash and he *really* wants this.'

DON'T DRINK AND BID ... OR DO

I said, 'Is that his Ferrari downstairs?'

McGrath said, 'Yes.'

I said, 'Fucking wanker.'

The huge balcony was crowded, and I remember thinking, 'WOW, if I can fit *this* many people up here I'm going to have the best parties!'

There were a lot of locals there just to watch. This apartment was big news, and if it got to $200,000 it was going to be a record-breaker for Bondi.

I wasn't going to get involved till the end of the auction, that was always my plan. Let everybody else wear themselves out, then I'd jump in.

The price got to $210,000 very quickly, and this blew most of the bidders away. It was just Wanky Wealthy Guy left and the hammer was about to fall.

Bourbon made me do it! Just as McGrath was saying, 'Going three ttttttttttt ...', I jumped in with $212,000.

Everyone had sort of thought it was over and the apartment was going to Ferrari Dude, then all of a sudden Sandy-Footed, Boardshorted, Shirtless Drunk Surfer jumps in and it's on.

Ferrari Dude and I were at opposite corners of the balcony; McGrath was standing in the middle of us. Ferrari Dude and I didn't even refer back to McGrath, we just made eye contact with each other.

It was a stare-off. It felt exactly like a shootout in the Wild, Wild West.

When *he* bidded $215, *I'd* jump in with $220 without even waiting for McGrath to offer. It was kind of like we were yelling at each other. *He'd* yell $225, *I'd* yell $230, and each time the gathered crowd would gasp.

He started to say '$245', but before he even got the number 'five' out, *I* barked '$250'.

We are now very much in uncharted territory, I have half a bottle of Wild Turkey in my belly and a soggy blank check in my pocket, and if this auction isn't over soon that blank cheque will be just a blob of papier-mâché.

My sober limit for the day was probably $210; I knew that was about $10,000 more than the apartment was worth, but I desperately wanted to live here. I was a Bondi surfer boy and this was the ultimate Bondi surfer-boy beach pad and I *really really* wanted it …

We're now up to $260, and the intensity of it all is incredible.

We've been going up in $5000 jumps, but now he tries to slow me down with a $1000 bid.

'$261,000.'

You know how they say when you're about to die your whole life flashes before your eyes? Well, in that split second, everything that unit meant to me flashed through my mind.

Climbing up the stairs with the newspapers, seeing the view for the first time, eating pizzas with my mates in the park below, jumping off the rocks and into the surf, parking with a girlfriend watching the submarine races, and how I felt when I first saw the FOR SALE sign.

'*$275,000!*' I yelled, looking Ferrari Dude straight in the eye.

Now, $200,000 was a ridiculous price for a unit in Bondi at the time, so $275,000 was *beyond stupid*. I could tell by the look on Ferrari Dude's face that it was a ludicrous bid, he was like: '*Wwwwwwhat???*'

Going once, going twice …

SOLD to the man in the wet boardshorts with no shoes, who's maybe just a little bit drunk!!!

I still own it, and it's still one of the coolest beach pads in Bondi. I've had some absolutely ridiculous offers for it, especially in the last few years, when the Bondi market has completely exploded.

My little pocket of Ben Buckler has become one of the most valuable precincts in Australia, those three little streets where I used to push my rusty wheelbarrow full of newspapers is now the playground of billionaire tech wizards, billionaire property developers and a heap of record-breaking property deals.

Thank you, Wild Turkey.

My First Time

1992

I'd only met this guy about ten minutes ago, and now here I was, lying face-down in a strange back room somewhere in Kings Cross with my pants down.

I'm not going to lie, I was pretty scared. I was trying to clench my butt cheeks as he touched me round there.

He came across as aloof, like this was no big deal for him. He was bald with a long beard, he was heavily tattooed and he was wearing a leather vest with no shirt underneath, faded jeans and worn-out biker boots.

I'd never really considered doing this before. We hadn't been for a coffee, we didn't know each other, we'd hardly even spoken.

My mind was darting between 'Get up, pull your pants up and get the fuck out of here!' and 'Hurry up, bald man with leather vest and no shirt, just get it over and done with!'

He was saying things like 'Relax, mate, it's only going to hurt at first', and 'After the first few minutes, most guys start to enjoy it.'

I couldn't see what he was doing as he stood above me, but I could certainly *hear* stuff. I heard rubber stretching, then contracting with a SNAP!, I heard him shake a bottle full of liquid then pop the top off, and it sounded like he was liberally applying the liquid to I don't know where.

My butt cheeks were in utter turmoil by this point.

Will I regret this for the rest of my life? Will I ever tell my family, or will this be a dirty secret I'll take to the grave?

'OK, here we go ... I'll start slowly, let me know if the pain is too much. It'll all be over in about twenty minutes ...'

He put his hand on my bum. I instinctively, defensively clenched my butt cheeks as tight as I could.

I felt him pull back, then he said: 'Mate, if you do that I'm just going to have to push harder ... We're committed here, it's happening, just relax a bit ...' he said as he slapped my arse playfully.

He was right. It only hurt at first.

So ... exactly why was I here getting my first tattoo?

It was all because I'd been sacked a few days earlier.

Now, being sacked, or axed, or boned from a primetime TV show is a bit different from being sacked, or axed, or boned from a normal job.

They're talking about it on the radio, they're writing about it in the newspapers, and *everyone* knows you've failed. A lot of my axings have been shit shows, so it's been way out of my control as to whether the show could ever have succeeded. Regardless, it's always reported as 'Larry Emdur's *Celebrity Dog School* Axed', or 'Larry Emdur's *Cash Bonanza* Axed'.

Here's how TV works: when the show is a success, it's *the programmers or producers* who take the credit. When it's a failure, it's *the host's* fault.

After about a year and a half of riding high, the ratings of *The Main Event* had started to dip and concern had set in. Now, I wasn't really privy to what was happening behind the scenes, but I knew we were getting to the point where the show was going to be wound up.

In this situation, the host is usually one of the last to know. That makes sense to me; you see, if they'd told me the show was finishing in, say, three months, it would've been really challenging for me to keep bouncing out there every show full of enthusiasm and positivity.

So I only found out not long before the taping of the very last episode.

It was a Thursday night, and I already had it in my head that after the episode I was going to go and drink away my sorrows. We'd finished recording late, so by the time I got to the city it was past midnight, and the only precinct where I could find a vibe, some greasy food and a Wild Turkey bourbon was Kings Cross. I gravitated towards the famous Bourbon and Beefsteak bar, open twenty-four hours for punters of every kind, including freshly axed TV wankers.

I was a man on a mission. I had some colleagues with me and we started drinking heavily. Soon we were screaming with laughter and my troubles were drifting away.

Friends came and went, and I just stayed there. They formed a bit of a relay team. New friends came in for breakfast, and we'd walk around, then drink some more. The breakfast crew handed me over to the lunch crew, then the heavy artillery arrived late arvo for the evening shift. I have *such* great friends.

At one stage, we ended up at Harry's Café de Wheels at Woolloomooloo, got pie and pea floaters and fell asleep on the wharf for an hour or two, then walked back up the hill and started drinking again.

I felt putrid, I stank, but I was still on my mission. I remember taking off my shirt and having a wash in the bathroom sink at the Bourbon and Beefsteak before heading back out to the roadside table and ordering more drinks. I didn't want to go home, I just wanted to get smashed.

One mate even brought me a shirt on the second night, and another went to the chemist and bought a toothbrush, toothpaste and deodorant so I could continue my epic bender.

End of Day Two, and I was feeling like the walking dead and ready to announce my victory after a legendary forty-eight-hour bender.

Then one of my friends handed me a newspaper, open to a page with a big picture of my smiling face and the headline 'EMDUR AXED'.

'Five bourbon and Cokes, please,' I said to the waiter, as I settled in for the next leg of the marathon.

Now, there were tattoo parlours all along the Kings Cross strip, and more than a few times over those two days I'd been drunk enough to consider getting a tattoo to mark this shitty occasion. I'd actually spent many hours visiting some of these tattoo parlours and going through their books to see if any design jumped out at me. But I knew I was drunk and exhausted and couldn't see straight, so I'd always walk out again and return to my drinking, then go back in, then chicken out again, and round and round we went.

I walked into one tattoo place where the guy behind the counter coincidentally had the newspaper in front of him open on the 'EMDUR AXED' story. He recognised me and yelled: 'Hey, fucker, I've got the *perfect* tattoo for you!'

He furiously flicked through the design book, and when he found what he was looking for, he rotated the book so I could see.

The tattoo he was proposing was a skull with an axe in it. He said he could do that and then write the word 'AXED' underneath it.

I thought it was clever, laughed, and left to drink some more.

At some point I had to finish this marathon. I was sober – ugly, sad, hung-over sober – but I still wanted to get a tattoo. I'd told all my mates over the last couple of days that I was going to get a tattoo to mark this occasion, so now I was sort of committed.

While I was drunk I'd been looking at massive, angry, multicoloured tattoos, but now I'm looking in the book for the smallest, quickest, cheapest tattoo.

I turned the page and saw a half-eaten apple.

It spoke to me. I was twenty-seven, and in my discombobulated state I reckoned this half-eaten apple meant that half my life was over and only half my life was left.

At twenty-seven, I thought that by my fifties my career would be well and truly over. Now, as a fifty-seven-year-old, I've adjusted that thinking ever so slightly.

Now, if you're sitting there thinking, 'Hang on, Lazza, I feel sure I've seen a half-eaten apple somewhere, and I've definitely never seen your arse', well, turn your phone over and you'll see that you're right.

Apple products definitely weren't as prominent then as they are now; none of us had iPhones in the palm of our hand every day.

But I essentially, coincidentally, have the Apple logo tattooed on my arse.

Sylvie jokes that now my arse is ageing and saggy, that tattoo isn't as fresh and crisp as it used to be, but that tatt will always be a funny reminder of a particularly silly few days when I really put my public decency clause to the test.

And even though I have their logo tattooed on my arse for life, I still have to wait a week to get an appointment at the Apple Genius Bar, which just doesn't seem right to me.

Maybe if I flash my arse at the concierge at the Apple Store next time, I'll be able to jump the queue?

PART III

THE BONDI BOY AND THE POLISH GODDESS

WHEN LARRY MET SYLVIE

1990s–2022

'Now, you listen to me, Larry, you little fuck, I have a hundred people in this network who would crawl over broken glass and eat their own shit to do your job for free.'

David Leckie

Legendary former CEO of Channel Nine and Channel Seven

I Should Be So Lucky

1992

Sylvie and I have two wildly opposing stories of the first time we met. We both believe beyond all reasonable doubt that *our* version is true and correct, and the other's view is totally wrong – but seeing as *mine* is the only one now printed in a HarperCollins book, I believe that makes it the most ethically sourced version and places it right on the border of biblical. You know the old Pharaoh jive talkin' 'So let it be written, so let it be done'? Well, mine be written!

I've always believed in fate, and how I met Sylvie kind of confirmed it for me. A sliding-door moment, or a series of strange events, that led me straight to staring down Sylvie's blouse and on to a life of endless love and wonderment.

On this particular afternoon, I was flying from Sydney to Melbourne to host a show called *Tonight Live with Steve Vizard*. Every now and again Steve would hand his baby over to me, and filling in as host was a huge deal for me. *Tonight Live* was a terrific show, in the mould of some of the great American late-night talk shows. An opening monologue, celebrity guests, stunts, a show band … it was massive. I've always had a deep love of this genre, so this was me in a very happy place.

But on this particular day, there were violent thunderstorms, the traffic was horrible on the way to the airport and I was running late. Added to which, I was doing breakfast radio at the time on 2UW (now KIIS FM), so I'd been awake since 3.45 am. I loved my time on radio – I didn't have to wear a suit, didn't have to streak my hair. (I didn't *have* to, but I may have still done so.)

When I finally got to the airport, the lady at the Qantas desk was pretty flustered. You could tell she'd had a crappy afternoon, as flight after flight had been cancelled due to the thunderstorms. She'd been tasked with telling angry travellers the bad news and she was copping abuse from everyone.

I was behind two businessmen in the queue, and they were giving her hell.

Dickheads! Honestly, how can someone in a suit and tie with a briefcase flying business class look so smart but be stupid enough to abuse *the lady at the desk* for the flight cancellation?

Did she create the storm? *Probably not, dickhead.* Did she make the decision to cancel the flight? *Probably not, dickhead.* Was the decision to cancel the flight made to potentially prevent the plane from crashing and killing everyone on board? *Almost certainly.*

So yeah, let's all yell at the poor lady at the desk, because she probably has the power to overrule the company's safety protocols, step out from behind the desk, jump into the cockpit of the plane, start it up and personally fly us all to Melbourne if we abuse her loudly enough.

Shut up and piss off to the bar, you dickheads.

But there was a chance I wouldn't get to Melbourne to host the show, and that was a huge deal for me and the staff at Seven, who'd have to find another host at the very last minute. I was as frustrated and angry as everyone else, but not for a moment would I have considered raising my voice at the woman at the desk.

Dad's lesson was always with me: '*Be nice to everyone.*' The woman was pretty rattled, so when it was my turn, I just kind of smiled and said, 'Wow, rough day at the office, huh?', and politely asked if there were any planes likely to get through to Melbourne over the next few hours.

She explained that a lot of planes hadn't been able to get into Sydney during the afternoon, so there weren't even planes here ready to go when the storm passed.

Then she leant over the desk and said, in hushed tones, 'Look, I'm not really supposed to say this, but maybe Ansett will be able to get some planes away sooner than us when the storm passes.'

This lady with her sneaky little secret tip had just changed my life forever. I'm glad I was nice to her – who knows where I would be if I was a colossal tosser like the guy in front of me? I could be thrice divorced and working in a food truck in Tijuana. But no, I was now on a collision course with destiny – destiny with an undone top button.

The Ansett terminal was on the opposite side of the airport. If you know Sydney airport, the Virgin terminal used to be Ansett and there was no big car park in the middle. There was no way of getting across under cover, and the rain was torrential.

I have longish thickish hair and I'm wearing a greenish woollish jacket, and now I'm bolting across to the Ansett terminal through torrential sideways rain.

OK, so now I'm wet – not as in damp or moist, but as in I've just jumped into a swimming pool and climbed out and walked into Ansett.

My shoes are full of water, my jeans are soaking wet right through to my boxers, my super-absorbent woollish jacket has absorbed three to five times its own weight in stormwater, and my hair ... don't get me started on my hair.

I'd love to tell you that I looked like Ryan Gosling in that kissing scene from *The Notebook* – you know the one where Rachel McAdams looks like she's going to dislocate her jaw to eat his face, because he looks *that* good dripping wet?

But in reality I probably looked like a meme of a long-haired guinea pig that accidentally fell into an inflatable kiddies' pool, so all you can see through its saturated, now-flat hair is two beady little eyes and a couple of buck teeth.

I was a sight to behold – a sad, soggy, beyond-moist sight at that. The lady at the Ansett desk took pity on me, I think. She said the reports were that the storm would pass in the next thirty minutes or so, and there was a delayed plane that would be first to go. It was currently full, but one business-class passenger hadn't checked in yet, obviously caught up in the horrible traffic on the way to the airport. So she suggested I step off to the side, start to drip-dry, and wait. If that person didn't show, then I could get on the plane.

Aaaaaaand ... BINGO! I'm on, and I'll get to Melbourne in time to host the show. BEST DAY EVER!!!

But wait, there's more!

I sat down in seat 3B. I was soaking wet, cold, uncomfortable and pretty miserable.

Then it happened. I looked towards the galley and out she walked.

My heart skipped a beat, doves cried and angels wept. She was the most beautiful woman I'd ever seen, a flight attendant by day and a sexy Disney princess by night … (Hmmm, maybe that sounds a bit creepy, so I guess I mean a grown-up Disney princess, who's no longer in the movies so her public decency clause has expired so she's no longer contractually obliged to be nice after dark so now she can be naughty.)

An incredibly beautiful, sexy smile, blue eyes so blue and so warm they could defrost AND perfectly cook a steak from frozen, a deep tan that *screamed* European heritage, and she was heading straight for me.

There were little bluebirds and red balloons in the shape of hearts swirling around her head as she walked towards me. I think she was walking in slow motion, similar to Jason Donovan when he got out of the limo at my place for a surf, but much more sexily and yummily. (Just so we're clear, that will be the last time in this book I compare my wife to Jason Donovan.)

I was torn between a volcanic feeling of love at first sight, and the discomfort of wet boxer shorts riding up my arse.

Her first words to me – I swear – were: 'What happened to you? You look horrible.'

It was the best pick-up line I'd ever heard – and right here is where Sylvie's story and mine start to separate and splinter into a million tiny, mutually unrecognisable fragments.

Sylvie to this day maintains it was in fact *not* a pick-up line at all. She was merely stating the truth, that I looked horrible.

Ha ha ha, yeah, whatever, Sylvie, whatever.

Then she said: 'Can I get you anything?'

'Your phone number, two cans of whipped cream, a game of Twister, some fluffy handcuffs, a bottle of Baileys, a bearskin rug, an open fireplace and your boyfriend's address so I can have him knocked off?' I thought to myself.

What I *actually* said was: 'Noooo, thanks, I'm fine, I'm just going to sit here in my wet boxers and be my horrible self.'

She laughed and kept moving.

So, let's review, shall we, before we proceed? She flirted with me openly, then laughed at my terrible joke.

This proved to me beyond doubt that she was totally into me – as in, she loved me, she'd never met anyone like me, and she probably wanted to spend the rest of her life with me frolicking naked around the pool at our villa in Majorca.

Now, the best thing about flying business class and trying to flirt with the flight attendant is that there are only a few seats, so I was going to get another shot at this, like, every minute or so.

This was flirtation on high rotation – or, as *Sylvie* remembers it, *aggravation* on high rotation.

Not far into the flight, and after five or six brief interactions, I felt like I was in a committed monogamistical relationship with this goddess. In my head I was debating whether we were going to have floating floorboards or shagpile in our marital home. I'd already decided we'd have a king-size waterbed with a slippery slide at the end that ran straight into a spa bath with underwater disco lights and a generous number of cup holders. I was planning a trip to Myer in Melbourne the next day to buy us matching bathrobes, and we'd get tattoos of each other's faces just above our pubic bones, which would serve to scare off any future lovers who might be sniffing around.

In other words, I was TOTALLY committed to her. I would've given her the world right then and there.

She stopped right next to me for the sixth or seventh time. 'OK, you have to make a choice.'

'Fine, I'll leave TV, I'll walk away from my career and family and everything in my life I love, and I'll get on the next plane to whichever strange European village you're from. I'll harvest beetroot to sell at the markets for the rest of time, and we'll have twenty children and they can help me harvest the beetroot – however the hell you do that – and you can grow your armpit hair as long as you like, I don't even care, I just want to spend every minute of every day of the rest of my life with you. YES, I have to make a choice, and THAT is my choice!'

These were the thoughts that were swirling through my brain before she'd had a chance to go on.

'The chicken or the fish?' she asked.

Oh, really, we're doing *that* thing?!

When the chicken arrived – according to my version, the one printed in a HarperCollins book, and I say this with my right hand *on* the book – I believe that Sylvie had undone her top button, and when she laid down the tray carrying the chicken and those funny little carrots, I was staring straight down her blouse.

I was just looking straight ahead, Your Honour!

I maintain, Your Honour, that this was entrapment at its most conniving.

As I looked straight ahead, there were two things I desperately wanted to grab: those cute little salt and pepper shakers, I always stole them. But because Sylvie was really making a big move on me, I thought maybe I should leave them this time, as I didn't want her first impression of me to be that I was a horrible, moist thief.

There wasn't much more interaction PC.

(I was going to divide our budding romance into two separate timeframes, PC – Pre-Chicken – and PC – Post-Chicken – but because they're both 'PC' it's a little confusing.)

Post-Chicken, I was slowly reaching the sad conclusion that this lofty, hyper-romantic tale was, like the chicken, plucked.

Once the 'We've now commenced our descent into Melbourne' announcement was made, it seemed to me that Sylvie began to prioritise her work over me. Paying attention to *me* had taken a pitiful second place to clearing drink glasses, and ensuring hand luggage was stowed securely in the overhead lockers or under the seat in front of you, seatbelts were securely fastened, tray tables were safely stowed, salt and pepper shakers were recovered and all the passengers on board were generally safe and secure.

This eternal bond of two hearts, two minds, two lives and one undone top button was dissolving before my very eyes.

As the flaps went down for landing, I whispered gently into my chest, 'Brace brace brace', so my broken heart could ready itself for a little crash landing of its own.

I couldn't believe it. We could have had it all! You had my heart in your hands, Sylvie, and you played it perfectly, right up to the 'flaps down' bit.

There would be no long kiss goodnight, no 'Fare thee well, my naughty Disney princess!', no 'Am I ever gonna see your face again?' I'd put it all on the line in the last one hour twenty – not including runway taxiing time – and my return on investment was zero.

I just wanted to disappear into some dark, miserable cave and hide from the rest of the world, sort of like my wet boxers had done up my arse for the entire flight.

I was releasing her into the wild for her next flight of fancy, where she'd probably be chatted up by some weatherman from the *Today* show, someone who played a bit part on *Neighbours*, or worse, a pilot.

I caught one last glimpse of her as she walked across the galley to 'disarm and cross-check' the doors, then I heard the door open and the other flight attendant say, 'Bye, Sylvie.' *Oh wow, now I know her name, I'm like a spy! Now I can just find her on Insta and slip into her DMs … Oh whoa, wait, slow it down, Marty McFly, it's 1992.*

Turns out she was running off to catch a connecting flight and that was that.

I was racked with regret. Regret because I should've tried harder, regret because I should've let her know how I felt, and deep regret because I hadn't stolen the salt and pepper shakers when I had the chance.

I stood up and tried to pull my wet boxers down without looking too strange, then glanced down and saw my seat had a big wet patch. I'm one hundred per cent sure it was from my wet jeans – actually, let's call it eighty-nine to ninety-four per cent sure.

I was off the plane and onto the moving walkway. Looking forward, I could see people jumping awkwardly off to the left and right as they got to the end.

There was an obstruction, and that obstruction was the breathtaking, blue-eyed, slightly unbuttoned love of my life (well, the last one hour forty-five of my life) …

Sylvie was crouching down at the end of the moving walkway, looking for a ticket in her bag.

Now, Melbourne airport is huge, and either side of the moving walkway there must be thousands of square metres of low-traffic space.

Space where, hypothetically speaking, anyone who needed to stop and find something in a bag could retreat and not force three hundred already late passengers to have to jump dangerously over them as they knelt at the end of the moving walkway.

OMG OMG OMG, is that *Sylvie* at the end of this moving walkway? OMG OMG OMG, did she literally just find what she was looking for in her bag literally at the exact moment I literally reached the end of the moving walkway???

> ENTRAPMENT: To catch as in a trap; to ensnare; to catch by artifices; to involve in difficulties or distresses; to entangle; to involve in any difficulties from which an escape is not easy or possible.

She got me good. Escape was not easy or even possible.

I was trapped – like when you go to Aldi for bread and milk and they trap you into buying a sewing machine, a ten-pack of hi-vis thermal work socks and a Bluetooth karaoke microphone from the middle Specials table.

I did a quick look over my shoulder to make sure there were no pilots behind me, in case she'd set up this trap for one of *them*.

So now we're on the next moving walkway together and we're chatting away happily, but *I* know and *she* knows this moving walkway will soon meet the non-moving bit and that may be a pivotal point in this relationship.

It was speed dating long before speed dating was a thing.

'Do you live here in Melbourne?'

'No, I live in Sydney, but I'm flying up to Brisbane now for the big Ansett Christmas party and I'm staying up there with my parents for a while.'

'Oh, whereabouts do you live in Sydney?'

'Double Bay.'

'No way! I'm just five minutes away in Bondi. Next time you're back in Sydney we should get a coffee ...'

Quick confession ... during the flight I'd written down my contact details on a piece of paper, hoping I'd get the opportunity to pass it to Sylvie, but I never got that opportunity, and I'm sure you'll agree it would've been totally lame anyway.

But this was that moment of *'If not now, when?'* This was where the rubber met the road – or at least, where the moving walkway met the other walkway that *didn't* move.

So I reached into my pocket and gave her the scrap of paper. On it I'd written my home number, my work number, my mobile number and, just to drill home how adorable I truly am, my mum's number.

She laughed out loud when she saw Mum's number and I was back in the game.

Bear in mind that this was all happening at breakneck speed. Sylvie said, 'I'll never call you, but let me write down my mum's number, and if you can get past her, maybe, just maybe, you can take me out for coffee.'

End of moving walkway, end of discussion. Sylvie went left to catch her connecting flight, I went right to the exit door, and that was that.

Tonight Live finished at 11.30 pm, and there would've been some after-show drinks, so I reckon I got home about 2 or 3 am. Even so, I was up early and warming up my voice for Sylvie's mother. Should I go soulful and low, like Barry White? Or high and playful, like David Beckham?

I couldn't get that Dr Hook song 'Sylvia's Mother' out of my head. I mean, seriously, what if I rang and Sylvie's mum said she was too busy to come to the phone?

Because I was working on breakfast radio, I'd developed a good range of voice delivery tones and techniques. Obviously I'd use a slightly different voice when introducing Michael Bolton's 'When a Man Loves a Woman' from the one I'd use introducing Right Said Fred with 'I'm Too Sexy'.

I opted for the voice I'd use to introduce Boyz II Men's 'End of the Road'. A gentle fusion of upbeat breathiness, a whispered curving of the non-pivotal words with an overall smooth, creamy tone similar to the sound expensive Swiss chocolate would make if it were slowly melting on a French silver platter on an Italian yacht cruising the Greek islands at low tide in mid-July. You know the sound, yeah?

That was the voice I would use to win over Sylvie's mother.

It was 7 am, which I thought was probably a reasonable time to call. I cleared my throat and rang – forgetting it was daylight savings in *Melbourne* but not in *Brisbane*.

A 6 am call to win over the mother?

Nice move, idiot.

'… Hello?'

WOW, Sylvie's mum sounds very young, and *very* cute.

'Um, good morning, sorry to call so early. You must be Sylvie's mum …'

'No, this is Sylvie.'

'Well, oh, ummmm, hey Sylvie, unless you gave your mum's number to someone else last night …'

'Good morning, Larry,' she immediately said in that gorgeous Polish accent.

This threw me; I was still in FMILCOM (Future Mother-in-Law Charm Offensive Mode). I dropped the melting-chocolate voice and accidentally fell into nervous-thirteen-year-old-boy-whose-testicles-are-about-to-drop-but-haven't-fully-committed-yet voice. A voice like one ball is down but one ball is still up. Wobbly and zigzagging between high and low, like Barry White having a conversation with Michael Jackson but you're doing both voices in one sentence.

Somehow, that didn't seem to matter. The conversation went swimmingly.

We spoke for hours every day for the next month, before Sylvie finally agreed to fly back to Sydney and let me take her for coffee.

Our first date was ten hours long. Coffee turned into lunch, then the movies, then dinner, then dessert. But when I dropped her home, she refused to kiss me. As I leant in, she turned her head and offered me her cheek for a goodnight peck.

Maybe she didn't like me, maybe her mum had told her to 'treat 'em mean, keep 'em keen', maybe she didn't want to invite me in because she'd heard on the grapevine that I might try to steal her salt and pepper shakers.

Whatever the reason, it worked perfectly.

It turns out that while we were out, her best friend and flatmate, Helen, had actually called the police and reported Sylvie missing because she'd gone out with a strange guy for coffee and was supposed to be home nine hours ago. Helen thought Sylvie had been kidnapped.

I hadn't kidnapped Sylvie, but she had kidnapped my heart…

(On the strength of that last vomit-inducing sentence, all my future book deals have been cancelled. Worth it though, classic line.)

Whitegoods-Inspired Lust

1993

Getting the job as host of The Price Is Right was quite simply the greatest gift. It was a perfect job for a fun-loving, happy-go-lucky, perpetually smiling high-school dropout. It was never ever like being at work, it was more like having an epic adrenalin-fuelled day out with a bunch of hilarious people. I've hosted many different shows, but the energy and the vibe of a *Price* night has been virtually impossible to replicate. I'm eternally grateful to everyone who got me there and kept me there. I seriously doubt I would still be on TV today if I hadn't hosted *The Price Is Right*.

'*I love you, Larry!*'

Women young and old – and even some men – would say it to me all the time on *The Price Is Right. Spoiler alert*: I don't think they really loved me.

WHITEGOODS-INSPIRED LUST

Like real love, this experience was exciting. All your senses would be tingling, your toes would curl up and the hairs on the back of your neck would stand on end. Also like real love, this would only last about five minutes – actually, on second thoughts, I guess that means statistically it would often last *longer* than real love.

I called it Whitegoods-Inspired Lust.

On *The Price Is Right* we gave away a sexy smorgasbord of prizes, leading up to the showcase, which would usually include holidays, cars, jet skis and motorbikes. Most people, of course, wanted to win EVERYTHING. I used to say *The Price Is Right* was like Disneyland, just with no annoying mice and no huge queues, and the only thing you could ride was ME.

I'd get jumped on, cuddled, smothered, tackled to the ground, dry-humped and licked all over – and that was just in the change room before I came out.

At the start of the show, four contestants would famously be called to 'COME ON DOWN!!!'

Most people went out of their way to dress loudly, over the top. Maybe they thought it would increase their chances of being called down. Maybe sometimes it did.

The people who would Come On Down out of the audience and jump around the stage with me would be caught up in a surreal moment, potentially about to win a fridge or a cooktop or the elusive, highly sought after washer–dryer combo. And in that surreal moment, overcome with nerves, they would often tell me that they loved me.

It was a bizarre phenomenon. Normal people would never come up to me in the street and say, 'I love you, Larry.'

Now, Whitegoods-Inspired Lust would sometimes have a happy ending, and that would be awesome. As a host, it is quite simply the best feeling in the world to be standing next to someone who is just about to win something that you know for sure will change their life.

But at other times, like in real love, the end of the story was a humiliating, tragic letdown. As in, we're finished, we're done, I have nothing more to give. The contestant is left wanting more, feeling frustrated and unfulfilled, and reconsidering if I'm the right game-show host for her … Ring any bells? No? OK, let's move on.

Standing next to someone who had just won was fabulous, but as we all know, life is like a box of chocolates, and those chocolates can sometimes be half chewed, melted or attacked by ants.

A lot of people *didn't* win. Or, even better for television – but worse for them – won something they didn't want or couldn't give a shit about.

And herein lie some of my most memorable hosting moments.

I don't remember their names, but I'll never forget their stories. So I'm just going to give them random names I've chosen from strange-baby-name lists. There were so many thousands of prizes over so many series over so many years, so I'm not always sure whether it was a VHS recorder or a bar fridge that was up for grabs, but in each case, the essence of the story – the funny bit – remains true and correct.

'Candida, COME ON DOOOOWWWWNNNN!!! You're the next contestant on *The Price Is Right*!!!'

Shawn 'Cossie' Cosgrove's voice was so magnificently deep we used to joke that he had to wheel his balls into the studio in a wheelbarrow. That was *clearly* a joke, because if you remember his voice, you'll know it would've needed a forklift rather than a wheelbarrow.

My King and Queen of Bondi. Dad and Mum looking regal for a wedding in the late 1970s.

Me, age nine months, and Mum. Mum has always been there to support me, right from my very first steps.

Me, age eighteen months, and Dad. Dad was so cool and stylish. Me? Turns out I was more of a camel-toe kinda guy.

My sister Nicki, age seven, and me, age six, annoying everyone in the street by riding our mini-bikes up and down the footpath.

Me (thirteen), Dad, Mum, and sisters Martine (eleven) and Nicki (fourteen), spruced up for a big family gathering. This is how Dad would always wear his shirts; I don't even know why he bought shirts with buttons at all.

Nanny Leah and Grandpa Louis, admiring my fresh bowl cut. Mum would literally put a bowl on my head and cut my hair with craft scissors.

Me and my biggest fan, Nanny Minnie, in the early 1980s. Nanny Minnie would happily stand up at the front of a crowded bus at 5 pm, clap her hands and loudly announce, 'OK everyone, it's nearly 5.30, so go home and watch my grandson on *The Price Is Right!*'

The Greek islands, 1984, where my love of toga parties began and my relationship with ouzo ended forever.

You can decide what's more disturbing here: Dobbo and me walking around my twenty-first party with Candy, my mates' 'tasteful' birthday present; or the fact that I'm wearing a hat in the shape of a massive poo. It was a great night ... I think, I can't really remember.

Interviewing then Prime Minister Bob Hawke at the farewell party for the Seoul-bound Olympic team in 1988, as a young Channel Ten reporter. I said, 'You must be a happy little Vegemite,' and he laughed and replied, 'I've never been asked that before' ... You can tell by the eye contact that the interview went really well after that.

Broadcasting live from inside the Lucas Heights nuclear reactor on *Good Morning Australia*, with Tim Webster and Kerri-Anne Kennerley, in the late 1980s. I'm not sure why everyone else was wearing full hazmat suits ... Oh well, that probably explains my third testicle.

Behind the scenes of *The Main Event* in 1992, with the show's creator, soccer legend Craig Johnston; singing superstar Tina Arena; and the world's funniest bathmat, Agro.

When Agro is on your shoulder, that means Jamie, the man whose body is attached to the hand up Agro's bum, is kneeling somewhere around your groin. That could explain my raised eyebrow. This photo is also a flashback to a time when people on TV could actually raise an eyebrow.

Happy days at *The Price Is Right*, with a few of the models and announcer Shawn 'Cossie' Cosgrove (far left). (*Nine Network Australia*)

The day I asked Sylvie to marry me was quite the production, which of course we had to replicate for this *Woman's Day* magazine photo and story. *(Woman's Day)*

Our wedding day, 1994: 'Sylvie, despite this disgusting matching vest and cravat (with adjustable Velcro band), will you marry me …?'

Me and my co-host, Kylie Gillies, on one of our very first photo shoots for *The Morning Show* in 2007. 'Maybe it'll last six months,' they said. Well, we've won the national ratings for fifteen years straight, and it's been a fantastic ride and a very important part of my career. Kylie and I just clicked and we've never *un*-clicked. *(Katrina Tepper/Newspix)*

Me and Karl Stefanovic on supermaxi yacht *Perpetual Loyal*, which we crewed for the Sydney to Hobart race in 2013. Karl may have beaten me in the Sydney to Hobart and at the Logies, but I beat him in the title for Sexy Australian of the Year, so bite me, Karl!!! Not that we're competitive … *(Justin Lloyd/Newspix)*

The night in 2015 that Sylvie got to go to bed with a magazine cover guy, after I won *Men's Health* Celebrity Man of the Year.

Me, Martine, Mum, Dad and Nicki in the backyard of our Brighton Boulevard house, about 1990. Happy as … family.

People would always come up to me and ask me to say, 'Come On Down!' like I did on TV, but *I* never said it on TV. *Cossie* did.

Cossie's 'Come On Down!' sounded like twenty Harley-Davidsons towing an iceberg over gravel. Mine would sound like Fran Drescher from *The Nanny* after she sucked in a helium balloon. My version was sad, and always a letdown.

I show Candida and the other three contestants a starter prize and they each make a bid. Candida bids the closest without going over, so she wins the starter prize, then comes onto centre stage and plays for a major prize.

This is when I get to have a little chat with her. Nothing too serious – what do you do, do you have a family, what would you like to win, do you love me? Blah blah blah.

Then it's time to play. 'Good luck, Candida, I hope you win this!' I say bouncily.

The big doors fly open, to reveal a great-looking male model in Speedos and a gorgeous female model in a bikini, standing next to a terracotta birdbath with a variety of fake birds Blu Tacked around it.

Why we had sexy models in swimsuits in the middle of a Melbourne winter standing next to a terracotta birdbath still befuddles and excites me to this day. But you have to remember this is television, so it's not normal.

Cossie bellows in his amazing, earth-shattering mega-voice:

'IT'S A TERRACOTTA BIRDBATH!!! Lovingly crafted from timeless stone, this beautiful yet practical piece of art, inspired by the great gardens of Europe, will be the highlight of your entire neighbourhood and the envy of everyone in your street. The local birds will love and admire it almost as much as you do.'

OK, big fellar, you might want to rein that sales pitch in a bit, 'cause by the look on Candida's face, I'm not sure she believes this *will* in fact be the highlight of her entire neighbourhood, I'm not sure she can immediately identify which particular great gardens of Europe this was inspired by, and I'm not sure she's one hundred per cent convinced the local birds will be able to love and admire it in her thirty-seventh-floor inner-city apartment with no balcony …

I'm a Sagittarian, and that means I suck my energy from other people. If you're up, *I'm* going up with you; if you're down, *I'm* going down too. (Let me have another crack at that: if you're down, we're going down together …)

From an energy perspective, Candida was going down on the birdbath, but *I* was hosting an upbeat TV game show, so I had to fight off my Sagittarianalist instincts (which also include making up new words), so as not to go down with her. I'd have to double down on my upness to offset her down-ness.

I'd have to act like when you see a friend with an ugly baby that looks like a cross between Mr Bean and Shrek, but you still feel compelled to say, 'Oh, he's *so* gorgeous!' (Don't judge me, you've done that, you know you have.)

'WOW!!! WOW!!! This birdbath is beautiful, and absolutely unique!!!'

I would say this stuff knowing full well that the only unique thing about this birdbath was that it had two sexy models in swimsuits standing next to it, in a TV studio in the middle of a Melbourne winter. Apart from that, you could probably pretty much pop down to Birdbaths 'R' Us and buy one that was identical.

'Candida, all you have to do is put these grocery items in order from least expensive to most expensive and you'll win this magnificent birdbath.'

The items were a packet of Tim Tams, a jar of Moccona coffee, some dishwashing liquid, a ten-pack of batteries and some fly spray.

I've told this story for decades, gone over it in my head a million times, and it remains my firm, inescapable and undeniable belief that Candida wanted the Tim Tams more than the birdbath.

But the two biggest prize winners would go through to play in the showcase for more great prizes, so she had to commit.

I was so happy when she won the birdbath that I gave her the packet of Tim Tams. Reports from the prize warehouse years later were that the birdbath was never, ever collected.

But the following might be an *even better* story ... I'll never forget the look on Hyacinth's face when she won.

She'd applied to come onto *The Price Is Right* years earlier, but had moved from Melbourne to Port Douglas in the meantime.

She was so committed she applied to come in again. When she got the confirmation letter, she excitedly booked her flight from Port Douglas to Melbourne.

People's names were called out randomly on the show, so there was never a guarantee you'd be selected to play. But it was her lucky day. After waiting for years, and flying herself down from Port Douglas, she got called down out of the audience.

She was over-the-moon excited. She'd been dreaming about this for years, and now all the planets had aligned to make this dream of winning a reality …

'Good luck, Hyacinth, I hope you win this!!!' I say.

The huge doors fly open.

'IT'S A GREYHOUND BUS TRIP AND TWO NIGHTS' ACCOMMODATION IN … PORT DOUGLAS!!!!!'

OK, quick recap. Waited years to get into *Price Is Right* audience, buys flight from Port Douglas to Melbourne, pays for Melbourne hotel, comes in to show, wins three-day bus trip BACK TO HER HOMETOWN with two nights' hotel accommodation THREE MINUTES FROM HER HOUSE, then a return bus trip to Melbourne, where she'd need to catch a flight BACK TO PORT DOUGLAS.

And … SHE WON IT!!! THE WOMAN FROM PORT DOUGLAS WON A TRIP TO PORT DOUGLAS!!!!! Come on, that's better than anything you've ever seen on *MAFS*.

Thank goodness there wasn't a terracotta birdbath on the set, or I'm sure she would've picked it up and rammed it up my arse … sideways.

The next story is one of my all-time favourites.

I asked Winifred, the lovely ninety-year-old great-grandmother, what she'd like to win. She said maybe a cruise, or something nice for around the house. I'm thinking, 'Winifred, if you want a terracotta birdbath, just pop out to the prize warehouse in a year or two, it'll still be there …'

She was delightful, a tiny lady with white hair, a beautiful smile and a lovely, soft manner.

'Here we go … good luck, Winifred, I hope you win this!!!'

The huge doors flew open and the noise of the revving Harley-Davidson was deafening.

Cossie boomed in: 'IT'S A NEW HARLEY-DAVIDSON!!!!!'

The big, bald bikie, with a gorgeous bikini model seated behind him, revved the Harley to the max as he drove it right up next to me and Winifred.

It was hysterical. The audience exploded, Winifred couldn't stop laughing, the bikie kept revving … It was a truly beautiful television moment.

Once it all calmed down, I said: 'Well there you go, Winifred, what do you think about that?'

She just laughed again, shrugged her shoulders and replied: 'What the shit do I do with that?'

SO many monumental moments happening all at once. A ninety-year-old lady finding out she was playing for a Harley, a gorgeous bikini model on the back seat, and a great-grandmother saying 'shit' on an afternoon game show. *Could it get any better??!!*

HELL, YEAH!!!

She won it!!!!! Brilliant television, and I could just imagine her doing doughnuts in the car park of the nursing home.

But if any story could beat Winifred's for sheer ridiculousness, it was probably Dianella's.

During the starter round, Dianella bid the closest to the price of the matching his-and-hers tracksuits and excitedly bounced out to me on centre stage. During the chat I had with her, we established that she was living in a caravan in a caravan park, leading a very simple and happy life. She was *very* nervous and *very* excited: just the way we liked 'em! Frothing at the mouth, weak at the knees, eyes wide like a deer caught in the headlights, holding my hand so tightly I was worried she was going to rip the meat right off my phalanges …

She said maybe she'd like a holiday or a new car: our two most common answers to my most common question, 'What would you like to win?'

Surprisingly, or not, no one ever came out and said, 'I'd really like to win a twelve-month supply of haircare products' – although when the seventy-year-old bald man won that, it was pretty funny.

Surprisingly, or not, no one ever came out and said, 'I'd really like to win an assortment of female fluoro-coloured Lycra aerobics outfits', although when the hundred-and-fifty-kilo, heavily tattooed male truck driver won that, it was pretty funny … and great television.

Dianella was very sweet, and I thought it would've been lovely if there'd been a car behind the big doors.

I rarely knew what the major prize was; there was too much else happening for me to worry about that. I also found it was more fun if I was as shocked or surprised as the contestant when the doors opened up. I could honestly share that moment with them.

But I *did* know if it was a car. I'd get a secret cue from the floor manager, because a car would warrant a slightly more dramatic buildup before I threw to the prize. I might drag out the conversation with the contestant a bit more, and try to find the perfect moment to throw to the car. Like:

Me: So, tell me about your family.
Contestant: Well, I've got three kids and I'm a full-time mum.
Me: So you're just ferrying those kids around all day?
Contestant: Pretty much.
Me: Well, maybe you could start ferrying them around in THIS …

Doors fly open. Cossie hollers: 'IT'S A NEW CAR!!!!!'

Audience explodes, contestant explodes. 'I love you, Larry!'

No, you don't, you just want the car!

So anyway, it's the moment of truth for Dianella from the caravan park.

'Good luck, Dianella,' I say, 'tonight you could win THIS …'

Doors fly open, Cossie roars: 'IT'S A ROLLER DOOR!!!!!'

Now, there's nothing Cossie could say in his spiel that could possibly make a roller door appealing to someone who lives in a caravan.

'This modern and sleek roller door will make a wonderful addition to your home …'

No, it won't, Cossie.

'It has extended remote-control range, so you'll never have to get out of your car in the rain again …'

Yes, she will, Cossie.

'Its advanced technology will add a new layer of protection to your home …'

Cossie, step away from the microphone … Cossie, blink three times if they're making you say things you don't believe …

'So keep your car out of the rain, hail and shine …'

Wait, did he say 'car'? Is there a car coming??? Nope.

'With this new roller door, you'll be the envy of everyone in your street ...'

Hang on, hang on! Did they cut and paste that from the terracotta birdbath script? OK, that's enough, can I see the writers in my office after the show, please?

'And this could be yours, Dianella, IF THE PRICE IS RIGHT ...'

Thanks, Cossie.

'OK, Dianella, what about that?'

It was completely stupid question. It took me a while, but I eventually learnt not to ask questions I didn't want the answers to.

'Well, Larry, I live in a caravan, so I don't *have* a garage, actually.'

Hey, Dianella, Diiiiiiianellllllaaaa, don't suck my energy, I'm a Sagittarian, don't rain on my parade, don't bring me and my popular show down with tiny trivial stuff like that, how selfish! Maybe you should think more about ME AND MY SHOW and less about YOURSELF.

The last contestant told me she loved me AND dry-humped me, and SHE was only playing for a pair of corduroy beanbags! And now you're dragging my show down with negative answers like THAT. I can feel TV sets around Australia right now turning over to Wheel of Fortune, *maybe you'd rather be over there buying a vowel than standing here next to me winning a roller door!*

Come up here with me, Dianella, up here on the game-show rainbow, in the exciting, rarefied air above the clouds where EVERYONE is excited about a roller door. I'm Willy Wonka, you're in the Chocolate Factory, where's your Whitegoods-Inspired Lust??!!

Let's win this ...

Dianella *did* win the roller door, and I often think of her sitting with a Bundy and Coke on a fold-out camp chair outside her caravan, with her garage door wedged between two trees, pushing the button on the technologically advanced, extended-range remote control and watching this fabulous roller door just go up and down, up and down, up and down, waiting patiently for someone to invent the internet, then invent a website where you can sell shit you don't want.

Hang in there, Dianella, it's coming!!!

The Price Is Right meant different things to different people. For all its bright lights, loud bells, buzzers and wonderful whistles, sometimes, just sometimes, this mish-mash of madness actually changed lives. It wasn't always about the jet skis, the holidays, the cars and the roller doors. As this next contestant proved, sometimes *The Price Is Right* was able to make a huge difference even with the little things.

Sally and I were having a great time. She was fun, and a perfect contestant. We'd had a great, nervous, giggly chat, and now it was time for the major prize reveal.

'IT'S A NEW JET SKI!!!!!' screams Cossie.

But Sally didn't look as excited about the jet ski as we'd hoped. Remember when fireworks were legal and you'd light them and stand back in anticipation, waiting to see them shoot into the air and explode into a million different colours, lighting up the night sky with excitement and magic – but instead, just as the wick ran out you'd hear *FFFFfffZZZZZzzz. z zz zzzz z* and the whole thing would just kind of fizzle out? Sally's reaction was *just* like that.

(OK, smartarse, your challenge for the day: write the sound a wick makes as it fizzles out. See if you can do it better than me.)

'Now, Sally, to win this jet ski, you have to correctly price these two items …'

Doors fly open to reveal a lovely shagpile rug with a male model on top, and a pretty ordinary-looking microwave oven.

Suddenly, to my surprise, Sally was beside herself, jumping up and down, holding her hands to her face, squealing. There was something in this minor prize reveal that had reignited her rocket. Naturally I thought it was the sight of the male model sprawled out on the shagpile rug, but then I noticed she wasn't looking that way.

'Sally, what's going on?'

She stopped squealing and jumping and excitedly told me: 'Larry, I'm a single mum with four young kids. I've wanted a microwave forever, my house is *so* hectic at mealtimes. But I don't have a job at the moment, and I just can't afford one. Gee, I'd love this *sooooo* much!'

I remember thinking: 'But they are, like, a couple of hundred bucks.'

With no money coming in, having paid the rent, bought the groceries, and been a great mum to her young kids, Sally couldn't even save up a couple of hundred bucks to buy a microwave.

The tension was mounting in the studio. Sally was so focused on the microwave it was ridiculous. *Everybody* wanted her to win, especially me. We'd all heard enough of her story to be deeply emotionally invested in these next few minutes.

The game played out with an unusually high level of drama.

'OK, Sally, if you've put the shagpile rug and the microwave in the correct order, then you win those AND the jet ski …'

'I just want the microwave, Larry!' she told me. She crossed her fingers tightly and looked towards the heavens: 'Please, please God, please …' She seemed to be on the edge of breathlessness.

We heard the error buzzer, *not* the winning bells. She had put them in the wrong order.

She was gutted, and so was the entire audience.

Now, in my head I had already decided to give her the microwave if she lost. I would've paid for it myself, or done a little deal with the network or the sponsor. But just as I was about to tell her that, the floor manager got word from the executive producer to instruct me to give it to her.

'Sally, you've been a great contestant, and we're going to give you that microwave.'

The tears of joy flowed thick and fast. Like I said, sometimes it's the small things.

That was a *great* day in the office.

Placki Kartoflane

1993

Eventually, Sylvie and I had kissed, and I wasn't actually too bad. I'd learnt a lot from the Raquel Welch poster on my wall as a teenager, and all those games of Spin the Bottle.

Now, after about six months of shamelessly pursuing my Polish goddess, I was ready to tell her I loved her.

This was a big deal for me. I was never very good at this stuff – as any of my old girlfriends, who have probably found this book in the $1 bin and are using the cover as a dartboard, will tell you.

I wanted to tell Sylvie I loved her in her native language. It was either going to be an incredibly romantic gesture or the tackiest thing she'd ever heard. But I was willing to roll the dice and roll some Rs and perfect my nonexistent Polish.

Surely the mere fact that I was even prepared to commit to this fanciful plan was proof that I really did love her.

I was willing to attempt to learn three whole words in a foreign language. THREE. WHOLE. WORDS. If that's not love, I just don't know what is. You with me, fellars?

If only I'd been this committed to learning English back at school!

This was many, many years before Google and Siri, so I called my best mate Robbie's dad. Fred spoke a few different languages, including Polish. So I told him I'd booked a really nice restaurant for Saturday night and I wanted him to teach me how to tell my Polish girlfriend that I loved her. I was hoping 'I love you' in Polish would be something easy like 'I loveski youski.'

He asked me if I was sure about this. In his thick Hungarian accent, he told me it was three Polish mathematicians who ended World War II after cracking the German Enigma Code. So you needed to be careful with Polish women, because they were *very* smart.

'*Placki kartoflane,*' he said.

'Is that "I love you"?' I asked.

He repeated it: '*Placki kartoflane.*'

I thought, 'Wow, he's right, the Polish *are* very smart, the way they've condensed the three words "I love you" into the two words "*Placki kartoflane*".'

I grabbed a pen and paper and asked him to say it one more time. I wrote it down like this: 'Plarts-key cart-o-flarnee.'

I rehearsed this all week in front of the bathroom mirror – sometimes with the emphasis on the 'Plarts', sometimes with the emphasis on the 'flarnee'. I practised raising an eyebrow for dramatic effect when I hit 'cart-o'. I even chucked in a bit of gesticulation, and tried to choreograph my face to the syllables.

It must have been a pitiful sight: me, standing in front of the mirror, articulating and gesticulating all over the place.

I wanted to get it *exactly* right. I wanted this moment to be burnt into her memory forever.

I wanted my hands, my tonsils, my eyebrows and the angle of my chin to all work in perfect harmony when I delivered the all-important message.

Like Ronan Keating singing a ballad, I would extend my arm gently upwards, then twist my wrist till my palm lovingly faced the heavens above, then, in slow motion, I would close the wrist and pull it back towards my heart.

Plarts (extend arm)

key (raise left eyebrow, quarter smile – no teeth – open palm and twist skyward)

cart-o (close hand)

flarnee (de-extend arm and draw closed fist back to chest as if to rest on heart, soften eyes with a gentle blink, tilt head playfully to the left)

I'd spent most of the week on this, and by Saturday I was ready. The waiter poured the wine, the candle flickered, Sylvie looked so beautiful and I was hypnotised by her blue eyes (still am today; they're *blue* blue, like a Bora Bora lagoon at low tide).

I leant across the table and took her hand in mine. This was the moment to tell her I loved her – and not in some yobbo Aussie way:

Hey, darl', I know we've been hangin' out a bit lately, and I really love the way ya get me a VB outta the fridge when I get home from work and open it with ya belly button. I love the way ya drive me and the boys to the footy and wait for us in the car till it's finished. I love the way ya let me use ya Netflix account. I love that huge tramp-stamp tattoo on ya back just above ya jeans that says 'No Ifs No Butts'. I love the way ya don't yell at me for leaving me dirty socks and undies on the floor like me mum used to. In fact, I think I love ya, but I still want to go to the pub with me mates on Friday nights …

Oh, no no no no-ski. *I* was going to do it in her native tongue. Yes, I'd learnt two words in Polish (and please remember I was prepared to learn three, so the fact that the Polish had condensed 'I love you' into two words was just a beautiful bonus). If that doesn't scream commitment, then I don't know what does.

So I looked deep into her piercing blue eyes and said it *perfectly*, even better than perfectly.

'*Placki kartoflane* …'

She didn't say anything, just looked slightly confused.

I'd thought about this moment all week, and to be honest, in my head I'd seen it going a little differently. I knew I'd nailed the delivery: I'd said it exactly how Fred had told me to say it, and with all the perfect little pauses and gestures I'd passionately rehearsed. I didn't have any food in my mouth, so it wasn't like I was masticating while articulating and gesticulating.

I started thinking: 'Bloody hell, what have I done wrong???'

So I said it again, with less Ronan Keating and more of a Barry White kind of vibe, slow and smooth. But now I was desperate, and there's a chance all my rehearsal references had got mixed up.

It was quite likely I had Lauren Bacall, Ronan Keating and Barry White in my mouth all at the same time.

Which may well be the first chapter in my next book: 'Sentences I've Written That Didn't Look So Good Out of Context'.

Then Sylvie started laughing, loudly. My first thought was, 'OK, what a bitchski. I never want to see you again. Just because your people cracked the Enigma Code, doesn't mean you get to be so nasty.'

Suddenly I urgently wanted a girlfriend with a tramp stamp that said 'GET SOME!' who could open my VB with her belly button.

I asked: 'What's so funny? I thought telling you I love you in Polish would be special.'

Potato pancake, *that's* what *placki kartoflane* means. Potato fucking pancake.

When his secretary put me through to Fred on Monday morning, all I could hear was his hysterical laughter. He'd got me good and proper! I told him the whole story and we laughed about it for a long time.

Just before I hung up, he reminded me never to lie to or cheat on my Polish girlfriend, because the Poles cracked the code that won the war.

When I finally flew to Brisbane to meet Sylvie's parents, the Lipczynskis, they also reminded me about that – a few times, in fact.

My first dinner with her mum and dad was a true test of my love for her.

Sylvie had told me that when she explained who I was to her dad, he'd said: 'Oh, no, you're not going out with a TV bimbo, are you?' But both her parents were so warm and friendly it made me immediately fall in love with them, and love Sylvie herself even more.

Ela and Wlodek had brought Sylvie to Australia from Poland in 1981 in search of a better life. They'd had relatives already settled in Brisbane who over the years had convinced them Australia could be a better place for the family.

Fourteen-year-old Sylvie, speaking barely a word of English, arrived pasty-white from a European winter, smack-bang into a Queensland summer.

Her early days at school here were full of stories of being bullied, teased and called a wog. Some of the girls accused her of putting on an accent just to impress the boys. (I think she did this when she first met me, and it worked a treat!)

Back in Poland, Wlodek had had a successful ski business and Ela had worked in a foreign exchange bank, but when they arrived here they had to take whatever work they could get. Ela was a cleaner in banks and hospitals and Wlodek was a welder in a steel factory. They both worked long, hard hours, but they wanted a good life here so they just did what they had to do.

Ela was also a talented seamstress, and she ended up working closely with famous Queensland designer Keri Craig.

Meanwhile, Sylvie ploughed through school and went to university to study Medical Laboratory Science. She was destined to be a research scientist who would probably marry a Nobel prize–winning professor who probably would go on to cure some previously incurable disease – but then a friend dared her to apply for a flight attendant's job at Ansett just for shits and giggles. That, of course, led to her trapping and marrying *me*, so *I* am now the 'just for shits and giggles' part of her life.

Once we got the ancestry.com stuff out of the way, it was time for dinner.

As we've well and truly established, I was a Bunny in a Hole, Nino's Hawaiian Pizza, and Big Ben pie and Coke kinda guy. My tastebuds were like politicians: they were always there when I needed them, they did what they had to do, but they were incredibly boring.

Chlodnik – cold beetroot soup – is a beloved Polish dish. Basically, everything you need to know is in the name. It's cold, it's beetroot and it's soup.

This was a test, I was sure it was a test. I loved their Polish daughter, but would I love their Polish food?

I'd been a TV host long enough by this point to have perfected the fake smile and fake enthusiasm. '*Mmmmmmmmm, this is just beautiful!!!*' I said with a huge smile after trying to get the cold beetroot soup past my tastebuds without giving each of them a heart attack.

I finally got through it. 'OK, that's done,' I thought, 'now bring out the chicken or the steak.'

I didn't immediately recognise the next dish that was lovingly placed in front of me. I said to Sylvie, '*Hmmmm*, this looks interesting, what is it?'

Sylvie said, 'Don't worry, try it, you'll love it.'

I knew that really meant 'YOU *WILL* LOVE IT' (even if you don't).

The knife went through it surprisingly easily. I tasted it, and everyone was watching for my reaction.

I dug deep and called on Generic Game-Show Host Face #84647: a gentle, convincing smile, a subtly raised eyebrow, and an ever-so-slight nod of a tenderly tilted head.

'*Mmmmmm*, wow, that's lovely! Come on, Sylvie, what is it?'

I almost spat it straight back out when she said, 'Ox tongue.' And she said it with a smile – as in, 'Ox tongue, you love it, yes?'

There was something about eating the brains, the livers, the kidneys, the heart, the scrotum or the tongue that just didn't do it for me or my unsophisticated facehole. Who knows *what* was in those Big Ben pies Dad and I used to eat – but at least it was conveniently hidden in an appealing package of soggy pastry drowned in tomato sauce.

Now I just had a naked ox tongue on my plate, looking up at me, staring me down, ready to jump into my mouth and hump my tongue.

I suspect this is how my first Spin the Bottle victim felt when she saw me coming towards her, tongue flapping everywhere.

But I ate it, all of it. And it was actually very nice, although I have never *ever* ordered it again.

We had a fabulous night, full of embarrassing stories about Sylvie as she was growing up and Ela's famous struggles with the English language. When she was applying for her first bank loan, Ela said to the manager at the end of the meeting: 'I love you from the heart of my bottom.'

Ela and Wlodek reminded me so much of my own parents: warm, friendly, funny and completely endearing. Wlodek is such an impressive and intelligent man, always ready, willing and able to talk about anything from sport to world politics. He's also a fine father-figure who has never ever raised his voice at his daughter, and the best father-in-law a boy could hope for. And he knows not to try to serve me ox tongue again.

Ela passed away in 2018, and we lost an incredible lady, a flirty, funny and cheeky woman, and a deeply involved and caring mother and grandmother. When Ela walked into a room, it was like someone had set off a beautiful display of fireworks. I've never met anyone quite like her. Everyone who met her loved her, and I feel truly blessed to have had her in my life.

As I said at her memorial gathering: 'We miss her dearly, and we will always, always and forever love her from the heart of our bottom.'

There's Something About Mary

1990s

'Who's your favourite contestant?'

It's a question I've been asked a gazillion times, after hosting so many episodes of so many game shows over so many years.

It's true that the contestants tripping and tumbling down the stairs on *The Price Is Right* were pretty funny, and yes, the woman in the boob tube who jumped to her feet and threw her hands above her head so the boob tube became a belly-button tube was also a highlight.

But the answer to my favourite-contestant question always has been and always will be …

Mary.

Mary was excited to be called down. Not normal-excited, but way-way-way-over-the-top, through-the-roof, fireworks-going-off-in-every-part-of-her-body excited.

This can be an issue, because at this stage you haven't won anything, you've just been called down. I was always concerned when they peaked too early. Would they be able to top that if they actually won anything? But it always made for *great* TV.

Mary bid the closest without going over the starter prize, and it was GO time. She was off like a rocket ship. She shocked me by digging deep and finding a new level of excitement, the likes of which we hadn't seen on the show before, or maybe on *any* show before, *ever*.

Mary snorted when she laughed and laughed when she snorted, so she got herself into a perpetual self-saucing spin cycle of laugh–snort–laugh–snort–laugh–snort. She was laughing at her snorting and then snorting at her laughing, it just didn't stop.

Everyone, and I mean *everyone*, was in stitches.

I think we managed some sort of little chat, then I threw to the prize package. It was a camera, a calorie tracker and a holiday.

The game was called Make Your Move. Basically, it was a big, brightly coloured board featuring a row of numbers: *1 6 0 1 5 1 0 7 5*. Under that there were three small boards, each with one of the prizes printed on them. All Mary had to do was slide each board under the numbers that represented its price.

So, between the screaming and the snorting and the laughing and the snorting and the snorting and the laughing, she did.

She slid the camera under the numbers *75*, the calorie tracker under the numbers *160* and the holiday under the numbers *1510*.

We always revealed the minor prize first, which would obviously help build the drama before the reveal of the major prize. But Mary was a mess, and we hadn't even started the reveal yet.

She was gripping my hand with pressure similar to that of the jaws of life used by police rescue squads to cut trapped people out of car wrecks. *Her* mascara was running, *my* mascara was running. Her eyes were popping out of her head, and her neverending cycle of laughing and snorting had escalated to ATOMIC Mode. It was like Cirque du Soleil was performing just under the skin of her face.

'Geez, I hope you're not faking this,' I said, and off she went again.

At this point the floor manager leant in and handed her a glass of water. Her mind said, 'Yes!', but her hand said, 'No way, I'm too busy having fun to stop dancing and drink water!' So as she accepted the glass, the water sploshed and splashed everywhere. She tried to get it to her mouth using the old second-hand-to-steady-the-glass method, but there was just too much going on for even *both* hands to steady the water in the glass. So she gave up on that, and it was time to play the game.

'Mary, you said $75 for the camera. IS SHE RIGHT ...???'
REVEAL!!!

Bells, buzzers, lights, dingers ... YES!!!

Mary jumped out of her skin, and this was just for a $75 camera! Now I had to reveal whether the *other* prizes were correct.

God help me. I'd never worked so hard to keep a show on track.

At this point the audience was in hysterics, Cossie had lost it, the models were crying and laughing at the same time, and the crew was pissing themselves. This was magical television.

Somehow we calmed down enough to reveal the other two prizes.

AND ... SHE WON!!!!!

The reaction was off the Richter scale, SUCH a memorable, funny moment.

All her family ran down, audience members were wiping tears from their eyes, I collapsed on the studio floor, and Mary knelt down over me and started fanning me.

I threw to the commercial break with the few scraps of words and energy I had left.

Cossie went up to Mary during the break and asked: 'Mary, are you OK?'

She snorted and laughed some more and said: 'That was better than sex!!!!!'

*

When Sylvie and I were getting serious, I explained the pitfalls of my business, how it was never predictable or reliable. I'd already been axed plenty of times, but I promised her whenever I got axed from now on, we'd go on a big adventure. I promised I would never sit around and wait for the phone to ring. When the first series of *The Price Is Right* was wound up, about a year after Mary's memorable appearance, I immediately booked us one-way tickets to LA. We found a beautiful waterfront apartment on Marina del Ray, packed up the house, grabbed Jye and all his Wiggles paraphernalia and went on our adventure.

Days before we left, we found out Sylvie was pregnant with Tia, so this wasn't only going to be a nice break from work, it was also going to be one of the most exciting and wonderful times as we counted down to this magnificent new arrival.

I was walking along Santa Monica beach. A woman rollerbladed past me, then suddenly stopped and circled back to me.

She said, 'Hey! Hey! You're that guy!'

I said, 'What guy?'

She said, 'You're that guy!' Then she did the snorting–laughing combo Mary impersonation. 'You're THAT guy!'

Turns out a few nights before, Mary had featured on some huge TV bloopers show in America. It was such a good clip they'd started with it and kept going back to it during the show ... 'And let's see how Mary is going on *The Price Is Right* in Australia ...' run clip ... 'Yep, she's still going!'

Today people *still* talk to me about Mary. I've learnt that clip has appeared on TV bloopers and blunders shows all over the world.

I've got to say it's actually difficult to put Mary's story into words, it's such a visual all-you-can-eat combo of madness and mayhem.

If you feel like a good laugh and a good snort and a visual experience that's maybe better than sex, I urge you to google 'Mary on *The Price Is Right*', and you'll see what I mean.

Three Weddings and a Femoral

1994

OK, so I'd told Sylvie I loved her, and even met the parents. The next big move was to lock her down. Sure, she was pregnant with our child, and that was a sweet enough bond, but it was time to put a ring on it, before she realised she'd made a huge mistake in choosing to be with me.

I considered getting down on one knee, then thought, 'NAH! I'm gonna go big.'

So I began to concoct a plan of Hollywood-blockbuster proportions. You remember the little show-off from the marching competition at Rose Bay Public School? He was still alive and well.

No one knew anything about it except my mum and my best mate, Robbie.

Sylvie's parents were down from Brisbane and staying with us in Bondi. Just confirming Candy, my twenty-first birthday present, was long gone from the TV bench by the time they arrived. Sylvie was about three months pregnant. That bit is all true … here come the lying and the cheating, very dangerous activities around a Polish woman.

I said I had to stay at home and do my tax, knowing my mum would offer to take Sylvie and her parents on a bit of sightseeing round Sydney, as I had instructed.

I put them into a cab bound for Rose Bay Wharf, where they planned to jump on a ferry and head in to Circular Quay for a stroll around the Opera House.

As they got out of the taxi at Rose Bay Wharf, Robbie *just happened* to pull up at the wharf in his big boat. Fully rehearsed, he saw them and yelled: 'Hey, guys, what are you doing?'

My mum, just as rehearsed, replied: 'We're just taking Sylvie's parents for a look around the harbour.'

Robbie responded, 'Why don't I take you around on my boat?' He suggested they cruise around to Watsons Bay then head down the harbour to the Opera House and Harbour Bridge. It all seemed very organic and unplanned at this point.

Sylvie's parents were thrilled with this plan. It's a lovely boat, and *much* better than a ferry. (Coincidentally, Robbie *may* have had some champagne in the fridge. Good boy, nice touch!)

As they pulled up at busy Watsons Bay, a limousine driver in full grey suit and hat, carrying a sign saying 'Miss Lipczynski', materialised at the end of the wharf.

The boat was probably still ten metres off the wharf when he started looking around and calling, louder and louder, 'Miss

Lipczynski? Miss Lipczynski?' Like he might at the airport arrivals terminal when trying to find a passenger.

Everyone heard Sylvie's name being called, and they were all – except for Robbie and Mum – slightly confused. In that silly moment, I think they concluded that I had put a limo on for them to have a nice drive around the city. Whatever was going on inside their heads, Robbie reported back later that the whole thing was *very* funny.

He backed the boat up to the wharf and they all got off. Sylvie asked the driver what was going on, and he replied, as rehearsed, 'We're just going for a nice drive around the city and then to the Opera House.'

This next bit had to work with military precision or it would all fall in an expensive, embarrassing heap.

I had rented five Harley-Davidsons and riders, and had three signs made up – bright yellow with bright-red writing. Sign one, on Harley Number Three, said 'SYLVIE'; sign two, on Harley Number Four, said 'WILL YOU' and sign three, which *I'd* be carrying on the back of Harley Number Five, said 'MARRY ME?'.

I'd carefully planned this with the limo driver and the Harley riders, and it would all happen on New South Head Road, along the Rose Bay foreshore. A straight stretch, double lanes.

The Harley riders and I were hiding, in formation, in a back street just off New South Head Road.

As the limo went past, we revved up and sprang into action.

The limo was to travel at forty ks an hour, then Harleys One and Two would rev obnoxiously, pull in front of the limo and slow it down. Harley Three, with the sign 'SYLVIE', would pull up next to the limo and cruise along until Sylvie saw the sign, then move in front with the others.

Sylvie remembers seeing the sign and saying to our parents: 'Hey, look, someone has the same name as me!'

Then Harley Number Four pulled up alongside the limo – all at forty ks an hour and running out of runway – with the sign 'WILL YOU'.

Mum later reported that at this point the penny started to drop.

Harley Four moved in front of the limo, then Harley Five, with me on the back in a tuxedo and bow tie, carrying a sign that said 'MARRY ME?', pulled up.

I reached into my jacket pocket, grabbed a ring box and very carefully and quickly passed it to Sylvie through the window at forty ks an hour, then we pulled in front and formed a five-Harley arrow-formation escort for the limo.

OK, master plan executed; now I guess I just needed some sort of response.

I understand there was laughing and cheering in the back of the limo, before Mum prompted Sylvie with: '*Well???*'

Sylvie said YES!!!!!!!!!!!!!! (Well, technically to *Mum*, not to me ...)

We were still on the move, and I looked back at the limo driver and kind of raised my arms and shrugged my shoulders, as if to ask him: '*Well, what did she say???*'

I'll never forget the huge smile on his face as he lifted both hands off the steering wheel and gave me two big thumbs-up.

We stopped at the next set of lights, and it was a particularly cool-looking scene. The riders were revving the Harleys like crazy. It was noisy and fabulous. A car pulled up next to us and honked, then the female passenger wound down her window and screamed: 'Did she say yes, 'cause if she didn't, *I'll marry ya!*'

We escorted the limo and family back to a suite I'd booked at the Swiss-Grand (now QT) hotel in Bondi, where all our friends and extended family were waiting. I was over the moon that she'd said yes – but if she hadn't, I'd planned to cut the free drinks off at 3 pm.

Our wedding day was beautiful. We got married in a huge marquee on the water's edge in front of the Opera House.

My best men Mark, Mark and Mark and I had finished a bottle of Wild Turkey bourbon in the back of the convertible Chevrolet on the way to the wedding. So now we were a little bit sunburnt and just a little bit pissed.

The Price Is Right was a pretty big show in 1994, and the promo at the time had me bouncing around the set of the show as the song 'We're Just Wild About Harry!' played in the background, then I'd jump up and yell: 'It's Larry!' It was on high rotation on the network, so at this point in my life, everywhere I'd go people would sing to me, 'We're just wild about Harry!'

As we all mingled on the forecourt waiting for Sylvie to arrive, a huge police boat came towards us with my good friend John Whitehead at the helm. He was a senior officer with the water police at the time. They came in pretty close, blasted all the sirens for a few seconds, then all sang loudly over the police-boat PA: 'We're just wild about Harry!' It was a bloody funny moment.

Sylvie, with her bridesmaids – her best friends Audra and Helen, and my sister Martine – arrived in a horse and carriage that trotted all the way down Macquarie Street and along the side of the Opera House to the marquee overlooking the harbour at the front. Sylvie and her bridesmaids all wore beautiful dresses hand-made with love by her mother, Ela.

Everything was going according to plan, Sylvie looked breathtaking, and yes, I cried when I saw her.

It was a dreamy day. Somehow that thunderstorm and undone top button (disputed by Sylvie) had led to the most magical day of my life. How could a schmuck like me trap a goddess like this? I still regularly ask myself that question, and I think the only probable answer is because I put Mum's number on that scrap of paper I handed her at the airport. Have you ever heard a more adorable pick-up story? Let me answer that for you: HELL NO!

Organising a wedding was way out of my skill set, but I wanted the day to be amazing. My fabulous manager at the time, Rhonda Dawson, had helped organise a 'festival of Sylvie' and it was very special indeed.

It was a day full of love and wonderful memories – the only real glitch happened during the vows, when the celebrant said to Sylvie: 'Do you take Larry to have and to hold for the rest of your life?' The horse pulling the carriage, which was tethered just behind the marquee, started neighing, loudly and a lot.

We had the world's best MC, Shawn 'Cossie' Cosgrove, whose voice would've been heard all over the harbour. The speeches went really well. My great friend George Kapiniaris made a killer one. He's a very funny guy; if you remember the classic Aussie comedy *Acropolis Now*, George played the character Memo.

George wanted to make sure the Polish guests could understand his speech, so he basically put 'ski' on the end of every wordski. Everyone thought it was funny, except a couple of Polish dignitaries. Oh, wellski.

At the end, everyone stepped out of the marquee for a fantastic fireworks display on the harbour, ending with a big fireworks heart containing the words *Larry 4 Sylvie 4 Ever*.

(Yes, you're right, I saved money by using the number *4* instead of spelling out the word *for* twice in fireworks.)

We went to Bali for our honeymoon. I'd already been about fifteen times on surfing trips, but this would be the first time I would go and not buy a Bintang singlet, because Sylvie didn't like them – *that's* how much I loved this woman.

Sixteen years later, in 2010, we renewed our vows. I wanted to remind Sylvie how much I loved and adored her, and we'd always dreamt of going to Bora Bora. Cocktails on the balcony at sunset on bungalows perched over bright-blue water … it looked like a dream in the brochures. I mean, it was no fish and chips on Bondi Beach while being shat on by crazy seagulls, but it still looked dreamy.

Now, *so so* much had happened between 1994 and 2010, but without a doubt the most divisive and controversial moment in our marriage was the declaration of our wild cards.

Yep, we'd got to that mythical stage in a relationship when you think you feel so confident and comfortable with each other you can *actually* say out loud who else you'd like to sleep with.

'You go first …' she said.

'No, *you* go first,' I said, remembering what Fred had told me about how clever Polish women are, and convinced this was some sort of trap.

'C'mon … seriously, who would you sleep with?'

I'm like, *OK, let's do this.*

'I would sleep with Eva Mendes, she's my wild card, my hall pass …'

I closed my eyes and waited for whatever was coming next. To my relief, I didn't hear any hunting knives being drawn from their sheaths, or chainsaws starting up, or arrows being stretched back on their bows …

With both hands I felt my legs, my arms, my neck, my penis; everything appeared to be where it had been before I said the words 'I would sleep with Eva Mendes'.

I couldn't feel any mortal wounds … *Hmmm, THAT went OK.*

'And you?' I asked nervously.

'Nathan Fillion,' Sylvie said. At the time he was playing a crime-solving writer on her favourite show, *Castle*; more recently you might have seen him on *The Rookie*. And there I was, thinking she watched *Castle* because she liked trying to solve the crimes!

So … our marriage had survived *that* game, we would definitely be together forever.

Many months later, we checked in to our breathtaking overwater bungalow in Bora Bora, the deep fluorescent blue of the water matching Sylvie's sparkling eyes. The waves lapping at the stairs off the balcony, the champagne on ice, the sexy lingerie already unpacked on the bed (mine, not hers, hers was still in the suitcase) … The Love-o-Meter was reading 'EXTREME'.

We poured a glass of champagne each – it was complimentary so tasted extra-yum – and stepped out onto the balcony. It was straight off a postcard, utterly spectacular. Then I looked to the right, and there on the balcony next to ours was a guy in a tight pair of Speedos.

What the fuck??!! I looked closer – not at his tight Speedos, but at his face.

Nooooooooooooooooooooooooooooooooo!!!!!!!!!!!!!!!!!

NOOOOOOOOO FUCKING WAY!!!!!!!!!!!!!!!!

Nathan Fillion, the dude I'd given Sylvie permission to have sex with, was ten metres away from Sylvie in his tight Speedos, in the most romantic place on earth!!!!!!!!!!

Nooooooooooooooooooooooooooooooooooo!!!!!!!!!!!!!!!!!!!

'Hello, reception? Yes, it's Mr Emdur in Bungalow Twelve, could you please bring me a speargun, URGENTLY??!!'

Anyway, our romantic holiday turned into a sad game of me watching Sylvie twenty-four hours a day. I slept with one eye open and didn't let her out of my sight.

Renewing our vows fell into second place behind keeping her away from the communal breakfast area, where no doubt old Lover Boy would be lounging, smearing himself with tanning oil and gently licking freshly peeled mango pits in slow motion … Just like in Sylvie's dreams and *my* nightmares.

Right then, vows renewed – let's get out of here!!!

OK, let's try this *one* more time, third time lucky … 2015, and my femoral artery is working overtime pumping blood around my lower body every time I look at Sylvie. (I know the femoral artery pumps blood to the groin, among other areas, Sylvie still excites me, and I really really wanted to use the title 'Three Weddings and a Femoral', so that's that!)

I'd organised a surprise party for Sylvie's forty-fifth birthday, and then I thought, 'Well, everyone will be there and we've got catering, why don't I marry her again in front of all our family and friends?'

Remember, they weren't at the Bora Bora renewal; it was just the celebrant, Sylvie, Nathan and me.

The party was all organised, everything was in place. It was going to be the greatest surprise Sylvie had had since looking at the balcony of the bungalow to our right in Bora Bora. Except *this* surprise was going to involve *me*, instead of that sexy, mango-licking, oiled-up Hollywood superstar.

My family and Sylvie's friends were helping organise the surprise party, but I hadn't told anyone about renewing the wedding vows. That was going to be a big surprise for *everyone*.

The day before, I crumbled and had to confide in my sister Nicki. She is my rock and my go-to problem-solver, always has been, always will be.

So I told her that I had a celebrant coming and was going to surprise Sylvie with a wedding-vow renewal.

'Oh, NOOOOOOOOOOOO you're not!' Nicki said.

'Are you telling me Sylvie's going to walk into a room in her jeans and T-shirt, after being out at a bogus girls' lunch all afternoon, and then you're going to spring a *vow renewal* on her? Most girls would want to have a nice dress on, have their hair done, put on some make-up for such an occasion …

'Oh, NOOOOOOOOOOO you're not, and … what if she says NO?'

I hadn't considered that – that's how adorable I think I am – but Nicki was right, always has been, always will be.

She made me promise I would tell Sylvie, even though it meant losing the surprise. I reluctantly agreed.

Sylvie and I were in bed the night before, watching TV. I turned it off and said: 'Sylvie I've got something to tell you, I didn't *want* to tell you but I have to.'

Sylvie remembers this moment very well. It must've been the way I said it, but she immediately thought the next sentence was going to include either the words 'divorce', 'affair', 'trial separation' or 'Nathan Fillion has lost his penis in an unfortunate spearfishing accident in Bora Bora'.

I told her that her lunch the next day was a smokescreen to get her out of the house so I could get ready for her surprise birthday party, and that I'd had the vows from our wedding reprinted, and after dinner I'd organised a celebrant to come in and help us renew them. I'd thought it would be really special doing it in front of our family and friends.

My confession went down well; I think compared with the divorce announcement she'd thought was coming, this was a reasonable result.

It was a terrific party – although Sylvie had modified her vows to read:

'He is my lover, my best friend and my ATM.'

Oh great, I'm your automatic teller machine? So in summary, Sylvie only wants me for money and sex! I feel so used – happy, but used.

The Lighter Side
1997

For as long as I could remember, Dad had yearned for a cabin on a river. *Any* cabin, on *any* river.

He was actually a pretty good artist, maybe that's where Martine gets it from. His desk would always be covered in drawings and sketches – and some of those drawings would be of a cabin, painted in vivid colour.

Dad had a clear vision for this cabin – what it would look like, but more importantly how it would make him *feel*. How relaxing it would be, how easy it would be to catch fish from his front lawn, how warm the sunshine would feel on his face, and how much more freely the fresh air would flow through his terminally damaged lungs.

I don't know if he ever really thought he'd own one. Maybe just the thought of it was enough for him. His mindful, meditative destination, where he'd go in his head to avoid what was *really* going on.

His lifetime of chain-smoking had finally caught up with him. My very best mate in the universe, my handsome, funny, popular, strong mentor and idol was now struggling for virtually each breath through a long, narrow tube that ran from an oxygen bottle into his nostrils.

We'd go on long drives, with the oxygen bottle in the back seat of the car and the tube running up over the back of his neck. The conversation on these drives was often limited – not boisterous and funny and full of life like back in the days when we'd go fishing or to the beach, but measured by the number of words he could get out between breaths from the oxygen bottle, his voice croaky from the medication he was taking. Some days he felt better than others, and we could have a relatively normal conversation, but as he deteriorated, he would literally have to pre-plan the number of words he was about to say to coincide with his shallow breaths.

He'd spend hours at home going through ads for river cabins, and when he found one he liked, he and I would go and inspect it. Boys' trip.

Mum and Dad still lived in Bondi, in the house at 20 Brighton Boulevard where we'd moved when I was thirteen. So a trip to any river house was at least a couple of hours away.

We went on quite a few of these trips. I was never sure whether Dad was really that interested in the cabin, or just wanted to get out of the house and go for a long drive with me.

We'd have a pie somewhere for lunch, just like we did when we were fishing on our little superyacht, *Siesta*. Didn't have to be a fancy pie, even a shitty one from a petrol station was enough to bring back the memories we wanted to relive.

It probably sounds strange, but anyone who has spent time with a person on oxygen will know that when their mood changes, when their excitement level increases or decreases, you can hear their breathing change. The oxygen exchange between bottle and patient sounds a bit like Darth Vader breathing. When it slows down or speeds up, there's an obvious change in sound.

On one particular occasion, after a couple of hours of driving and calmly chatting, we pulled into the driveway of the Torrens Water Ski Gardens at Wisemans Ferry, on the Hawkesbury River northwest of Sydney.

I heard Dad's breathing speed up. Something had just happened, and I didn't know what.

He took a deep breath. '*This is it.*'

'This is what?' I asked

'This is like the place in my dreams. This is the place I've always drawn.'

He pointed to a huge tree, casting long, cool shadows over a bright-green lawn that ran right to the river's edge.

'*This is it.*'

He became quite overwhelmed and breathing became difficult. He simply couldn't get the air he needed into his lungs. This happened a lot, and I always felt helpless, but there was nothing anyone else could do. He had to calm *himself* down, using the breathing techniques his lung specialist had given him.

Instinctively I'd want to say, 'Are you all right?' or 'Can I help?' or 'What's wrong?' But if I did that, it just made the moment worse, because then not only would he be struggling to catch his breath, but he would also feel compelled to try to answer me.

So whenever he got a little breathless, I'd kind of look the other way and not say or do anything, and eventually he'd get some air back into his lungs and calm himself down. Not saying or doing anything felt totally counterintuitive, but it was the right thing to do.

Even writing this now, it makes so much sense, but I can tell you that in a moment of panicked breathing it was both very challenging and extremely distressing just to sit by.

I suppose the really sad part of this physical reaction was that it would also often happen when he was happy or excited. So he would experience the same sort of frightening breathing battle when he was stressed as he would when he was cuddling his grandchildren. As he ran out of breath, he would panic; can you imagine cuddling your grandchildren and having that beautiful interaction trigger a panic response?

It was beyond heartbreaking.

On this occasion, after the panic had subsided a little, we drove a bit further into the cabin park. I looked at him and could see his eyes were filling with tears. Even before the lovely manager came down to meet us, I somehow knew we weren't leaving here today without buying this cabin …

It was in the front row of cabins, looking straight over a lawn stretching to the river. It was old, very modest, and not in good condition at all. It smelt a bit mouldy and was long overdue for a proper clean.

When I said to Dad, 'Let's just buy it, right now', he was hesitant. Perhaps simply *dreaming* of being somewhere like this was more realistic than actually owning it and coming here.

'Let's just do it, let's buy it,' I encouraged him. 'Enjoy it for a while and then we'll sell it. You've always wanted it, and here it is. Let's buy it!'

I was probably being a bit gung-ho, but I knew he deserved this, even if it was only for a year or two.

Dad had been a salesman since he was a kid, so every transaction had to be a deal. The manager told us the price, Dad negotiated a bit, then we shook hands.

I reckon he ripped through an entire oxygen tank on the way home; his excited breathing tempo was *so* fast. We didn't talk much, as he had to concentrate, but we looked at each other and smiled a lot, and I mean *a lot*, on that drive home. Perhaps it's only when words are hard to come by that we realise the power a simple nod and a smile can generate.

The whole family had several working bees up there. We cleared everything out, ripped up the mouldy carpets and cleaned the place from top to bottom. We bought a new fridge and TV, a comfy couch and, of course, some outdoor furniture so Dad could just sit and relax on the balcony all day, staring out across the river.

It was set up exactly the way he wanted it; it was his man cave, his shed, his castle. Mum understood the whole 'escape' concept – Dad needed a place to relax, breathe and just sit quietly, and Mum was very supportive of him going there on his own to do just that.

There were some lovely neighbours there. Every time Dad pulled up in the car, someone would come over and help him in with the groceries. Then he'd sit on his balcony and people would walk past with a coffee or beer in hand and stop for a chat. He was great company as long as his breathing was in order, and he could still tell great yarns.

To talk to people at home in Bondi, he'd have to get up, get dressed and somehow get down to the beach; now he could just get out of bed and take five steps to put the kettle on, and five more to sit on the balcony, where the constant procession of passers-by all had time for a chat.

So this cabin was perfect for him. He felt relaxed, and the fresh air and the beautiful river made him happy. He still loved his fishing, and he could walk slowly across to the river's edge; he hardly needed his oxygen tank when he was in a relaxed state moving at his own pace. He'd sit there in his picnic chair and cast the rod out. But if, heaven forbid, he actually caught a fish, he'd have to yell out to someone to run down and reel it in for him, which of course someone always did.

He loved it there, but he was dying. It was sweet, but it was sour. Predictably, getting there and staying there became challenging after a few years, and we had to call an ambulance for him a few times. Finally, as a family, we deemed it a bit too dangerous for him to be in a cabin on his own so far from help.

He reluctantly agreed, he knew. But I'm so glad he bought it, I'm so glad he got the time there.

Anyone who ever met him will remember how funny he was. Towards the end, his doctors and nurses would always comment on how hard he'd work to make them laugh. He still had yarns to tell.

A few years earlier, I'd urged him to start writing these funny stories down, and as I read them I kept thinking, 'These are *really* good, so personable, warm and funny.'

At the time he was receiving a thin magazine called *Lungnet News*, which featured all the latest medical news and views and updates for people suffering from lung conditions. It was a really valuable lifeline for its subscribers, reminding them all they weren't alone with this.

We convinced him to reach out to *Lungnet News* and see if they would be interested in a fun column from someone struggling with a lung condition. He wrote them a little test story, called 'Have a Laugh, with David Emdur'. They loved it, and next thing we knew, Dad was a columnist. The title soon changed to 'The Lighter Side, with David Emdur', and that was perfect, it was *so* him. He would always look for the lighter side of life.

After that he was always searching for funny stories for the magazine. He would write about his grandkids, he would write about trying to do wheelies on his mobility scooter, and he would write about how in hospital he'd begged the doctor to put Viagra in his drip.

My favourite column was about one time when he rode on his mobility scooter, with our daughter, Tia, his trusty co-pilot, by his side, towing our son, Jye, on his skateboard by a piece of rope along a very busy Bondi Beach promenade. Tia was in charge of the scooter's horn as they zigged and zagged along the promenade, all the tourists were taking photos, and it was a blast until they got stopped for dangerous behaviour by the lifeguards.

Dad went to a seminar organised by the magazine once, and was greeted like a bit of a rockstar, with many readers coming up to him and thanking him for brightening up their darkest days. He was showing them the lighter side of living with lung disease, and they loved him for it.

Dad passed away in 2004. When we were clearing out his office, I found a folder full of all his columns.

I sat down and read them all, backing up over certain words and phrases to enjoy them again and again because they were just '*so* Dad'. I could hear his voice as I read them. Through my tears, I read and read until they made me smile, which of course is exactly what they were designed to do.

Here's Dad's very first column for *Lungnet News*, dated December 1997:

HAVE A LAUGH, WITH DAVID EMDUR

It did occur to me the other day, as I tried to release my oxygen hose from under the lounge chair (it always gets caught there, have you noticed that?) that there are some very funny sides to all of this.

Not wanting to make light of any of our conditions, but whatever our respective conditions or diseases can take away from us, they certainly should not take away our sense of humour.

I've found a good laugh is still the best cure. A little bit of sunshine in what can otherwise be some pretty gloomy days.

I thought I might jot down some of these lighter moments in the hope you can raise a smile too. I'd like to share some of these experiences with you and get them off my chest. God knows the less I have on my chest, the better.

It was a quiet Sunday morning in our household – that means the calm before the grandkids storm. I have a few options.

Fake a few symptoms, close the door and stay in bed.

Get into my comfy chair and get settled before they arrive.

Get up, be as strong as I can, and for the next hour or so, show the family I'm feeling fine.

I wobble between options 2 and 3. Option 1 was OK for a while until the grandkids decided it was more fun jumping up and down on Grandpa in his bed than it was eating croissants with the adults out the back.

I'm lucky enough to have an oxygen concentrator at home. The oxygen hose reaches from one end of the house to the other. At first, I used to worry about visitors tripping over it. Now I enjoy seeing the shocked expressions on their faces when I point out they are standing on my lifeline. A two-metre-high jump is not unusual.

My grandkids are smart (do all grandparents say that about their grandkids?). They have found 101 uses for the oxygen hose. It can go from being a skipping rope to a blow dryer for the budgie in a matter of minutes.

They take it, invent a new game with it, and eventually give it back, albeit covered in sand, soil, toothpaste or tomato sauce. They even reckon it makes a great long-distance lemonade straw.

There was one day it didn't come back, the house was relatively quiet so I knew the grandkids were up to no good. After about an hour I thought I should go in search of my oxygen supply.

I tracked them the same way they track me wherever I am in the house. I picked up the hose and followed the track towards the giggling gaggle of kids.

Through the dining room, past the kitchen into the lounge room, down the hallway, the giggling was getting louder, past the bedroom, past the front door, BINGO … The hose went under the bathroom door. I had the oxygen bandits cornered. But what could you do with an oxygen hose in the bathroom?

I opened the door quietly and poked my head around the corner. Three granddaughters and a grandson in the bath together, giggling wildly at their new invention.

A spa bath, with one air jet, my oxygen hose.

So there you have it friends, the latest in family entertainment. All you need for a home spa.

A few cheeky and ingenious grandkids, a grandfather with a lung problem then just add water.

Smoking killed my dad, and every year, on the anniversary of his death, I post a photo of him on social media with a message trying to encourage people to stop smoking. I hope and pray that each year I can stop at least one person from smoking, and that that person gets to enjoy the love and adoration of their kids, parents, grandkids and friends for many years to come, because that's definitely what Dad would've wanted to do.

Mark Beretta is a fantastic guy with a massive heart, and he unknowingly offered me *another* way to make sure my dad's legacy has an impact.

Beretts is the sports guru on *Sunrise*, and he's always doing amazing charity work. In 2010 he helped found the Tour de Cure bike ride, which he still rides in each year. TDC has raised over $80 million, funded 580 vital research projects and produced over fifty significant breakthroughs in cancer research. He has received an Order of Australia Medal for his charity work, he's a major in the Army Reserve, in 2019 he was named Father of the Year by the Shepherd Centre (which supports children with hearing loss), and he's also an ambassador for the Raise Mentoring Program, aimed at young people across Australia.

Beretts is the guy who makes me feel very under-accomplished and insignificant – although he's never hosted *Family Double Dare*, so I still have that over him, I guess. I've said to him on many occasions that he's the human being I always meant to be, but never got around to it. He's turned his name and fame into a superpower, and I really admire him for it.

In 2020, Beretts put me in touch with the Raise Foundation, and they asked if I would write a letter to my mentor for their video campaign.

Dad had always been my mentor. He had died sixteen years earlier, but he was in my thoughts every day. Situations came up in my life all the time – business, family, on TV, off TV – where I'd find myself asking: 'What would *Dad* want me to do now?'

So I sat down to write a letter to Dad for the Raise campaign. It was very difficult to write, and it was *extremely* difficult to read on camera. I practised at home and cried each time, but afterwards I was very glad to have had the opportunity to be a part of this important campaign.

Here's my letter …

Dear Dave – Davo,
It turns out that what they say is true – that you don't know what you've got till it's gone.

You taught me so much – but it's the simple things you taught me that are so very powerful and still make all the difference in my world today. In fact, I reckon they're even more relevant today.

Be nice to everyone and look for the lighter side in every bad situation – that's what you always taught me.

When anyone around you is sad, you work hard to make them smile. And you promised me there is always light at the end of any dark tunnel. You promised me that.

I've tested the theory a few times – turns out you were right.

You were my dad and my best mate.

But it wasn't until after you left us that I realised you were also my mentor. You made me a better son, a better husband and father, and a better human being.

How can I ever repay you for that?

Well, actually, I know what you'd say.

You'd say be nice to everyone and help people see the lighter side in every bad situation.

Dad, I use your lessons every single day.

I'm sorry I never got to tell you this stuff – but I have saved this letter in the cloud.

Hopefully, it's next to your cloud so you get to see it one day.

With love,

from Larry

To see the video, just scan the QR code below, and if you can support the Raise Foundation in any way, it is a fantastic cause.

And if you feel like you want to try and give up smoking, I know it's really difficult, but there are plenty of great resources out there for you: icanquit.com.au is a good start.

Please try for you, for your family, and for all the people who love you.

This has been a *tough* chapter to write; it's taken me longer than any other in the book, and I've had to wrestle with some beautiful memories and some very traumatic moments. But I'm *so* glad I wrote it; I'm glad my family has this story in black and white to keep and hand down, and I'm glad I got to share it with you.

Funny thing: when I first sat down to write it, I knew I had to find something funny to finish with. Even before I wrote the first words, I knew I had to do what Dad would've done and find the lighter side to all of this.

It's sad that I never got to tell him this story, because he would've ABSOLUTELY LOVED IT.

We were all sitting in the hospital waiting room. Dad was in his final days; it was no longer 'if' or 'when', it was just 'anytime now'. We were literally camping out at the hospital.

We were all emotionally and physically smashed, slumped across the floor and various lounges at the back of the waiting room. There was an elderly gentleman in a big chair at the front, and his wife was standing next to the coffee urn, near the TV. It happened to be tuned to Channel Nine.

The Price Is Right came on. Neither of them had seen me up the back of the room.

As the intro to the show played, the gentleman yelled out to his wife: '*Oh, for God's sake, turn this shit off!!!*'

Dad would've loved that one.

Sniffing Molly

1998

It was always funny watching the overseas stars presenting at the Logies. They were usually presenting the Gold Logie, which meant it was the last award, which meant they had plenty of time to get pissed while trying to work out why they'd agreed to fly to the other side of the world to be part of this thing.

I think they were always told it was Australia's Oscars, but looking at them about an hour in to the ceremony you could always see they had concluded beyond all reasonable doubt it was nothing like the Oscars, as in POSITIVELY, ABSOLUTELY NOTHING like the Oscars.

The first few Logies I went to, I did the appropriate, expected and acceptable thing of getting drunk with everybody else. I don't do that anymore, but I can definitely say the Logies make more sense and are funnier when you're drunk.

They can go on for a while, then when they get to 'a while', they tend to go for a while longer. Here's what I've learnt, it's my Logies hack: if during a commercial break you need to race out to the toilet — and who doesn't? — then they lock you out in the foyer till the next commercial break. And what do you know? All the cool folks are hanging out in the foyer, more than happily locked out.

It was 1998, and *Friends* was one of the biggest shows on the planet, so having Matt LeBlanc (aka Joey) as the Logies guest of honour was HUGE. *Everyone* was going crazy, *everyone* was trying to get close to him, brush past him and even trying to sniff his aftershave. YES, Molly Meldrum, I'm looking at YOU!

I never knew how much of a great actor he was till he got up onstage and said, 'It's a pleasure to be here.' I'm like, 'Whoooaaaaa, dude, you're an *incredible* actor!'

As always, for the 99.9693 per cent of people in the room who *weren't* up for a Logie, it was all about the afterparty. They were legendary events: a great bunch of friends getting pissed and celebrating being part of the best industry there is.

Daryl Somers was hosting that Logies. I knew his style very well, so I could tell when he was about to launch into his closing spiel, and I knew *that* was the time to bolt out of the room and race to the afterparty. Scoring a standing position at the bar was even more prestigious than winning a Logie.

About half an hour after I'd arrived at the afterparty, in walks Matt LeBlanc, surrounded by an entourage of doting entouragey people doing what doting entouragey people do: surround and dote.

They casually went up to the bar and cleared a standing position for Matt.

Hang on, wait a second, back it up, boyfriend! One does not simply *stroll* into the Logies afterparty and take up a standing position at the bar!! *I* raced out before the end of the ceremony, and I've held this wee in for four hours so I could secure this spot!!!

Matt himself looked a bit bored, though I didn't understand why – I mean, these were our Oscars! Though admittedly, yes, the ceremony had gone on for ninety minutes longer than scheduled, and yes, the room smelt more of Lynx Africa than I'm sure the Oscars afterparty would.

For some unknown reason I thought *I* was the answer to all his problems, the happiness to his sadness, the sunshine in his storm, the wind beneath his wings, the icing on his doughnut (actually I take that last one back).

I had convinced the barman to give me a whole bottle of Sambuca and two shot glasses. He initially said no, then I said the Sambuca was for Matt LeBlanc so he gave it to me.

I was drunk enough to have the confidence to push my way through Matt's entourage, lean into him and say: 'Hey, man, you look really bored, wanna Sambuca?'

He lit up immediately, and asked: 'Are you Italian?'

I said, 'No, does it matter?'

He said, 'Hell, no, let's go!' He pushed through his entourage with the excitement of a young man who'd just flown to the other side of the world for the Australian Oscars, and having been bitterly disappointed, desperately needed a shot.

I poured two shots and we sculled them like two naughty schoolboys at the back of the dancehall, then the next shot, then the next, then the next. From there on in, my memories of exactly what happened are predictably a little blurry.

But more and more people were joining in the Sambuca Circle, and it was enormous fun. I remember at one point I felt like I had to throw up, and I definitely had to wee, but there was no way I was leaving this magical Sambuca Circle. There was no way I was handing my new best friend over to dazzling Daryl Somers or swooning soapie stars or terrific Tracy Grimshaw or sniffing Molly, who would've eaten him alive with some fava beans and a nice Chianti.

At some point I told Matt that Sylvie – who had gone back to our room with a headache and missed this entire festival of LeBlanc – was a huge fan of his, and she wouldn't mind me coming home very very very late, smelling of Sambuca, because she loved him so much.

The night ended somehow – either Melbourne Crown Casino ran out of Sambuca, I passed out, or a romantic fusion of both – but when I woke up the next morning (confession: it may have been afternoon), there was a glossy eight-by-ten-inch photo of Matt LeBlanc under the door with a handwritten message:

Dear Sylvie, your husband got me very drunk, love Matt xx

I thought it was very sweet he remembered, because *I* kind of didn't remember anything ...

'Emdur, You're a TV Slut!'

1998

'There are a couple of young guys doing a TV show out of a garage, and they want to come in to the set of *The Price Is Right* and film a little stunt – what do you think?' the *Price Is Right* publicist asked.

We'd get these requests all the time. By 1998, *Price* had well and truly burnt itself into popular culture with its kooky catchphrases and crazy contestants. We had regular set visits by people who wanted to include us in their quirky little projects.

One time, we shot a quick skit during a commercial break. They told me it was for a low-budget film, and if I agreed to be involved, I'd get paid something crazy like $126. Clearly the price was wrong, but I was up for anything fun. I was told all I had to do was play the host of *The Price Is Right*: a role that I, for your information, executed brilliantly.

Well, that little low-budget film was called *The Castle* and it's still considered one of the greatest Australian movies ever made, and my appearance in it is still considered one of the greatest and most accurate portrayals of Larry Emdur hosting *The Price Is Right* ever. Me playing me doing my job could only be described as thesbiatically poignant. (*Hi Larry, this is Zoe from Spellcheck. Unfortunately due to your continued blatant abuse of the system, we're cancelling your subscription.*)

I was absolutely and positively unforgettable. But I'm just reminding you in case you've forgotten about it.

So, yes, I was up for doing fun stuff on the side. The young guys from the garage got held up and never made it into the show to film their skit. I said to the publicist, 'Why don't I just go into their garage and be interviewed on their show?'

She was quite surprised by that, but I had quite a bit of downtime during *Price* recording weeks in Melbourne and I often didn't do much. I'd sit in my hotel room, maybe go to the hotel gym and pool, come back to the room, eat the Pringles from the minibar ... (Yes, I was making good money. That's always a measure of how wealthy you are: whether you eat the minibar Pringles for $8 or go across the road to the 7-Eleven and get them for $3. Yeah, life was gooooood.)

My limo pulled up to the garage and I tried to get out in slow motion like Jason Donovan. Not sure I nailed it.

'Hi, I'm Rove!' said the incredibly enthusiastic, smiley young guy who shook my hand at the garage door. If the Energizer Bunny had a long-lost human brother, this was him. 'Oh, my gosh, thanks for coming in, we can't *believe* you've come in! This is my friend Pete Helliar.'

The Loft Live was a fabulously cheap-and-nasty tonight show being produced in a garage at RMIT Uni in Melbourne and broadcast on community TV Channel 31. It was a tonight show with 'L' plates on it. Rove once told me his budget for the show was $50 a week, but I could tell the show actually ran on adrenalin, enthusiasm, naïvety, a truly wonderful sense of the absurd and a passionate love of television.

Rove and Pete followed no network rules, there were no grumpy TV execs saying you can't do this or you can't do that, no sponsors to appease. It was just crazy, freestyling, highly contagious fun. It honestly looked like a bunch of mates had got together in a garage, picked up an old desk and a scrappy lounge from a council collection pile, convinced some other mates to operate the cameras and were doing a cross between *The Tonight Show* and *Wayne's World*.

IT WAS *BLOODY FANTASTIC*!!!

I loved the concept, dished up with buckets of chutzpah and bravado.

We did the interview, and it was great fun. These guys were ON FIRE! It was clear to see that Rove as a host had The 'IT' Factor.

The very next day I made an appointment with the legendary boss of GTV9 Melbourne, Ian Johnson, specifically to ask him if he'd ever heard about this young guy Rove. He said he hadn't. I said you've got to hunt him down, he's a young Daryl Somers or Steve Vizard, very funny, very fast, good-looking, great hair. He's *really* good.

Now, I don't know if that particular conversation resonated with Ian or not. I'd like to claim that *I* discovered Rove in that garage, but if that were true, he would probably feel compelled to gift me between twenty and thirty per cent of every dollar he's ever made. And he's never offered to do that. #waiting

A few months later, it was announced that young Melbourne comedian Rove McManus was launching his own late-night variety show on Channel Nine, with the incredibly inventive and creative title *Rove*. I often wonder if the same creative geniuses who named Rove's show *Rove* were also paid millions of dollars to come up with that extremely clever name for Seven's new morning show, which they called *The Morning Show*.

In a strange twist, when I recently called Rove to ask about his memories of that *Loft* appearance, to my delight, he said he still had the email I wrote to him just after his show debuted.

Here it is ...

McManus, Rove

From:	emdurtain [emdurtain@█████]
Sent:	Tuesday, 28 September 1999 10:28
To:	rovemcmanus@█████
Subject:	bastard

Hey dickhead,

When I went to work the day after my Chan 31 interview and told them all how funny and clever and fucking wonderful you were, I didn't mean for them to give you your own show while I search through rubbish bins to try to feed my family, starving coz' their dad can't get a TV gig.

I've been away for the last month otherwise I would've written earlier to wish you all the luck in the world. Peter Ritchie says it's going great.

Your now part of the greatest TV family in the country, having been through most of them now (literally) I'm qualified to tell you that GTV is by far the greatest place to work.

Can't wait to see the show. Good luck with it all, I wish you all the success you deserve.

And remember in 20 years time when you're sitting in the jason lazy-boy recliner rocker in your cigar room in the western wing of your 23 room Toorak Mansion, running your fingers through your transplanted hair, while you watch a video tape of you and Jamie Packer catching a Marlin off your 68foot cruiser that he bought you after your 16th Gold Logie. Remember me.

Kill 'em

Larry E

Fast-forward a million years, and I refuse to acknowledge that Rove got me my current job on *The Morning Show*, otherwise he'd be entitled to twenty to thirty per cent of every dollar I've ever earned from that show, and that's never gonna happen.

It was 2006, and I was hosting *Wheel of Fortune* on Channel Seven. Rove and I were on rival networks – about a year after debuting on Channel Nine, the show had moved to Channel Ten – but we had become great mates. We were at one of our regular long lunches, and had consumed enough wine to consider how funny it would be if I came in and appeared on *Rove Live* (as it was now called). I was on Seven, Rove was on Ten, and while that cross-network promiscuity is common in the US, it's an absolute no-no here.

But we thought it was a fun enough idea to pursue, so I proposed it to the Seven publicity team. Why *shouldn't* I break the Golden Rule and appear on another network if it was going to be great publicity for *Wheel*?

Surprisingly, they agreed!

So I went on *Rove Live* and we had great fun.

Shortly thereafter, *Wheel* was axed. Naturally, I blamed it entirely on Rove. And so began our long-running 'feud'. We've sumo-wrestled, we've taunted each other on social media, we've had a boxing match which only ended when I punched him in the dick. But I still consider him one of my great mates.

So I was floating between jobs, but it was no big deal. I had property investments and a lot of corporate work. Remember, I am the most axed man on television, so by this point I was quite good at being 'between jobs'. It was the way it worked in the jungle.

Early one morning, Rove took it upon himself to appear in the big window behind Kochie and Mel Doyle on Channel Seven's *Sunrise* with a huge handwritten sign that said:

SAVE LARRY

This earth-shattering campaign had people holding up signs in the strangest places and even graffitiing SAVE LARRY on freeway walls and bus stops. Now, I was already doing bits and pieces with *Sunrise* so I was kind of on their radar, but about the same time I was called in to host a pilot for a cleverly named concept called *The Morning Show*.

Bear in mind that by this stage, I'd hosted or been the fill-in host on over twenty different shows, on all three free-to-air commercial TV networks. The big fill-in gigs had been on *Hey Hey It's Saturday*, *Tonight Live with Steve Vizard*, *IMT* (the late-1990s revival of Graham Kennedy's legendary *In Melbourne Tonight*), and others you probably don't remember – *I* didn't until I googled myself! Shows like *Uncle Tobys Super Series* (Ten), *Chance and Coincidence* (Seven), *StarStruck* (Nine), *Surprise Wedding* (Seven) and *The Very Best of the World's Best Ads* (Nine).

As one TV exec once put it: 'Emdur, you're a TV slut!'

I'd done countless auditions and even more pilots. So *The Morning Show* was just the latest in a long line. (I probably had another pilot audition the following week at Channel Nine for a show where contestants get married after only just meeting each other, but that'd never work …)

To my surprise, *The Morning Show* was actually given the go-ahead, with me and Lisa Wilkinson as hosts. But Lisa decided it wasn't for her so I started auditioning with other potential co-hosts. The directive was: 'Put a stranger on the couch next to Larry and tell them to act like best friends.'

Within minutes of starting her audition, Kylie Gillies was chatting away to me and we were laughing and carrying on like old mates. We just clicked, and we've never *un*-clicked. It would be impossible to fake this kind of connection for two and a half hours of live TV, five days a week for fifteen years. We make each other laugh, we 'get' each other.

I'll never forget the call I made to Kylie to congratulate her. I was on a motorbike ride through the New South Wales Snowy Mountains.

The executive producer of the pilot, Adam Boland, had called me earlier and we'd agreed that Kylie should get the job. He said, 'Give me an hour to sort it all out and talk to her, then *you* can call her.'

An hour later, I stopped at a truck stop to do two things: wee, and call Kylie to congratulate her. I can't remember which one I did first, but they were both *very* satisfying.

It's a powerful relationship. We rarely agree on stuff: *she* likes the Royals, *I* like The Rock; *she* likes reruns of *Keeping Up with the Kardashians*, *I* like reruns of *Baywatch*; she *liked* being on *Dancing with the Stars*, I *hated* being on *Dancing with the Stars*.

But all those differences are exactly what makes this relationship so great. We hear a lot of people say they see their own relationships mirrored in ours – *she* likes this, *he* likes that, *she* pays attention, *he* doesn't. It's yin and yang, it's how most relationships are. We may disagree, but we know where each other is going, when each other is going to start or stop and, most of the time, what each other is thinking.

'EMDUR, YOU'RE A TV SLUT!'

It's often described as a TV marriage, and that's fair: some days I spend more time with Kylie on the couch than I do with Sylvie at home, and Kylie and I have been through a lot together.

Initially we were told *The Morning Show* would probably only be a three- to six-month trial. It was coming into a crowded market, with both Channel Nine and Channel Ten having established similar shows in that timeslot, so we just didn't know if it would work.

Well, from day one it won the ratings, and since then we've been the top morning show every year for fifteen years. That's an incredible thing to be able to say in this industry. The little baby TV show we gave birth to is now a feisty, pimply teenager with three mothers – Kylie, Director of Morning Television Sarah Stinson and Executive Producer Chloe Flynn – and one goofy dad, me. We're very proud of our fun little slice of television, and of course of our fabulous team.

Over the years, when Kylie and I do something particularly ludicrous, funny, silly or off-the-wall, Sarah, our rockstar boss, will chime in over the comms with: 'I love you two!' So we aim for that.

People always ask me what are my favourite or most memorable *Morning Show* moments. There've been *thousands* of fabulous moments over fifteen years on live television – I've got them all written down ready for my next book! So here are just a few ...

The late great Joan Rivers was sitting on the *Morning Show* couch, and just as the interview started, she said, on live TV: 'Can I say "vagina" on this show? Is this the sort of show where I can say "vagina"?'

I wouldn't have thought so ... Hang on, let me phone a friend. 'Hi Lindy Rama-Ellis, it's Larry – can you say "vagina" on *The Morning Show*?'

We were interviewing Meat Loaf on the show and Kylie started calling him 'Meat'. Yes, she felt *that* familiar with him! Both Meat and I lost it.

We were beginning our interview with Michael Bolton and he appeared to fall asleep as we were introducing him. This story went around the world; he denied it but it was bloody funny.

The Morning Show has also allowed me to continue doing the sort of TV I used to love as a young reporter: getting out into the street and interviewing ordinary people about stupid stuff. It's always funniest when they're drunk; that's when the best TV happens.

Once, in the back car park at the Melbourne Cup, a young lady who'd had a wonderful day on cheap champagne and no food ran over to us and yelled: 'I don't have any underpants on!'

'Why not?' I asked her.

She pointed to a drunk guy lying on the grass and said: 'He ate them!'

Another time, exploring the topic Country Versus City Love at the legendary CMC Rocks country music festival in Ipswich, Queensland, a happy young lady with a can of VB in a stubby holder approached us. I put a microphone in front of her and I asked: 'What would you do if your boyfriend cheated on you?'

Without skipping a beat, she answered: 'I'd suck his best mate's cock! *That'd* teach him!'

You see, *this* is why I love being in television. OK, I'll never win a Walkley journalism award with interviews like that, but geeeez, I'm making memorable TV.

'Two Hundred Cheeseburgers, Please, and YES, I'd Like Fries with That!'

2001

I've never really thought of myself as famous, and I've never wanted to be. Even the concept kind of bemuses me. But if the dictionary definition is just 'Known about by many people', then I guess I've become that.

Not famous enough to go on *MAFS* or *Love Island*, then start up an OnlyFans site, then get paid to sell stuff I don't use; I'll never be *that* famous.

Fame doesn't make you a good person, or better than anyone else. It's just a thing, like a pimple or a receding hairline.

But at least, unlike a pimple or receding hairline, you can use this fame thing for good.

The clichés are all true – better seats at restaurants, free drinks at pubs, cushy deals with hotels and car manufacturers – but some people *also* choose to use their famosity for the betterment of humankind.

For a while there, I was leaning more towards the hotel upgrades and better restaurant seats than the betterment of humankind. But then something happened to change all that.

We were living on the Gold Coast, Jye was about seven, Tia was two, I was filling in on a morning radio show for a few weeks, and we were having a ball. Living in a beautiful hotel room, eating out wherever we wanted.

I'd go off to the radio show at about 5.30 am and be home by 9.15 am, then we'd just do that Gold Coast thing of pool, beach, surf, theme park, lunch, beach, pool, dinner out and repeat.

I'd finished my first run on *The Price Is Right* in 1998 and was now working on a big new show called *Cash Bonanza* on Channel Nine. It was a game show linked in with scratch lottery tickets and it was being filmed on the Wild Wild West set at the Movie World theme park on the Gold Coast. All you really need to know about *Cash Bonanza* is that I had to wear a vest and a puffy shirt, sort of like a cowboy, a cowboy from the American Wild Wild West who did his cowboy clothes shopping at the Pacific Fair shopping centre on the Gold Coast.

The radio station had made quite a big deal of my coming to town to do the show, so we were very well received at the fancy restaurants and all the attractions.

The four of us were driving through Broadbeach one day when I saw a small circus set up in a park – nothing too flash, just one of those classic travelling circuses that go up and down the coast and pop up in a park or sports field for a few weeks then move on.

It was called CIRCUS SUNRISE SPECTACULAR, and it was the total opposite of the places the radio station had lined up for us to visit with our VIP passes and chaperones. But we were just cruising with nothing in particular to do, so we pulled over, made our way to the ticket office with the singlet-, shorts- and thong-wearing masses, grabbed some popcorn then headed into the big top.

We were sitting on foldout chairs right next to the aisle, and in the aisle itself were two young children with intellectual disability in wheelchairs who had been brought in for a big day at the circus.

It was *such* a fantastic show: old-school, high-energy, beautifully corny and heaps of fun. But I can't give you too much detail, because I just couldn't take my eyes off these two kids in the wheelchairs. They would squeal with excitement and delight at each trick or event, laugh loudly at every funny thing, and be the first to clap when a new act came out and the last to stop clapping when an act had finished.

Their reactions were deeply moving, their enthusiasm mesmerising, powerful and contagious.

'Are you crying?' Sylvie asked, looking at me.

'Noooooo, I think I have some dust in my eye,' I replied.

We'd been going to all the big events and big shows, and maybe, just maybe, I'd lost sight of the fact that it's sometimes the simple things that can bring people, especially kids, the most joy. As simple and quaint as I thought this circus was, to them it was massive.

At the end of the show, as the performers did their final dance around the dusty centre ring, everyone was hooting and hollering – except one of these two kids was crying. She'd had the most exciting two hours ever, and now the show was over.

The ringmaster had paid extra-special attention to these two kids during the show. He'd seen this young girl crying, and bounced over to give both of them a special tip of his hat and a bow.

All afternoon I couldn't stop thinking about how much fun those kids had had. So at about three o'clock, I drove back to the circus. It was closed but I could see people still working around the tents and grounds, so I climbed under the barrier and asked someone if I could see the boss.

David was a very nice guy. His wife and kids were all in the show too. I told him I'd been at the show that day with my family and we'd all had the best time. Then I described the joy on those two kids' faces, how they'd been bursting out of their skins the whole time, even more than the other kids. I congratulated him on having made their day so special.

I'd already started to imagine three hundred kids with disability and from disadvantaged backgrounds in that huge tent – kids who usually don't get to go to the circus, kids who usually don't get to scream and yell, laugh and let go like that … I'd wondered if I could make that happen.

So, after a bit of a chat, I asked David how much it would cost to rent the whole circus for a day – everything, the whole shebang. I explained I'd like to treat a bunch of kids with disability and from disadvantaged backgrounds to a day under the big top.

He said he'd have to think about it, they hadn't done anything like that before. The money was one thing; the wheelchair access and safety considerations were another. Remember, all the kids in wheelchairs would have to sit in the aisles, so that would greatly limit the numbers we could have.

Later that evening, David called me. He'd come up with a figure of $3000 for an exclusive show, the whole deal, and capacity ended up being around two hundred, because of the limit on how many wheelchairs he could put in the aisles for safety reasons. But he told me they could remove the front row of chairs around the ring to fit more wheelchairs in.

OK, so the money was fine – in fact, much less than I'd anticipated! – but now came the challenge of finding and inviting the kids and actually getting them there.

The next morning at the radio station, I told the boss I'd just hired the Sunrise Circus at Broadbeach. I told him the story of the two kids in the wheelchairs, and how I wanted to fill the tent with kids who maybe didn't get to go to those sorts of things very often, and would enjoy it as much as those two kids had.

He loved the idea and jumped all over it! He suggested we link up with local community groups that would have connections with all the special schools in the area.

People in radio are always so well connected. I had a great idea, but no way of pulling it off, and now, with a few phone calls, it was all coming together brilliantly and at lightning speed.

Everyone thought it was a beautiful plan, and I've found over the years that projects fuelled by heart and good intentions tend to move faster.

The community group organisers called around and got us to capacity quickly by contacting schools and individual carers around town. The number of kids who could attend dropped again because – silly me – I hadn't thought it all through: many of the children needed carers with them. But this was now all being carefully managed by people who knew exactly what to do and how to bring such an event together.

The next suggestion from the radio guys was to call the boss at the local McDonald's.

It was my favourite 'I'm famous' call ever. And this is one of the occasions in my life when I'll admit I used my fame for good.

One of the radio team had called the local Macca's owner and told him I'd be ringing him soon.

Then I called. 'Hi, it's Larry Emdur here, I'd like to order two hundred cheeseburgers, please, and YES, I'd like fries with that!'

In no time, it was game day. All the kids started to arrive in vans and buses, and there was *such* a great vibe. Imagine around one hundred and fifty happy faces, covered in huge smiles!

A big van arrived with two hundred super-sized Happy Meals, and Sylvie and the kids and I ran around, along with circus clowns and carers, handing them all out. Even two-year-old Tia managed to deliver a few boxes.

And then we were treated to two amazing hours of circus fun. There was nonstop laughter, applause, screaming, cheering ... the excitement felt like it would blow the roof off the big top! That sea of little happy faces is burnt into my memory forever.

David and the team were brilliant. I'm sure it was their normal degree of brilliance, but this performance seemed extra special.

A million laughs and a million memories.

As the ringmaster took his final bow, he said, 'And thank you to Larry and Sylvie!'

But none of the kids knew who we were, or even cared, and that was just perfect.

I'm not famous enough to know how it feels when you finish a reality show and start your OnlyFans page, but to me, this day felt pretty damn good.

Larry Time

1994

'Hi Larry, nice to see you!'

Said the friendly lady as she came up to me. I was just about to walk through Bourke Street Mall in Melbourne, and she matched my steps and kept walking with me.

I'm terrible at placing names and faces. It's one of the main reasons why I wanted to write this book: so in a few years' time, when I'm in the nursing home and someone asks me, 'What did you do?', I can just hand them a copy of this book.

Well, when I say 'hand them', that's after I've signed it, and when I say 'signed it', that's after I've swiped their credit card on the machine conveniently Blu Tacked to my Zimmer frame.

So I'm nice to everyone – that's what Dad always drilled into me – but sometimes there's that extra layer of forgetful fog: 'What if I actually *do* know this person? What if they're an old workmate of mine or Sylvie's, or a long-lost family member, and I can't immediately place them?'

That's why my hellos are always engaging and curious at the same time, and 99.67 per cent of the time done with an initial smile of somewhere between a sixty-eight per cent and an eighty-four per cent intensity rating. Once I've confirmed I know them, I will ramp that up to a smile intensity rating of between eighty-eight and ninety-two per cent.

I once read somewhere that at least 86.3 per cent of statistics are made up on the spot and that really stuck with me.

'How are you?' asked the friendly lady, as we continued through Bourke Street Mall.

'I'm really good, thanks, how are you?' I replied.

'Yeah, I'm really good too, thanks! Hey, how is Jye going? What a little cutie, Sylvie said he's not sleeping.'

Jye was still a little baby, and it was true, he *wasn't* sleeping. I couldn't place this woman but she seemed very familiar with my family, so we just kept walking and talking.

Wherever I'd go, either a guy or a girl would come up to me and say, 'Hi, I work with Sylvie.' I'd hear that on every plane, in every hotel foyer, every restaurant, every pub, every café. They were everywhere. Sylvie finished with Ansett over twenty years ago and people *still* come up to me and say this stuff.

So, this woman was fitting into that well-worn pattern.

'Oh, congrats on the house!' she said.

We'd just moved into our marital home on the cliffs at Dover Heights, just north of my beloved Bondi.

'Sylvie finally dragged you out of Bondi, huh? It must get so windy up on the cliffs there …'

OK, chill out, Laz, this has all the bones of a mid-flight conversation between two flight attendants.

So I'm now relaxed, as this woman is clearly a friend of Sylvie's. I've adopted my full charm mode and I'm now dazzling her with a ninety-one per cent intensity smile.

'Yeah, we're all settled now, and it's only up the road from Bondi, so it's all good.'

'Do you think you'll end up renovating?'

'Yeah, we're talking about it, but we'll just settle in first and see how we go.'

'Yeah, renovations can be tricky with young babies,' she observed, before adding: 'When will Sylvie head back to work?'

'Not sure, I know she misses all her friends.'

'Yes, it's that social aspect that she'll miss. But those hours are tough, those early flights – my gosh!'

'I know, I know …'

'Gee, it looks like you're having fun on the show!' I was into my second year on *The Price Is Right* at the time.

'Oh, yeah, it's *so* much fun! We're filming this afternoon, in fact.'

'Is Sylvie down with you?'

'No, no, not this time.'

'I guess it wouldn't be that nice for her if you're working and she's stuck in a hotel room with Jye not sleeping.' Then after a pause she continued: 'Anyway, the last thing she'd probably want to do as a flight attendant who lives in hotel rooms is jump on a plane and stay in *another* hotel room!'

'Yep, that's very true,' I said.

I kid you not, the conversation went on like this for about ten minutes. It was running out of steam, but of course I didn't want to be rude.

Then I spotted a big shopping centre and just said: 'Well, this is me, this is where I'm going.' To finish up the conversation I asked, 'What's your name? I'll tell Sylvie you said hi.'

'Oh, no no, she doesn't *know* me.'

WHHHHATTTTTTTT????? 'How did you know all that stuff??'

'I've just read everything about you over the years, all the magazine and newspaper articles, and I heard you being interviewed on the radio last week.'

OK, this was incredibly creepy – sweet, but creepy. It seriously made me consider *never, ever* leaving the house again.

But the *average* day of Being Me is a little more predictable. It goes something like this …

I get out of bed, and look disappointedly at my wrinkling, busted fifty-seven-year-old face in the bathroom mirror, a face that spent its first thirty years floating around Bondi Beach without sunblock. I run my hand over my prickly scalp where my hair used to be – hair formerly so beautiful it looked like George Michael's hair and Billy Ray Cyrus's hair had a drunken one-night stand and *my* hair was the glorious offspring!

I have a wee, which used to sound like Niagara Falls after days of heavy rain but now sounds more like a drippy attempt at Morse code. As I walk out of the bathroom I glance back at the mirror and catch a glimpse of the apple tattoo on my left butt cheek that used to look colourful and crisp and tight and bite-worthy but now, as my wife often reminds me, appears to be fading, rotting and sagging in sync with my arse skin.

I pull on my jeans – ripped jeans like all the cool kids are wearing. I whisper to myself: 'Am I too old for ripped jeans?' It's a rhetorical question; I know deep down that I'm approximately three times the acceptable ripped-jean-wearing age!

I leave the house and I feel good for the first few steps. I'm wearing the jeans of a twenty-two-year-old, I feel the arse apple tattoo firming up with each step, I stop at the coolest coffee shop I can find and loudly order a double macchiato, just because I like saying the word 'macchiato'. This day is going great ...

Then it happens, like clockwork. Sometimes it's a bunch of tradies, sometimes it's a nicely dressed office worker, sometimes it's a homeless person – but here it comes, as if someone's thrown a dart at me and it hits me in the eyeball every time ...

Someone yells it from across the street even louder than I yelled my macchiato order:

'*Come on down, ya wanker!!!!!*'

Sylvie and I were in Harvey Norman many years ago looking at a new TV. We were standing in front of a wall with fifty TVs on it, and a young sales guy walked up, put his hand on my shoulder and said: 'OK, Smarty Pants, now put them in order from least expensive to most expensive.'

Another fairly regular one at the supermarket checkout is the girl will finish scanning everything and say, 'OK, it's between $125 and $132 ...'

Now I could hate it, it could upset me, but I like it, it makes me smile. As a wise old TV exec once said to me, 'As a TV host, it's when people *don't* recognise you that you should be upset.'

I love it that people always think it's the first time I've heard it. It makes me laugh when I walk past a bunch of tradies and one yells out, 'Come on down, ya fucken wanker!!!!!', then checks back with all his mates and they crack up and high-five each other as if to say: 'Yeah, we got him good.'

Truth is, I've probably heard that many times already that day, and each time it's made me smile.

But without a doubt, my VERY BEST experience of being recognised happened many years ago when I was visiting my Nanny Minnie in her nursing home.

We were all sitting together in the café there when a young lady walked up and sheepishly asked if there was any chance I could come over and say hello to her elderly mother, who was sitting at a nearby table – which of course I immediately did.

The elderly lady was enjoying her cup of tea and her cheese blintz. She looked me over and said: 'It's *so* nice to see you in person, you're much shorter in real life! I'll have you know that my Larry Time is my favourite part of the day.'

'Your Larry Time? What's your Larry Time?' I asked, puzzled.

It was her time every afternoon when she watched *The Price Is Right*. One half-hour in the day when she could forget about her troubles and just get lost in the colour and noise of a crazy game show.

Her daughter explained she had a terminal illness and was on large amounts of medication, and in constant pain and discomfort. During *The Price Is Right* she'd laugh and play along and shout the answers at the TV, like a kid at Disneyland. She'd giggle and shriek, throwing her arms about, cheering loudly when a contestant got the answer right, and yelling things like 'You idiot!' when they got it wrong. All to the consternation of her neighbours in the adjoining rooms.

Her dinner was not permitted to be delivered until six o'clock when the show had finished, and nursing-home staff weren't allowed in her room between 5.30 and 6 pm under any circumstances, unless they wanted to enthusiastically play along.

If there were visitors in her room while the show was on, they were only allowed to talk to her during the commercial breaks. These were the strict rules for Larry Time.

Her daughter told me one time, when someone on the show was trying to lock in the BMX bike ahead of the VHS machine, her mum was yelling, 'NOOOOOOO, NOOOOOOO, YOU IDIOT!!!' so loudly at the TV that the nurse had to come in and ask her to keep the noise down.

The three of us had a really lovely conversation, and I stayed with them till my Nanny Minnie came over and tried to steal me back.

'Isn't he cute?!' my nan said as she pinched my cheeks.

I had to keep smiling, despite the fact I could feel the capillaries in my face bursting as her arthritic thumb and forefinger squeezed my face with the force of a great white clamping down on a baby seal.

In some ancient unwritten law, this appeared to give the other lady licence to go ahead and pinch my *other* cheek. 'Yes, he's *very* cute!' she said as she squeezed.

I was stuck in the middle of a nanna cheek-o-war!

Of course *my* nan won the battle, no one could out-pinch *her*. The other lady came a reluctant second, and my cheeks a sore and sorry last.

I wistfully said goodbye and left the table. This had been quite a bittersweet moment for me. It was *so* lovely to hear that, in her words, my show was the highlight of her day, but I already knew this series of the show was about to wrap up. It had recently been axed, but that hadn't been made public yet.

The Price Is Right was a big successful show, but it would always come and go in spurts; a few good years, then they would rest it, that was its history. I remember this particular axing, and I felt OK, because I knew there was nothing I could've done to save the show. I was doing my best as host, we were giving away huge prizes, the contestants and crew were awesome, but for one reason or another the audience started to shift, and that's television.

But I dared not tell the lady the show was about to end; she needed to know that I would be there every day at 5.30 pm for her Larry Time.

It's funny, a few weeks later, when they finally announced that *The Price Is Right* was being axed, she was the first person I thought of. Not my wife or kids, but her. I wondered if there were many others out there like her; was a show like *The Price Is Right* THAT important?

It's often said – and it's very true – that as TV hosts we're not saving lives or curing cancer. But we *can* make a real difference to a few people every now and then, and for forty-odd years that has made me feel great about what I do. Even going back to the beginning of my career, when I was The Dog Reporter, doing all the light and fluffy stories at the end of the news. I always loved doing those stories because I knew they would cheer people up, particularly at the end of a heavy news night.

I never forgot that lovely chat with that lovely lady, and in fact, in 2019, it inspired me to produce a short film called *Larry Time*. In essence, it tells the tale of two young girls who are very – perhaps *overly* – devoted to their dying grandmother, and reveals the lengths they go to, to keep her happy after her favourite game show is axed.

Yes, like this book, it's 'inspired' by true events – potentially a little short on fact, but fun nonetheless.

Larry Time won plenty of awards on the short-film-festival circuit. And I was very proud to be able to include my niece Anneliese and my goddaughter Mitzi in starring roles, both wonderfully talented actresses and very convincing evil angels on screen.

As for me, it was the first time I'd ever really tried to act. All I had to do was play a TV game-show wanker, so it wasn't really that much of a stretch. But I was so worried I wouldn't be able to do the 'just been kidnapped' acting bit that I thought I at least should *look* the part, so I set my alarm clock to go off every forty minutes on the two nights before filming, the idea being by the time I got to the set I would look horrendous.

When I arrived on set, my friend, co-writer and director Dan Krige said, 'You look shithouse,' and I was like, 'Perfect, let's go.'

It was SUCH a fun project! If you want to take a look you can just google 'Larry Time', or simply scan the QR code below and it'll take you straight to the link for the movie.

I've always *loved* hearing stories like the one the elderly lady told me that day. How lucky am I to have worked on something that could bring such joy to a ninety-year-old lady in a nursing home, making her forget her constant pain if only for thirty minutes a day?

I feel so deeply privileged by that thought it's difficult to put it into words.

Those Tattoos Over My Heart

2017

There is nothing in this universe that will ever mean more to me than my two children. Like any dad, I know I embarrass them sometimes – maybe *all* the time – but they are my everything.

There's no way in the world I would write a book without mentioning them. They are, after all, the main reason why I wanted to do this.

They know I'm a high-school dropout who's barely read a book in his life, but I wanted to show them that you *can* chase things that scare you and climb walls that seem impossibly high. Although, to be honest, they've already both worked that out themselves, and they're both beautiful human beings with the world at their feet.

Tia is a prolific reader – the big stuff, history, philosophy, you name it – and I'm not sure if she's ever watched an episode of *The Morning Show* or *The Chase Australia*. So this book is a sneaky plan to show her that all those words that have scared me my whole life, well, I've done my best to tackle them in the hope that I can even mildly impress her. And maybe now she'll be as proud of *me* as I am of *her*. Although I don't think that is possible.

My dad and my wonderful Grandpa Louis always used to say, 'Maybe one day there'll be four generations of Emdur men roaming this planet at the same time' … well, when Jye was born this became a reality. I knew at that moment I had a new best friend for life.

In the hospital, my teary Grandpa Louis held Jye tight and looked over at me and said, 'He's perfect, I'm so proud of you.'

I said, 'Grandpa, I didn't actually do much, in fact my part in this whole thing took only about five minutes.'

Quick as a flash, Dad chimed in with: 'Five minutes? Now you're just showing off!' (SO Dad!!!)

Jye and I have always been incredibly close. I've wanted us to have the same kind of relationship *I* had with *my* dad, including sneaky trips away for pies when Mum wasn't looking.

A few years after Jye was born, I bought a small boat of my own, because I wanted us to have those same times my dad and I used to have on *Siesta*. Unlike on *Siesta*, the engine of *this* boat worked and the toilet flushed, and it had marine carpet, not shagpile, so it was quite a different experience in some ways. But it helped forge a bond between Jye and me that was just as strong as the one between me and my dad. Once Tia was a little bit older, she also loved spending time with me on the boat, fishing, laughing and talking, just like Dad and I used to do. These were precious hours indeed.

Jye became a rower at school, and one day we were watching some boys from his school compete. Their team was coming third, and their coach was riding along the shore on a pushbike.

He started yelling: 'Come on, boys!!! If not now, when??!!

IF NOT NOW, WHEN???!!!' They lifted their performance and they won the race.

This stuck with Jye and me, and we spoke about it all the way home in the car.

We agreed to adopt this as our mantra. We would say it to each other all the time, in the face of any big decision, or any dilemma.

A few years later, when he turned eighteen, we decided to get matching tattoos. There was never any question about what those tattoos would say:

if not now, when?

It's hard to believe that little poo machine is now just shy of thirty years old. He is a fine young man with a big, warm smile, and he's inherited that bit of the Emdur DNA that makes you '*Be nice to everyone*'.

When he turned twenty-four, I wrote the following tribute on Instagram (which, by the way, is where I do some of my best work – and for the record, writing a few sentences with a silly photo is SO much easier than writing a whole book!):

I used to be his superman, now he is mine.

He used to look to me for motivation and inspiration, now I look to him for that.

I felt like I always protected him, now I feel like he protects me.

I used to have bigger hands and more hair than him, but now ... whatever.

#ThunderBuddies4Life

#IfNotNowWhen?

I didn't know if I had any more love to give, I didn't know the capacity of my heart until the day Tia was born. As I held her for the first time it was like a volcano was erupting in my chest, as my heart exploded with feelings I'd never felt before.

This little human doll brought me to tears just by looking at me with her smiling Vegemite eyes. And the love I felt at that moment, I've never grown out of it, and I never ever want to.

The 'bringing me to tears' would be a constant in our relationship. Big tough dad??? Ha ha, no way.

I'd cry when I saw her fantastic school reports, I'd cry watching her at school sport, I sobbed like a baby at the daddy–daughter school dance, and *of course* I cried at her graduation. I don't know what it is, maybe it can't be defined or properly explained by ordinary little me and my limited vocabulary. Maybe her philosopher buddies Plato or Nietzsche would have a better chance.

Our favourite thing to do together is go antiques hunting. We get lost in 'Imagine a family sitting down in these old chairs' and 'Imagine an old man winding up this record player … what was he like, and what did he do for a job?'

These trips are *so* special; they bring our weird sense of the absurd to the fore. We can spend *hours* walking around antique stores – not looking for anything to buy, just imagining and reimagining stories full of wild 'What if?'s.

Sylvie and I are so very proud of Tia, particularly her humanitarian pursuits – from volunteering to teach underprivileged kids to read, to raising money for various charities, to regularly donating plasma. (If you've donated plasma, you'll know it's a big commitment, but she says it directly saves lives, and she loves that she can do that.)

Tia has a power over me that is indescribable, and I love it. She has a beautiful old soul who's maybe been here a few times before. She contemplates, understands and solves life, even through its most complex and complicated challenges.

She remains one of the most intriguing and fascinating humans I've ever known: brilliant and beautiful, a poet, a philosopher, a warrior.

Every day when I look in the mirror I see my *if not now, when?* tattoo on my chest to remind me of my special relationship with Jye. But I also needed *Tia* over my heart, that heart that exploded for her the day she was born.

Now, I know *most* daddy–daughter days would never involve going to a tattoo parlour. But that was what we did together in 2017, just like I'd done with Jye.

We already had a pretty good idea of what we wanted when we stepped into Bondi Ink, and it wasn't a tiny half-eaten apple – I mean, what *lunatic* would choose that?!

Instead, I got a tattoo of the waves of Aquarius, her star sign.

Tia chose the design: one wave above *if not now, when?* and one wave below. Perfectly framed, perfectly balanced.

Tia and I agreed that the waves of her star sign would, for the two of us, represent life's peaks and troughs, and remind us there will always be another wave to pick you up and push you through every stage of life.

Now and forever, whenever I look at my saggy old chest, I have a constant reminder of my two favourite things in this universe, right on top of the place where they've been since the very second they were born.

Mum's Menu

2021

My mum, Faye, has been a constant presence in this book, but I decided to save this final chapter *just* for her.

A chapter for Mum is difficult. Not difficult to think up, or difficult to write, but difficult to condense into JUST ONE CHAPTER. Mum deserves a whole book – nah! Mum deserves a whole *library* of books about her!!!

My mum is beautiful, tiny in stature, with huge blue eyes and a warm caring smile that says: 'I'm right here, I'm never *not* here, I'm *always* ready to listen. How can I help, what do you need, is there anything I can do?'

Growing up, I honestly cannot remember a raised voice or an angry moment, just a calming, positive, healing guiding light for me and my two sisters, and any of her family and friends who needed her.

Sure, my fun, breakaway Man time was spent with Dad, but he was also a travelling salesman. While he was away – which was a *lot* – Mum was the gorgeous, strong, resolute one who would never let us think for a moment that anything was wrong, or that things weren't going to plan.

Whatever we were doing, Mum was there, supporting and encouraging us. To see her now with her grandkids and great-grandkids, you can tell those traits run deep. They're nothing she has to bung on, she is just that beautiful soul.

I feel so blessed that these seeds of positivity, inclusiveness and yearning to seek out the good answers instead of the bad were the building blocks of who I am. I've learnt SO much from her, impossible to list or even measure – things that have just been burnt into my nature and my thinking.

Growing up, our meals were never complicated; they were basic and they were perfect. Lamb chops, roast chook with veggies, toasted sandwiches, spaghetti bolognaise, chicken soup, and of course Bunny in a Hole.

I'm a simple eater. I'm not much into Polish *Chlodnik* or ox tongue, and on the rare occasions when I end up at a fancy restaurant with friends or colleagues, I usually wait till everyone else has ordered so I can say to the waiter, 'Oooohhhh, *that* sounds good! I'll have what *he's* having!'

I'm not very adventurous and tend to order the same thing every time. We've been ordering the same three dishes from our favourite Thai place for decades.

I think my one-track mind when it comes to food dates back to primary school.

Quite simply the best bit of the school day was lunchtime – or, as I used to call it, Devon Time.

MUM'S MENU

Devon is the seafood extender of the meat section. It's called different things in different parts of Australia. In Queensland they've tried to elevate its standing in society by calling it Windsor Sausage, which sounds quite regal and leads us to believe this is enjoyed by the Royal Family while picnicking by the lake in the magnificent gardens of 950-year-old Windsor Castle. Windsor Sausage was also apparently what Wallis Simpson called Edward VIII.

The South Australian equivalent is the Bung Fritz – yeah, so *they* appear to have given up on the romance of it all completely. It's made from a certain part of the sheep's appendix known as the bung, but why the South Australians didn't try to disguise that fact by calling it literally *anything* else we'll never know.

The appendix is the thing that fights infections in the small and large intestines and helps us recover from diarrhoea. So let's just go ahead and pull out this bung that's been holding back all this infection and diarrhoea, and make that into a sausage and feed it to our kids ... yeah, let's do that.

Devon's ingredients label reads 'Meat including pork', which I think is very clever, leading us to believe that there's probably meat in there somewhere.

Back in primary school, none of this mattered to me. I didn't know, and I wouldn't have cared. It was my favourite meal and my favourite part of school and my mum made the *perfect* devon sandwiches.

Two perfectly cut slices of devon on the whitest of white bread, with a generous smudging of butter, top and bottom, and a perfectly measured splash of tomato sauce. Too little tomato sauce and I would have complained to Mum when I got home from school; too much and it would have oozed and seeped right through the bread. (BIG PROBLEM.)

Mum's application of the tomato sauce was brilliant, bordering on scientific. I don't know how she did it, but between lovingly building this Bondi delicacy in the morning and the lunchtime unveiling – on the bench under the tree opposite the bell, in the corner of the playground where the cool kids sat – the sauce would penetrate *most* of the way through the whitest of white bread, giving you a complete, sauce-infused bread experience.

Somehow the sauce had pulled up *just* short of full penetration. How did Mum make the sauce stop just before it broke through the outer layer? She was a genius! I felt sorry for the other kids.

There were posters of the Food Pyramid all over our school – in each classroom, on the wall of the canteen, in the hallways, and at one point even on the backs of the toilet doors.

Mum, within this heavenly sandwich, had provided me with everything I needed from the Food Pyramid to grow into a big, strong man. Carbohydrates in the bread, a tomato is a vegetable so obviously tomato sauce filled the vegetable requirement, dairy in the butter, and meat (potentially) in the devon.

The only thing that could make this lunch better was the addition of a small glass bottle of warm milk. At the start of every day, a bunch of crates would be delivered to primary schools across Australia containing small, very cute bottles of milk. Every child would be handed one at lunchtime.

Long before we'd heard about El Niño and La Niña, we'd measure the day's temperature on the Milk Scale. As in: 'Oh, no! Today our free milk is going to smell like spew after sitting in the thirty-five-degree morning sun for four hours!'

You'd struggle to grab the tiny flap on the foil top, then you'd peel it back to find a thick layer of creamy yuckiness floating across the top. You'd fold the foil top in half and use it as a scoop to shovel the cream off the top, then drink the milk while trying to give yourself the best milk moustache in the playground. Which was always funny, but you would sadly be stuck with a rotten dairy stench right under your schnozz for the rest of the day.

Back then we didn't have the fancy Wiggles cooler lunch boxes or fancy Little Mermaid icepacks. Mum would make my sandwich from a meat-related product that had 'Keep Refrigerated' on the label, put it in a plain paper bag and send it off to school on a hot summer's day, and my gut microbiome would prepare for its daily battle against warm sheep's appendix and possibly off milk.

The paper bag hopefully offered some protection against salmonella, but not enough protection to stop your school bag from smelling of devon. Fortunately, though, the devon smell wasn't strong enough to out-stink the smell of the rotting banana skin that had been dissolving at the bottom of the bag for a few days.

I don't know if anyone at the CSIRO has ever worked out how long it would actually take salmonella or a similar infection to blossom in a devon-and-sauce sandwich in a paper bag in thirty-five-degree heat, but it's probably four hours and five minutes. Fortunately I always ate mine at the four-hour mark, so it was all good.

Sure, there were fancy kids with their fancy Vegemite sandwiches, or the real snobs with Vegemite AND cheese.

Bloody wankers, losers. *My* devon sambo was the best.

If there'd been a *My Kitchen Rules* back in the '70s, Mum would've won it hands down with her devon-and-sauce sandwich. Manu would've completely fritzed his bung upon tasting this Faye Emdur speciality.

When we were kids, Wednesday night was a big night: it was Pizza Night. We'd take the short walk down to Papa Giovanni, a pizza joint on Campbell Parade. We thought we were going there because it was closer to home than Nino's, but Papa Giovanni had a secret weapon: Enzo.

We'd go pretty early, and often Dad would still be at work. We'd walk in, and each time Enzo the manager would race up, take Mum's hand and kiss it. Call me a possessive, cynical kid, but looking back I believe Enzo's kisses went for slightly longer when we'd arrived at the restaurant without Dad.

We'd share a pizza and a pasta dish. In the middle of the table was a small dish of parmesan cheese – at least I think it was parmesan cheese, it had the texture of shaved timber but it was yellowy and smelt like cheese, so who knows? There was a teaspoon sticking out of the dish. We *loved* our parmesan cheese, and there never seemed to be enough in the little dish, so every Wednesday Mum would bring a secret stash from home that she'd smuggled in in her handbag.

And I thought my devon sandwich left a bad smell in my school bag …

Mum *never* wanted anyone to see her taking cheese out of her handbag, for good reason. Even if I *hadn't* ended up working in the public eye, even if I'd become a toilet cleaner in Antarctica, I still wouldn't want anyone to know that my mother smuggled cheese into restaurants. I only feel comfortable writing this at this point in the book in the hope that Mum won't read this far. I'm tipping she'll only get to the chapter about Nanny Minnie and my twenty-first birthday and put the book down in disgust, then get up and put more pics of the great-grandchildren up on the corkboard.

The smuggling operation was always SO funny; we all had a role to play and we all knew exactly what we had to do. *I* would stake out the pizza-making area to ensure no one was watching; *Nicki* would keep an eye out for Enzo and any other staff likely to walk past; *Martine* would double-check that none of the other diners were looking our way; and *Mum* would whip out her bag of cheese and sprinkle it very generously over the pasta.

One day Enzo busted us. 'Faye, Faye, my darling! Would you like more cheese? I can get you some more, my darling …'

Mum embarrassedly, apologetically agreed.

Enzo brought over a new dish of cheese, lovingly placed it on the table, took Mum's hand and kissed it again. 'Anything for you, my darling …'

OK, OK, back off there, Italian Stallion. Enough with the cheesing and the kissing. If Mum's wedding ring isn't telling you everything you need to know, then maybe the fact that she's sitting here with her *three children* should raise some red flags, Enzo, no???

This story had a very happy ending: we only used about half of Enzo's freshly supplied cheese, so what's a caring Mum with three hungry kids and an empty cheese-transporting bag in her handbag supposed to do? Obviously pour the cheese into her plastic cheese bag, stuff it in her handbag and run.

We three kids resumed our observational tactics as Mum reversed the procedure from a cheese smuggling-IN operation to a cheese smuggling-OUT operation. (Or, as a police officer, lawyer or judge would call it, 'stealing'.)

It seems Mum was willing to break all the rules back then to feed her family. And some things never change. We are now in our mid- to late fifties, and Mum is *still* willing to break the law to feed us ...

In any crisis, during any issue in our lives, Mum would be on our doorstep in minutes if required. As a family we've been through A LOT – nothing exceptional, same as most other families, I suppose, but A LOT. Over the years there's been your normal buffet of births, deaths and marriages, car accidents, sackings, long illness, a family member who tragically took his own life, and many personal challenges in all our careers and relationships.

I don't know how, but Mum has always had an answer for everything. Mum has been the one we'll instinctively, without hesitation, lean on. It doesn't matter why or when or how or what, we just will. Even if we don't immediately go to Mum in a crisis, we've always known she was right there, just a quick car trip or a quicker phone call away. We all know she can talk us through the direst of situations, and of course she's the first one we call to share good news with.

It's like she has an invisible shield that protects us, and that shield knows no limits: it just keeps on expanding with every new grandchild and great-grandchild.

So, when the world is in the grip of coronavirus, Mum faces the biggest challenge in our family's history. How will she continue to spread the love and comfort, at a time when restrictions and fear are keeping us all apart?

Now, probably deep down, Mum knew her famous chicken soup could not prevent or cure COVID-19. But she also knew that even though we were apart, we could still stay connected through its magic.

When we were growing up, it was the first cure for everything – and I mean *everything*. *Of course* it cured cold and flu, but Mum's chicken soup also had broad-spectrum healing powers. Mum would make it if we had a headache, sunburn, allergies, a sore neck or pimples, even if we were anxious before a big exam or job interview.

When I came around after a relationship breakup or a TV-show axing (both more common than I'm comfortable talking about!), Mum would make me a batch of the soup and the soup would fix my life.

Thor had his hammer to save the world, and Mum had her big pot of chicken soup.

So, why *can't* it fix coronavirus?

Once again, the big pots come out. Part of the same set Mum used to make Bunny in a Hole in the '70s.

Loose screws only just held in place on cracked handles. Bottoms warped and blackened from hundreds, perhaps thousands, of hours on the high setting to bring that chicken soup, that magic cure-all potion, to the boil.

They don't look like they did in the '70s brochure with the happy family on the cover, that's for sure. They look more like something that should be in the next council pick-up – or, more precisely, a council pick-up about twenty or thirty years ago.

When Dad originally brought these pots and pans home for Mum, he made a big deal of the fact that they came with a lifetime guarantee. So Mum was NEVER, EVER going to throw them out. They were going to last a lifetime!

It wasn't that they cost a lot. Dad was a salesman and was selling them at the time, so they were probably free – OR, he nicked them.

(OK, so far in this story we've got Mum stealing parmesan cheese and Dad stealing pots and pans. Just FYI, neither of these crimes has ever been proven in a court of law. Anyone know the statute of limitations on crimes against food and cookware?)

It wasn't even that they were non-stick; they were just the opposite. EVERYTHING stuck. There was just some sort of sentimentality deep in that steel.

During the height of the COVID-19 pandemic, Mum was living in a house next to a small laneway. Her dastardly and probably illegal plan was to create a sneaky little drive-through soup pick-up zone for her children and grandchildren.

She spent days making industrial quantities of the famous soup, she dug out all the Tupperware in the house. (Yep, Dad used to sell that too. Don't get me started on the Tupperware, though, because I've already used most of my good words to describe how old and broken the pans and pots were.)

Each child or grandchild – most of them fortunately living within the allowable five-kilometre radius – was given a specific time to drive through the alleyway. Like the old parmesan-smuggling operation, this was a precisely planned procedure executed with stealthy criminal cunning.

Mum would stand in her garage – which by law she was allowed to do – and as each beloved relative drove past under cover of darkness, she would jump out and pass a Tupperware container full of soup through the car window.

There were a couple of blocks of flats overlooking the laneway, and for anyone looking out of their window and seeing a small lady ducking in and out of her garage, handing strange packages through the windows of cars as they slowly drove past after dark – well, there was no way known to man that this didn't look like my mum was running an illegal drug operation.

My fab and fun nephew Asher, Martine's son, is our most nimble family member, and we thought he'd be the least likely to get caught or arrested, so he was the favourite pick to attempt the stealthy moonshine soup run. We only discussed it, though, I don't think he ever did it ... Your Honour.

Here's the thing: Mum knew we technically couldn't come around and see her, and this broke her heart, so she used the most powerful weapon in her arsenal to lure us over just so she could catch a glimpse of us, just so she could say hello, and tell us face to face that she loved us and was proud of us. So we could all see those beautiful, blue, happy eyes and know that, even in the midst of a global pandemic, she was right there and ready to care.

She was pretty lucky she didn't get busted for interacting with others – or for appearing to peddle drugs from her garage.

And maybe the soup didn't stop coronavirus, but it magically kept us all together.

Months later, Mum moved house and we had to physically prise the pots and pans away from her. She reluctantly let us replace them with a new set for her new home – but only after I convinced her that maybe the lifetime guarantee was in relation to *Dad's* life and not hers. Because he'd passed away, maybe the 'lifetime' part of the guarantee had expired. (More of this behaviour in my next book, entitled *Bad Son*.)

We threw the pans in the rubbish pile in Mum's garage, but we're pretty sure Mum snuck in there and reclaimed them after we left, and is secretly still using them to quietly save the world!

I love you, Mum, I'm so proud of you!

AFTERWORD

Bye for Now, and Keep Smiling (Patent Pending)

2022

A TV legacy is like superannuation. You never really think about it when you're younger, then when you *do* start thinking about it it's often too late.

It was only recently, after a few tragic deaths in my circle of friends, that I started to ask myself: 'If I died tomorrow, what would I leave behind?'

Would I leave behind some kind of legacy? What would it say on my tombstone? I always thought 'He came on down' would be funny.

What will I be remembered for? Will I be remembered at all?

I've never considered myself to be clever or successful, or even particularly good at what I do.

If anything, successful TV hosts need to be bland, almost generic. The biggest names on American talk shows – Johnny Carson, David Letterman, Jay Leno, Jimmy Kimmel, James Corden – are all everyman, the guy next door. You feel incredibly comfortable with them, not threatened at all. Australian TV execs call it the 'beer-ability' factor: would an ordinary Aussie like to have a beer with that person?

I can relate to this 'bland, generic' theory, and maybe being kind of ordinary has played a part in my survival in this biz.

Hosting a game show is rarely about the host, it's more about the host's ability to let the game and contestants shine. I've always attacked the role in that spirit: the contestant is the star, the game is the star, and the host is the smiling yet unobtrusive mechanic who makes sure all the parts of the machine are working the way they should.

I've seen many, many hosts try to make themselves the star of a show, with devastating results.

I may *call* myself a TV wanker, but throughout my career I've tried really hard *not* to be too up myself. I've seen and worked with up-themselves people, narcissists, control freaks, and it's painful to watch and they're painful to be around.

I remember on *The Main Event*, we'd have a virtual rollcall of TV celebrities every week, and I got to see up-and-coming 'stars' who'd gone from obscurity to fame in a very short space of time.

Some were such arseholes and tossers it was hysterical. Many of the ones who were way over the top would have a pretty short run; I couldn't tell you many of their names today, as they just sort of fizzled out, and this was a great lesson for me and a powerful reminder how *not* to behave.

Sometimes during my career, when the show I was hosting was particularly successful, I've wanted to jump up and yell, 'Hey, my show's number one!', or (during *The Main Event*) 'WOOOOHOOOOOO, my show's beating *60 Minutes*!', but I deliberately have rarely behaved that way. (OK, sometimes I just can't help myself.)

And of course now I've been around long enough to know that ratings success can change so quickly that it's dangerously short-sighted to crow about that stuff.

But there was this one time when I remember feeling pretty special. So, if you'll please allow me a quick wank, as in, to tell you a wanky story about myself (because you probably haven't read any of those in this book yet) …

In early 2006, just before Channel Seven launched *Wheel of Fortune* with me as host, Channel Nine started running repeats of my old *Price Is Right* episodes in the same timeslot. For perhaps the first time in TV history, the same host was hosting opposing shows on opposing networks at the same time.

It was a thing! Anywhere you flicked at 5.30 pm, there I was, hosting the two biggest game-show formats on the planet.

A woman stopped me at the shops one afternoon and said, 'I loved that lady on your show this week who won everything!'

And I said, 'I'm sorry, *which* show?'

WHAT A WANKER!!!

That was a long time ago, but once a wanker … Ummm, I forget how the rest of that saying goes.

More recently, both Jye and Tia have mentioned to me that out there, after dark, where young people stay up past 9 pm and get *really really* drunk, people are using the name 'Larry Emdur' as rhyming slang for a bender.

BYE FOR NOW, AND KEEP SMILING (PATENT PENDING)

Wooohooo, my name is now associated with a wild drinking spree, I've finally made it! I have a legacy after all!!! In the eyes of my kids, this is HUGE!!!!!

All these years I've embarrassed them by hosting shows like *The Very Best of the World's Worst Drivers 1, 2* and *3, Celebrity Dog School, The Very Best of the World's Worst Drivers 4, 5* and *6* (Number 5 was surprisingly good), *Celebrity Splash, The Very Best of the World's Worst Drivers 7, 8* and *9* (should've stopped after 5 – or 1) and *Surprise Wedding*.

But that has all been forgotten, because now Dad is rhyming slang for a great night out that eventually leads to a 3 am kebab, a vomit in the back of a taxi and an inability to remember the name of the person who's just woken up next to you in bed.

I AM THAT!!!!!

I am now an important part of a really pissed Aussie's night ... *Boooooooyahhhhhh!!!*

I've joined some seriously legendary names on the Aussie rhyming-slang list: Kevin Sheedy for 'seedy', Jimmy Britts for 'shits', Gary Ablett for 'tablet', Charles Wheeler for 'sheila', Britney Spears for 'beers', Bob Hope for 'soap', Barry Crocker for 'shocker', Al Capone for 'phone', Westpac banker for 'wanker', Kathy Bates for 'mates', Reg Grundys for 'undies' ...

Last night I was on a Larry Emdur and this Westpac banker was giving me the Jimmy Britts, so I grabbed some Britney Spears and borrowed me Kathy Bates' Al Capone and called me Charles Wheeler, but she hung up.

The night turned into a Barry Crocker, I needed to get a dog's eye in me Ned Kelly, but it was MY Wally Grout. They didn't have to twist me Warwick Farm for another Britney, but luckily I'd hidden a lobster in me Reg Grundys.

You can't imagine how proud it makes me to be a part of that story. And, in a generally accolade-free career, I only have a few things that I'm *really* proud of.

Now, I know what you're thinking. 'Hang on, Lazza, hang on just a goddamn minute, didn't you beat the Hemsworth brothers AND Elle Macpherson to take out Sexy Australian of the Year in 2015, as voted by *RedHotPie* subscribers?'

(Do you like the way I shifted that to something *you* might say to avoid me saying it about myself? I think it worked well, you didn't even notice you did that, did you?)

Anyway, thank you for reminding me about the Sexy Australian thing, before you mentioned it I'd completely forgotten about it.

My phone went crazy as this news broke, I couldn't believe it – nor could anyone I've ever known.

How could *I* be voted Australia's sexiest person? I'm not sexy – just ask my wife. In fact when I told Sylvie I had just been announced as 2015's Sexy Australian, her response was as cold as a bowl of cold beetroot soup on a cold day: she laughed, as in out loud, coldly.

'Bub, seriously, it's true, I BEAT THE HEMSWORTHS!' I exclaimed, wounded.

She laughed out loud again, maybe even more out-louderer than the first time.

'Darling, that's gotta be a joke, it can't be for real …'

'OK!' I interrupted. 'OKKKKKKKKKKK, I get it, Sylvie, I'm not sexy, I get it. Just leave me alone, you dream-stealer.'

(But don't think I wouldn't use that moment to my advantage to lure my wife into the boudoir with the pick-up line: 'How *you* doin', can I interest you in a night of pleasure and passion with the Sexy Australian of the Year, no strings attached except marriage and two kids???')

It was a very silly and funny moment in time. Of course, beating the Hemsworth brothers was super awesome, but I also beat out Karl Stefanovic on that list and that made it even sweeter. SO BITE MY SAGGING APPLE ARSE TATTOO, STEFANOVIC!!!!!

'Laz, Laz, Laz, all this talk of an accolade-free career, and yet I seem to remember that same year you were the oldest guy ever to appear on the cover of *Men's Health* magazine, Hugh Jackman held that title at forty-five and you got it at fifty!'

Wow, you guys *really* have a good memory for stuff, I don't know how you're getting into my head with those crazy random memories and questions that then trickle down my arms and my fingers onto the keyboard, but WOW, yeah, I'd forgotten about that one too, thanks for reminding me.

Look, I don't want to make a big deal about this, but yeah yeah yeah, it happened just like you said – but I really don't want to make this book all about me ...

(*Note from publisher: please write us a lovely book all about you.*)

Yes, it was a real honour to win the *Men's Health* Celebrity Man of the Year title and appear on the cover – and don't think I wouldn't use that moment to my advantage to lure my wife into the boudoir with the pick-up line: 'How *you* doin', can I interest you in a night of pleasure and passion with the cover guy on *Men's Health* magazine, no strings attached except marriage and two kids???'

But none of this comes close to the gratification and pure delight I get from the thought of young people waking up in a gutter covered in vomit and kebab, saying:

'I just had the *best* Larry Emdur!!!'

If you're interested in getting into the TV game and your parents have bought you this book as a learning tool to help launch you on the path to your dream career, then take it straight back to the bookstore and demand your money back immediately.

But if I were going to give you any advice, it would be: if you *do* want to leave an everlasting legacy in the TV business, it's probably important you say NO to hosting shows in which contestants who get the question wrong have sixty litres of pink custard poured on top of them.

The *other* piece of advice I'd give you is: come up with a really cool sign-off. At the end of each show, you should sign off with some words that become such a part of your persona and your show that people watching at home might even say it along with you.

That's the dream, right there. Something people will remember forever. A wise old TV exec once said the perfect sign-off is the one that kids start to use in the schoolyard.

American hosts are big on their sign-offs. Guests on Jerry Springer's confrontational show were rarely, if ever, good to each other, so his classic sign-off of 'Be good to each other' was quite a creative juxtaposition. Legendary Australian newsreader Brian Henderson would end each bulletin with 'And that's the way it is.'

My idol and hero Ron Burgundy, would sign off with 'Stay classy, San Diego.' I've learnt more from that man about television than anyone else. Unusually, my *other* idol and hero Bob Barker, who was at the helm of the American *Price Is Right* for a record-breaking fifty seasons, always finished with: 'Help control the pet population. Have your pet sprayed or neutered.' Dave Garroway used to sign off from the US *Today* show simply yet powerfully with 'Peace.'

Back home, Don Lane, the Lanky Yank himself, used to finish his late-night show with the sign-language version of 'I love your faces.' That was really lovely.

But my favourite Aussie sign-off comes from my mate Rove.

'Say hi to your mum for me.' What an utterly ridiculous thing to close the show with! But boy oh boy, did it stick! Walking through the streets with Rove, I've heard this yelled at him all the time. It took hold, he'd done it! His signature sign-off had made the leap out of the television and onto novelty T-shirts, and people will be saying it to him till the day he dies.

I didn't have any particular sign-off on *The Price Is Right*. Sometimes I'd just say, 'Goodnight, see you next time', or 'Have a great night, bye for now!' No set piece, just whatever came out.

One night I said: 'Keep smiling, and bye for now!'

Well, the next week I received correspondence from *Sale of the Century*.

The letter basically stated that I should refrain from saying 'Keep smiling, and bye for now!' because that was Tony Barber's sign-off, and it was synonymous with him.

I was young and kind of cocky, but this made me laugh, loudly and a lot. My game-show brain was just randomly generating words and clichés each night, and one night I spat out 'Keep smiling, and bye for now!' This had somehow triggered an intellectual property breach: scandalous! It was like that time the Winklevoss twins said Mark Zuckerberg stole the idea for Facebook from them. This 'cease and desist' letter was on *that* level.

No disrespect to Tony, but I find the suggestion that he owned those words a little ridiculous.

I had a bit more fun with it on the show, then I let it go, mainly because it's *impossible* to keep smiling. You can't, try it.

What's more, if you try to force a smile for longer than is natural, research suggests it's actually bad for you. You are possibly trying harder to conceal negative emotions, and then there is the physical discomfort of trying to keep smiling.

So by suggesting that people keep smiling, Tony was actually making Australians feel shit. What a terrible thing to do.

Occasionally I threw in a few more funky ones: 'Goodnight, and remember, don't buy it unless The Price Is Right!', 'Hope you can Come On Down next time!', and 'Why buy a vowel, when you can win a jet ski?!' But none of them really hit home.

Then I drew on some inspiration from my childhood, playing the pinnies in Jimmy's Milk Bar. I remembered how I felt when I'd spent all my money and the last of the steel balls rolled between the rubber flippers and down the throat of the machine, and the big lights flashed up: 'GAME OVER'. I remembered that feeling of loss and despair, and that simultaneous feeling of hope that one day soon I'd be able to rise again from poverty and have another crack at this game …

So, 'GAME OVER' to close *The Price Is Right* each night was born.

Sure, I wasn't saving the world by urging people to get their pets neutered, and I wasn't reminding people to stay classy, or bullying them into smiling until their faces broke, but 'GAME OVER' was my thing and I was really proud of it. And I didn't get a single letter from any video or pinball game manufacturers, not to mention any other game-shows.

I've used it a few times to sign off on *The Chase Australia*. It doesn't feel a hundred per cent right, so I think soon I'll be introducing my new sign-off.

It's taken me a while to work up, and I reckon it'll stick. I really wanted to concoct a phrase that was short and sharp and that people could mime at home.

I think I'm going to start saying:

'That's all, folks.'

Whaddya think?

Acknowledgments

How the book came to be called *Happy As* is such a great little story. I was tossing around a few different names, and I called my oldest and dearest mate Robbie and told him I was writing a book. He was shocked – he knows I'm not a reader or a writer, or smart.

'What's it called?' he asked.

'I don't know yet.'

'Well, I reckon there's only one title for this book.'

'What's that?'

Without skipping a beat, he said, '*Happy As*. From the first day I met you, you've been the happy smiley kid, and you've never been anything else in the fifty-plus years I've known you.'

I love it that someone who has been such an important part of my life has named my book.

I feel very lucky to be surrounded by some incredibly fierce and fabulous women who I respect and adore, but two in particular have made a massive difference in my life. Sarah Stinson, my boss at *The Morning Show* for many years and now the Head of Morning Television at Seven, has been such a supportive friend and positive force both on and off TV. She is definitely one-of-a-kind, and a caring, thoughtful level head in what can be a rough-and-tumble TV scrum. Sarah has been instrumental in all my big career decisions over the last few years, including tackling *The Chase Australia* and even committing to this book. Last year, as my fortieth year in the business loomed, Sarah suggested I write a book about my time in this crazy biz. I'd certainly thought about it a lot over the years but never thought I could actually do it.

It was my manager, Lucie McGeoch (former *Morning Show* producer, now Director of Client Management with entertainment powerhouse the Michael Cassel Group [Hey Luce and Michael, does that mean *Happy As* could be made into a musical? Let's do lunch.]), who not only convinced me I could write a book, but more importantly convinced HarperCollins I could write a book. And here we are. Thank you, Sarah, for planting the seed and believing I should write this, and thank you, Lucie, for convincing me I could write this, even when you know I struggle with both reading and writing. You both have frightening powers of persuasion.

And then there's my tribe, the people I can't live without, the people I wrote this book for. The people who don't care about ratings, axings and silly headlines, we are just always there for each other, forever, no matter what.

My everlasting love and thanks to Sylvie, Jye, Tia, Mum, my father-in-law Wlodek, my sisters, Nicki and Martine, and Nicki's superman hubby and my legendary bro-in-law, Steve. To my brilliant and beautiful nieces who I absolutely love and adore: Bianca, our loving, caring, life-saving nurse; Madeleine, who is a gun young producer at *60 Minutes*, the very show that chewed up and spat out *The Main Event* and her favourite uncle in 1993 – how dare you, Maddz? – and Anneliese, our actress and calming little angel who spreads warmth and peace. To my big-hearted and always supportive nephews, Jake and Asher, who keep us all entertained and intrigued and are totally vying for my role as family MC at parties. And to Bianca's and Madeleine's perfect

ACKNOWLEDGMENTS

matches and solid additions to our family, Eden and Todd, and our brand-new little bundles of happiness and joy, Leon, Billy and Clementine.

It's my hope that one day you'll read this and see where it all started and understand the power of family.

Picture credits

Page 58: *The Morning Show* interview with Paul Hogan, courtesy of Seven Network. All rights reserved. ©

Page 66: Cassette tape and player by Enzo Tommasi/Unsplash

Page 81: *The Morning Show* interview with Lindy Rama-Ellis, courtesy of Seven Network. All rights reserved. ©

Page 103: Larry Emdur reporting on Seven Nightly News, courtesy of Seven Network. All rights reserved. ©

Page 121: Larry Emdur reporting on *News Overnight*, courtesy of Seven Network. All rights reserved. ©

Page 159: Beatles' albums by Nick Fewings/Unsplash

Page 187: Larry Emdur and *The Price Is Right* models, courtesy of Nine Network Australia

Page 216: Larry Emdur as host of *The Price Is Right*, courtesy of Nine Network Australia

Page 253: Mary and Larry Emdur on *The Price Is Right*, courtesy of Fremantle

Page 282: Daryl Somers and Matt LeBlanc at the 1998 Logies ceremony, courtesy of Nine Network Australia

Page 295: Circus acrobat by Miikkia Luotio/Unsplash